20.00

FIBRECRAFTS
STYLE COTTAGE
LOWER EASHING
GODALMING
SURREY GU7 2QD
TEL: 01483 421853

"Knitting By the Fireside
and on the Hillside"

Linda G. Fryer

"Knitting By the Fireside and on the Hillside"

A History of the Shetland Hand Knitting Industry c.1600-1950

The Shetland Times Ltd.,
Lerwick, Shetland
1995

© Copyright Linda G. Fryer, 1995
First published 1995

All rights reserved. No part of this publication may be reproduced, stored in a retrieval system or transmitted, in any form, or by any means, electronic, mechanical, photocopying, recording or otherwise, without the prior written permission of the publisher.

British Library Cataloguing in Publication Data
A CIP catalogue record for this book is available from the British Library.

ISBN 1 898852 01 4

Printed and published by
The Shetland Times Ltd., Prince Alfred Street,
Lerwick, Shetland, ZE1 0EP,
Scotland

To Mum

Who's always there to love and care.

Contents

List of illustrations viii
Author's note xi
Abbreviations xii
Preface xiii
Acknowledgements xvi
Chapter 1 Introduction 1
Chapter 2 The Shetland Method 1790-1872 13
Chapter 3 Truck & The Shetland Hand
           Knitting Industry 1790-1950 39
Chapter 4 The Origin and Development of Shetland Lace 67
Chapter 5 Dawn of Modernisation 1872-1918 93
Chapter 6 Modernisation 1918-1950 131
Chapter 7 Evolution or Repetition? 169
Appendices 182
Glossary 184
Bibliography 186
Index 188

List of illustrations

Illustrations marked with an * have been supplied by kind permission of the Shetland Museum.

Chapter 1.
Fig. 1.1 - Map of the Shetland Islands as a mercantile cross roads.
Fig. 1.2 - Map of the Shetland Islands.
Fig. 1.3 - 'Rooing' the sheep*.
Fig. 1.4 - Gunnister Man's hat.
Fig. 1.5 - Gunnister Man's gloves.
Fig. 1.6 - Gunnister Man's stockings.
Fig. 1.7 - Gunnister Man's purse.

Chapter 2.
Fig. 2.1 - Shetland knitter, c. 1900*.
Fig. 2.2 - Fisherman and knitter, c.1822.
Fig. 2.3 - Shetland population statistics.
Fig. 2.4 - Structure of the Shetland hand knitting industry, c.1872.
Fig. 2.5 - Dressing shawls, c.1894.
Fig. 2.6 - Arthur Laurenson.
Fig. 2.7 - Advert for Wm. Johnson's store.
Fig. 2.8 - Map showing Hay & Co.'s business dealings from 1844.
Fig. 2.9 - Table showing profit on hosiery, c.1872.

Chapter 3.
Fig. 3.1 - Map showing where the 1872 Truck Commission's meetings were held.
Fig. 3.2 - Pie chart showing the occupations of people who gave evidence at the 1872 Truck Inquiry.
Fig. 3.3 - Map showing Sheriff-substitute Mackenzie's route round the parish of Delting.
Fig. 3.4 - Jaw bone stand at the Edinburgh International Exhibition, 1886*.
Fig. 3.5 - Schoor & Co.
Fig. 3.6 - Schoor & Co.
Fig. 3.7 - Table showing prosecutions in Shetland under the Truck Amendment Act.

Chapter 4.
Fig. 4.1 - Sumburgh shawl, 1837*.

Fig. 4.2 - Mermaid poem.
Fig. 4.3 - The Ogilvy knitted lace christening cap, c.1833.
Fig. 4.4 - Advert for Mrs Standen of Oxford.
Fig. 4.5 - Modern Russian shawl.
Fig. 4.6 - Two stitch patterns i.e. Old Shale and Print o' Waves.
Fig. 4.7 - Bestway knitting pattern.
Fig. 4.8 - Paton's knitting pattern.
Fig. 4.9 - Lace shawl, c.1894.
Fig. 4.10 - Crepe shawl, c.1894.
Fig. 4.11 - Hap shawl, c.1894.
Fig. 4.12 - Diagram showing the construction of a Shetland lace shawl.
Fig. 4.13 - Extract from the Great Exhibition catalogue, 1851.
Fig. 4.14 - Bridal veil, 1851*.
Fig. 4.15 - Copy of the shawl presented to HRH Princess Alexandra in 1863.

Chapter 5.
Fig. 5.1 - Kelp burners, c.1907.
Fig. 5.2 - Steamer day at Lerwick, mid 1880s*.
Fig. 5.3 - Fishwives at work*.
Fig. 5.4 - Women delling, 1910*.
Fig. 5.5 - Advert for 'Shetland' wool made in Germany, c.1914.
Fig. 5.6 - Advert for the Mill of Aden, 1872.
Fig. 5.7 - Petrie family dressing shawls, c.1910*.
Fig. 5.8 - Chart showing marketing outlets used by private knitters.
Fig. 5.9 - Knitted veil.
Fig. 5.10 - Hand knitted underclothing.
Fig. 5.11 - R. Linklater, 1893.
Fig. 5.12 - R. Sinclair.
Fig. 5.13 - Anderson & Co.
Fig. 5.14 - Fair Isle knitting, 1894.
Fig. 5.15 - Letter from Mary Smith, 1882.
Fig. 5.16 - Mary Smith's household expenses, 1880.
Fig. 5.17 - Advert for John White & Co.
Fig. 5.18 - John White & Co.'s premises, 1904.
Fig. 5.19 - A knitted 'cloud'.
Fig. 5.20 - Shetland road plexus in 1864 and 1890.

Chapter 6.
Fig. 6.1 - Pie chart showing occupations in Shetland during the inter-war years.
Fig. 6.2 - Golfers wearing Fair Isle sweaters, 1920s*.
Fig. 6.3 - SWIA trade marks, 1925.
Fig. 6.4 - SHKA share certificate, 1944.

Fig. 6.5 - Kays of Shetland.
Fig. 6.6 - SHKA advert, 1947.
Fig. 6.7 - Advert for Shetland Spinners Ltd., 1940.
Fig. 6.8 - Structure of Shetland knitwear industry in 1950.
Fig. 6.9 - The Sutherland family carding, spinning and knitting*.
Fig. 6.10 - Logo and advert from HHI carrier bag.
Fig. 6.11 - Inside of hosiery store of Kays of Shetland*.
Fig. 6.12 - Stewarts of Shetland, 1947.

Chapter 7.
Fig. 7.1 - SHKA advert, 1949.
Fig. 7.2 - Jamieson's Naturally Shetland logo.
Fig. 7.3 - The SKTA's Shetland Lady trade mark.
Fig. 7.4 - The SKTA's Heritage Collection.

I would like to acknowledge and thank the following people and institutions for permission to publish material and illustrations: The Shetland Archives, Shetland Museum, Shetland Amenity Trust, Shetland Knitwear Trades Association, The National Museums for Scotland, Patons & Baldwins Ltd., Mary Downham, Marion Green, Mary Smith, Margaret Peterson, Peter Jamieson, David Pottinger and Sven Hovmuller.

Author's Note

THIS BOOK is based on the research work which I carried out on the Shetland hand knitting industry for the degree of M. Litt. in the Department of Scottish History at the University of Glasgow. The thesis entitled "The Shetland hand knitting industry 1790-1950; with special reference to Shetland lace" contains full references and an extensive bibliography. Both the Shetland Archives and the Shetland Library have copies of the thesis. As is explicit in the title, my research stopped at 1950. However, it was felt that some mention of the Shetland hand knitting industry up to the present time would be of value, and for this reason a postscript to cover the period 1950-90 has been added. It does not pretend to be more than a very brief review of the decades between 1950 and 1990 with a summary of the knitwear industry as it stood in 1990. Inevitably many people and firms worthy of mention have not been included in this postscript. No one person or firm was intentionally excluded and therefore I hope no slight is felt by my omissions.

As with the two World Wars, the social and economic changes brought about by the oil era of the 1970s, changed the nature of the knitting industry irrevocably. The impact of both oil and modern technology, coupled with events such as the creation of the Highlands and Islands Development Board and the Shetland Islands Council, make the period 1950-90 a massive and eventful one worthy of a separate study. I hope that someone will undertake this task and thus complete the history of the Shetland knitwear industry.

The title of this book - "Knitting By the Fireside and on the Hillside" - is a quotation taken from the 1888 Delting Truck Inquiry.

Abbreviations

AF	Agriculture and Fishery files (SRO)
c.	Around or approximately
Cd.	Command
CDB	Congested Districts Board
c.o.d.	Cash on delivery
HH	Home and Health files (SRO)
H.H.I.	Highland Home Industries Ltd.
MP	Member of Parliament
NFU	National Union of Farmers
NLS	National Library of Scotland
NMS	National Museums of Scotland
NSA	New Statistical Account
OSA	Old Statistical Account
PP	Parliamentary Papers
SA	Shetland Archives
SEP	Social and Economic Planning files (SRO)
SHIA	Scottish Home Industries Association
SHKA	Shetland Hand Knitters Association
SIC	Shetland Islands Council
SKTA	Shetland Knitwear Trades Association
SM	Shetland Museum
SNDC	Scottish National Development Council
SPRI	Scott Polar Research Institute (Cambridge)
SRO (WRH)	Scottish Records Office, West Register House
SWIA	Shetland Woollen Industries Association
ZCC	Zetland County Council

Notes.

1. Throughout the text 'The Second Report of the Commissioners appointed to inquire into the Truck System (Shetland)' is referred to as the 1872 Truck Inquiry.

2. The term 'South' is used by Shetlanders to mean the British Mainland.

3. All monetary values relate to sterling unless otherwise stated. The pound sterling was worth 12 pounds Scots.

4. The following decimal conversions cover some of the pre-decimal sums of money given in the text:

$$6d. = 2½ p \qquad 1/- = 5p \qquad 2/- = 10p$$

5. 1lb. = 16oz. and 2.2 lbs. = 1 kilogram

N.B. Words marked with an asterisk are listed in the glossary.

Preface

TRADITIONALLY the Shetland economy has been based on fishing, crofting and knitting. Generally speaking, the income from fishing paid the rent, whilst crofting provided food for subsistence, and the returns from knitting were used to clothe the family and help supplement the domestic economy. Yet despite this important role which hand knitting has always played in the Shetland economy, it has been undervalued and neglected by historians; there have been no comprehensive studies made of the Shetland hand knitting industry. Several reasons for this omission in Shetland's full and well documented history may be postulated. For example, knitting, regarded in Shetland as women's work, was rarely prosecuted as a primary or full-time occupation and, for this reason, the true numbers of women knitting for sale have not been adequately recorded by the decennial censuses which have never made provision for secondary occupations. Furthermore, unlike the Aberdeen or Sanquhar knitting industries, the Shetland hand knitting industry, continued without any structured organisation well into the twentieth century, making it difficult to attain hard statistics of the number of women engaged in it, their output, or the value of knitwear exported. Likewise, knitted goods were often bartered or exchanged for shop goods or sold to visitors for money; in either case, these transactions left little or no trace of having taken place, far less provided data for analysis.

Possibly the most important reasons for this oversight in the islands' history, is that fishing, a male dominated occupation, has always been regarded as the corner-stone of the islands' economy, whilst women and their work were looked on as secondary to men, despite their many skills and constant toil. Neither can it be overlooked that the vast majority of books, diaries and accounts written by early Shetlanders and travellers, were written by men. Few of these books fail to make reference to knitting but rarely give detailed information on the Shetland hand knitting industry. Two notable exceptions are the works by Mrs Eliza Edmondston, of the landed Edmondston family of Unst, and of Edward Standen, an Oxford merchant who was responsible for introducing fine Shetland hosiery to the London market. Fortunately, there is sufficient documented information from such sources as the Old and New Statistical Accounts of 1791 and 1845, The Poor Law Inquiries of 1843 and 1910, the Shetland Truck Inquiries, merchants' ledgers, Commissary, Sheriff Court, Procurator Fiscal, and Scottish Office Records, as well as contemporary diaries, newspapers and journals, to piece together a comprehensive history of the Shetland hand knitting Industry.

Truck, defined as payment in kind and not in the current coin of the realm, played such a large part in all aspects of Shetland's primitive, that is barter, economy, that the Government commissioned a separate truck inquiry for Shetland in 1872. This inquiry (which shall be referred to throughout the text as the 1872 Truck Inquiry), was entitled 'The Second Report of the Commissioners appointed to inquire into The Truck System (Shetland)' and is the single most informative source of Shetland life and work at that time, and in particular, gives a wealth of details regarding the running of the hand knitting industry, as well as throwing light on the social and economic conditions of nineteenth century Shetland knitters. Sixteen years later, a second smaller and less formal truck inquiry was held in the parish of Delting. The hand-written minutes of this inquiry (simply referred to as the Delting Truck Inquiry) are lodged in the Scottish Records Office at West Register House, Edinburgh. It was instigated by the Secretary of State for Scotland, following a petition sent by the knitters and makers of home-spun cloth from the Parish of Delting to Queen Victoria, complaining of the lowering of prices paid to workers after the passing of the 1887 Truck Amendment Act. Truck, with its many social and economic implications, was so enmeshed in the Shetland way of life and so inextricably linked with the hand knitting industry that a separate chapter has been devoted to an analysis of Truck and the Shetland hand knitting industry.

A separate chapter has also been devoted to the origin and development of Shetland lace. The term "Shetland Lace" is a misnomer, as true lace is defined as 'fine open-work fabric of three main types: bobbin or bone lace made by twisting threads; needlepoint made by looping and knotting threads; and machine made', not knitted. A more correct term for this form of knitting would be Shetland open work. Shetland lace appears to have evolved from a combination of events and circumstances rather than a single, specific event or influence. For example, the abundant supply of fine indigenous wool, the already highly developed knitting skills of local women, coupled with economic pressure caused by hard times during poor harvests, war and trade depressions, led to this beautiful textile-form evolving around 1835 and reaching its peak of perfection at the time of the Great Exhibition in 1851. This distinctive and highly skilled form of knitting rightly deserves greater attention than it has previously enjoyed, not only as a record of the dying skill of lace knitting, but as the important stimulus it gave to the islands' economy following the slump in the knitted hose market in the 1820s and 30s.

Any study of Shetland women and their work would be incomplete without an appraisal of the role they played in society and of their contribution to the Shetland economy. Women living and working in a crofting-fishing community frequently had to adopt the dual role of male and female, acting as surrogate fathers, bread-winners, and crofters, in addition to their normal role of mother, cook, housekeeper, and supplementary wage-earner, in the absence of their menfolk. In Shetland this absence usually ran from May to September, that is during the fishing season, and coincided with Voar* time, the busiest and most important time of year, as it was from those efforts and skills as crofters that the welfare of the family depended throughout the following winter. As in other fishing communities, Shetland population statistics show an excess female population, due in part to accidents and fatalities at sea, but one which precluded a proportion of the female population from finding a marital partner for support. The appraisal of the role of women found in chapters 2, 5 and 6, has been kept brief, as excellent work, including much oral history, has already been carried out in Shetland by both Ann Black, and the teams involved in the publication of both *Living Memory* and *Ahint Da Daeks*.

Finally the chronological divisions used in chapters 2, 5 and 6 have been chosen to coincide with major events affecting the hand knitting industry. 1872 was the year in which Shetland's major truck inquiry was held, 1918 the end of the First World War which marked a watershed in the organisation of the Shetland hand knitting industry whilst by 1950, hand knitters had to some extent been usurped by knitting machines.

Acknowledgements

AS THIS BOOK is based on the research work which I carried out at the University of Glasgow, I would like to thank Professor Allan Macinnes - my supervisor - for his guidance throughout the course of my research, and the staffs of the University Library and Scottish History Department, who have been consistently helpful and pleasant over the years. I am grateful to the staffs of the SRO at West Register House, Edinburgh; the National Library of Scotland and Commercial Library, both in Edinburgh; and the Mitchell Library, Glasgow, for their help in accessing material. I would like to thank Naomi Tarrant and Irene MacKay of the National Museums of Scotland, Edinburgh for the generous amount of time they spent in making archival material and artefacts available for my perusal, and Wilma Henderson (also of the NMS) for her speedy and efficient help with photographs.

One unforeseen bonus of researching in Shetland is the warmth and generosity of its people. I would like to express my thanks to all the very many people who have made my visits to Shetland both rewarding and pleasant, and in particular to thank Joan Mouat of the Heritage Centre, Mary Spence and Ida Sandison, Margaret Peterson of 'Nornova', all from Unst; David Pottinger of Anderson & Co., John Tulloch of Tulloch of Shetland, Pattie Anderson of Jamieson & Smith, Marion Leslie of Toab, Nancy Heubeck, Diane White of the Shetland Knitwear Trades Association, and Margaret Robertson (author of *Sons and Daughters of Shetland 1800-1900*). My thanks are also due to the staff of the Shetland Islands Council and Shetland Library for their assistance, and to Tommy Watt, curator of the Shetland Museum, who opened up the Museum early one Saturday morning to allow me to examine the Museum's hosiery collection before my departure south later that morning. Ian Tait was most helpful in assisting with illustrations from the Shetland Museum's extensive photographic collection. I am especially grateful to the Blacks of Toab for their help and kind hospitality, and to Brian Smith, Shetland archivist, for drawing my attention to numerous important sources, answering my questions and correspondence, providing support and encouragement, and with the funding provided by the Shetland Islands Council and the assistance of Angus Johnson, making the Shetland Archives such an excellent research centre.

After the submission of my thesis Mrs Mary Downham from South Africa wrote to Jim Wallace MP inquiring about the history of her great great grandfather's christening cap. Via Angus Johnson at the Shetland Archives, I received her letter and have enjoyed corresponding with her ever since. This correspondence led to the exciting discovery that it was Charles Ogilvy who was her great great grandfather and that the lace christening cap she referred to was none other than the cap to which Dr Robert Cowie traced the origin of Shetland lace knitting. This lace cap is shown by kind permission of Mrs Downham on the front cover and in chapter four. I can't thank Mrs Downham enough for sending me the photographs of this christening cap and thereby providing a such a tangible link with the past. I would also like to thank both Angus and Jim Wallace for the crucial part they played in this saga.

Special thanks are also due to Moira McAdam, Dr Sven Hovmuller from Stockholm University for supplying me with the photograph of the Russian lace shawl on sale in a Moscow market (fig. 4.5) and to Mary Smith (co-author of *A Shetland Knitter's Notebook*) for her kind permission to allow me to use her information on John White & Co.'s 1908 Mail Order Catalogue. Many firms and people have helped with my queries and I would particularly like to thank Mr H. McLean of Patons & Baldwins Ltd., Mr G. Stewart of Hunters of Brora Ltd., and my friend Ann Black for her enthusiastic interest and assistance with this project.

However, my greatest debt of gratitude is due to my long-suffering husband and son for their support, encouragement and forbearance throughout the ups and downs of researching and writing my thesis and this book.

Lastly to the many people whom I have not mentioned but have helped with my researches, thank you.

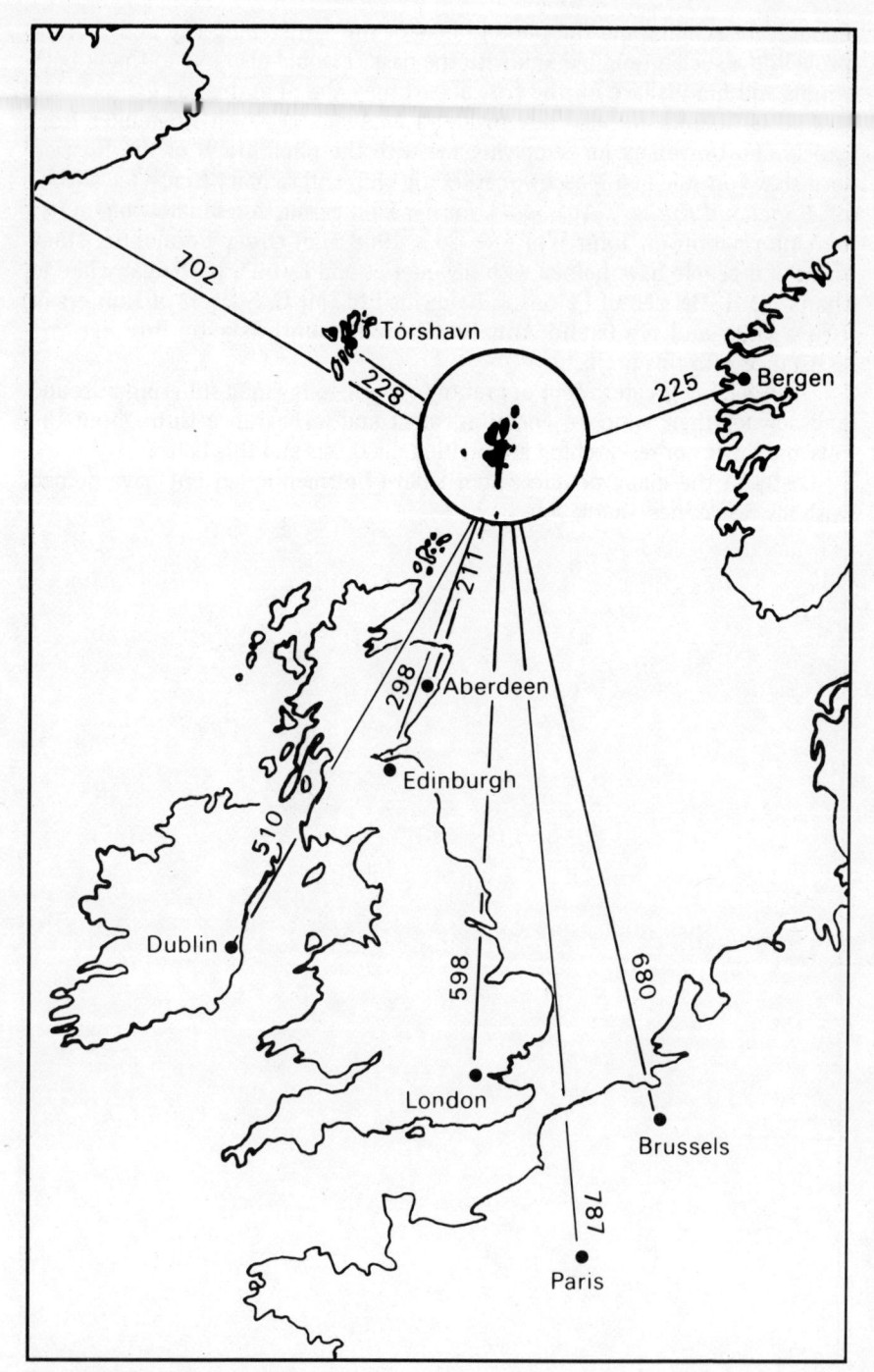

Fig 1.1 Shetland's geographical position.

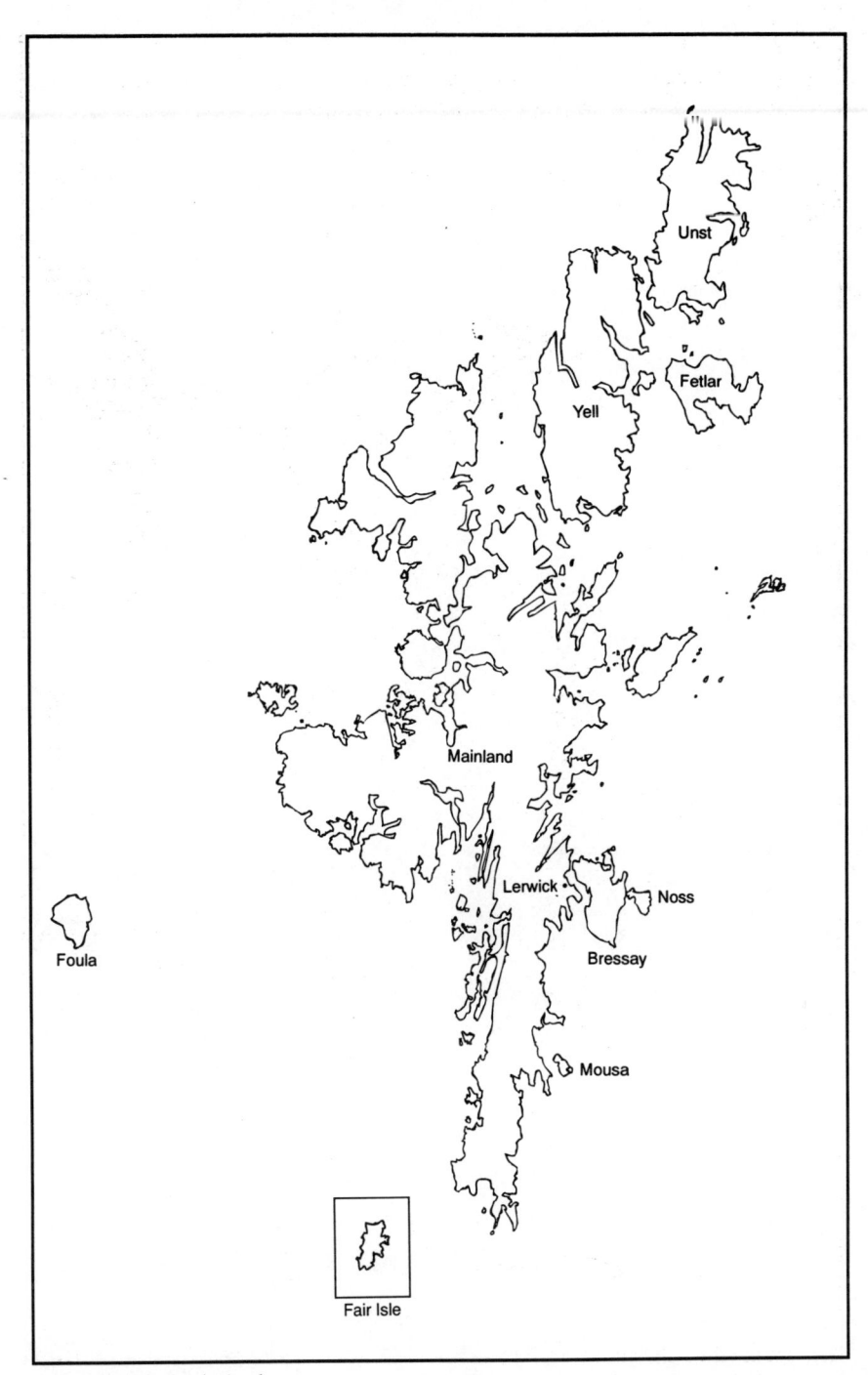

Fig 1.2 The Shetland Islands.

Chapter 1

Introduction

THE SHETLAND ISLANDS lie 184 miles (294km.) north of Aberdeen and 193 miles (308km.) west of Bergen (Fig. 1.1). They have been Scotland's most northerly territory since 1469, when they were mortgaged by Christian I, the Dano-Norwegian king, in part payment of his daughter Margaret's dowry on the occasion of her marriage to James III of Scotland.

The Shetland Islands comprise an archipelago of over 100 islands, only 14 of which are inhabited at the present time. The largest and by far the most densely populated of these islands is called Mainland, and it is on this island that Shetland's capital, Lerwick, is located (Fig. 1.2). These islands, lying between the latitudes 60 and 61 degrees north, are situated in the North Atlantic where the North Sea becomes the Atlantic Ocean, and are at the centre of the mercantile cross-roads between Germany, Britain, Scandinavia and the North Atlantic sea routes.

The area covered by these islands, which have a land mass of 550 square miles (1408 sq. km.), is approximately 70 miles (112km.) north to south, (excluding Fair Isle lying 25 miles (40km.) south of Sumburgh Head, the most southerly point on Mainland Shetland), and 35 miles (56km.) east to west; that is, from the Out Skerries on the east to remote Foula on the west. In common with other northern settlers, Shetlanders experience very short winter days and particularly long summer ones. Winter days have just under six hours of daylight at the winter equinox, whilst in June, July and August, the 'simmer dim' gives almost continuous daylight.

Despite the islands' exposed and northerly situation, Shetland enjoys a surprisingly mild climate with less snow and frost than mainland Scotland. This is due to the beneficial effect of the Gulf Stream. The North Atlantic depressions sweeping in from the west, do however, bring strong winds, and constant wind is a feature of Shetland's unusual weather pattern. Rainfall, on the other hand, is below mainland Scotland's average, because of its low geographical relief - Ronas Hill, at 1,550ft. (450m.) is Shetland's only 'mountain'.

The Shetland Islands, also called Zetland, Ultima Thule or Hjaltland, are often locally referred to as 'The Old Rock'. This vernacular term has its origin in the islands' great age of 2,000 million years. Much of the islands' extensive coast line is barren and rocky, whilst the interior is covered with a thick layer of peat, tussock grass, scrub vegetation and wild flowers but is devoid of trees. Many lochs abound and the ground is generally boggy with poor soil. This plethora of lochs, voes*, geos*, and water logged ground, coupled with the lack of roads, explains why boats have traditionally been the more usual method of transport.

Shetland's poverty of soil has, in the past, been compensated by the rich fishing grounds located round her shores; these explain why fishing has for centuries been the dominant economic activity for Shetland men, with crofting essentially a subsistence activity to support the family rather than earn money. Ironically, Shetland's exposed northerly position, poor soil and meagre grazing, are the ingredients which have been responsible for producing some of the hardiest sheep in Scotland, whose wool is exceptionally fine and soft; and it was from this indigenous supply of top quality wool, that the Shetland hand knitting industry evolved, making knitting the third strand in the islands' tripartite economy.

Shetland Wool

Few authorities can agree as to the breed from which the native Shetland sheep is descended. For example, Evershed in his paper to the Highland and Agriculture Society of Scotland, in 1874, reiterated Hibbert's belief that the breed which Shetland sheep most resembled was the Argoli, the wild sheep of Siberia, whilst O'Dell writing in 1939, suggested similarities to the Wild Mouflon of Corsica. Prophet Smith, a native Shetlander, addressing a Summer School run by the Education Department of the International Wool Secretariat in 1958, claimed that the most likely connection was with the mountain sheep of Northern Norway, and stated that: "Cut off for long periods from cross-breeding with other strains, the Shetland sheep slowly developed into an independent breed".[1] In a more recent study, Professor Wheeler of Newcastle University, stated that:

...it is generally agreed that the present animals show traces of primitive mouflon and urial (or turbary) blood, and indeed, in many ways the breed must be much the least "improved" of British sheep, retaining, for example, such anatomical peculiarities as having only 13 vertebral tail bones compared with the 20 or more in most breeds.[2]

There is however no doubt that the wool from these sheep is one of the finest wools produced in Britain. David Loch, the ardent promoter of the Scottish woollen industry, stated in 1780:

Zetland ... produces sheep with the best wool, not inferior to that of Spain, from which I have often had stockings manufactured much finer than any of the kind I ever saw; which were beautiful beyond description.[3]

The wool has a very short staple, is light, soft, silky and extremely warm but not hard wearing. The fineness of the wool is dependent on the part of the animal from which it is taken - the area around the neck providing the very finest wool. 'Rooing', rather than the quicker method of shearing, had been the tradition in Shetland until the 1950s (fig. 1.3). By this means the wool was plucked from the sheep and was said to aid the fineness of the fleece by leaving the longer, coarser hairs on the sheep and by not blunting the fine ends with clippers. It is believed to be a painless process as by the

INTRODUCTION

summer months the sheep's fleece is hanging off and easily removed by hand plucking.

A characteristic of this breed, and one which can be attributed to its primitive features, is the variations of fleece colouring. The most common colours are off-white, grey, and Shetland black. 'Moorit', a reddish-brown colour, 'shaela' a greyish-black, are just two of the many natural colourings common to these sheep. These natural colourings are used to advantage in traditional Shetland colour-stranded knitting* and in the subtle grading or blending of tones in Shetland haps*.

The average fleece weight of 1½ -2 lbs. from pure Shetland sheep, as compared to 5-6lbs from Black-face or Cheviots, led many agricultural improvers, like the famous "Agricultural Sir John" (Sir John Sinclair of Ulbister) and Thomas Mouat of Unst, to experiment with cross breeding in an attempt to increase fleece and carcass weights. The first cross-breeding

Fig 1.3 Rooing a sheep in Cunningsburgh in the late 1950s.   Photo: J. Peterson

experiments, advocated by Sir John in the 1780s, had the unfortunate consequence of producing an outbreak of sheep scab. This outbreak, first reported in 1786, had a devastating effect on the flock numbers. Edmondston, writing on the subject of sheep scab in 1809, remarked "There is not one left in fifty of the number that was a few years ago".[4] Other experiments have failed to produce sheep as hardy, or with a fleece as soft, as the pure native breed. Even less sophisticated measures, such as moving sheep to better pasture, have backfired. The nutritionally poor quality of their moorland feeding and the privation to which they are exposed during winter months - often having to forage for seaweed below high water mark when hill feeding had been exhausted - seem paradoxically to be the essential ingredients for maintaining the particular qualities of this primitive breed's wool. For example, Cheviot sheep reared in Shetland produce a finer quality of wool than the same breed reared in the North of Scotland.

Origin of Hand Knitting

This abundance of good quality native wool naturally lent itself to the development of a local weaving or knitting industry based on wool. A combination of circumstances seem to have favoured the development of the hand knitting rather than tweed weaving. Wadmal, a coarse cloth formerly woven for rent payment, was replaced by money payments during the first half of the seventeenth century, but continued to be made occasionally for home use until the middle of the nineteenth century. Against the weaving industry the following drawbacks are apparent. Firstly, weaving, traditionally a male occupation, required capital outlay on a loom and the space to work at this cumbersome object; secondly, Shetland men traditionally earned their living from the sea and apart from crofting, were not land based; thirdly, Shetland wool was found to be too soft for tweed weaving, giving a loosely woven cloth, which without a waulking* mill on the islands to finish it, quickly went shapeless with wear. Whether due to these adverse circumstances or to the fact that knitting fitted in with the rhythm of crofting life - being able to be combined with other activities - or to the higher ratio of women to men, forcing more women to support themselves or simply to the greater industry of women, it was hand knitting and not weaving for which Shetland and its wool became famous.

Knitted material is formed by using a continuous yarn and interlocking loops of yarn with the aid of two or more needles, or wires as they are called in Shetland; prior to the use of wires, sticks were used. There is no documented evidence to determine when the skill of hand knitting reached Shetland. As knitting spread through western Europe in the fifteenth century, it is probable that it reached Shetland during this period and, with the abundance of native wool available locally, rapidly developed. As far back as the fifteenth century, Shetland had established trade links with the Hanseatic ports of Hamburg, Bremen, and Lubeck; England and Scotland, whilst still retaining strong Scandinavian ties, even after 1469. Renaissance paintings of the 'Knitting Madonna' confirm that knitting was an established skill in fourteenth century Germany and Italy. Richard Rutt, Bishop of Leicester, states that Coventry cappers (cap knitters) can be traced back to the thirteenth century and were established by 1424, whilst David Bremner stated that in Scotland "About the middle of the fifteenth century peasants began to wear knitted instead of woven woollen caps".[5] This is very likely true as by 1496 the bonnetmakers of Dundee were sufficiently numerous to form a trade guild; within a hundred years similar incorporations had been established in Edinburgh, Aberdeen, Perth, Stirling and Glasgow (The Incorporation of Bonnetmakers and Dyers of Glasgow actually received their charter one

INTRODUCTION

hundred and one years after those of Dundee). The skill of knitting may have arrived in Shetland from the Continent or Scandinavia or from the north from Iceland or the Faroes, both countries having a well established export trade for knitted garments before 1600. 'Makkin', the Shetland dialect word for knitting, comes from the Norn verb 'mak', defined by Jakob Jakobsen as 'to knit woollen yarn'. This may indicate a Scandinavian origin. Unfortunately, there is insufficient evidence to accurately determine the origins of knitting in Shetland.

The earliest documented references to woollen stockings in Shetland are to be found in the *Court Book of Shetland 1615-1629*. Here three separate references are made to the theft of 'sockis' between the years 1615 and 1625; mittens and garters are also mentioned. However, although it is clear that these items were made from wool and were most likely knitted, there is no specific mention of knitting. The first direct reference to stockings being constructed by knitting is found in an early seventeenth century manuscript by Richard James, an Anglican priest. Accompanying Sir Dudley Diggs on an embassy to Russia in 1618, James visited Shetland and described the women as "...given to knitting mittens and stockings which the Hollanders and English do buy for rarity".[6] It is likely that the skill of knitting had been established well before this date, as for example David Bremner in his *Industries of Scotland*, in 1869, stated that "...upwards of three centuries ago, Scottish peasants were knitting hose".[7] However, as there is a total absence of evidence about its early development, no assertion can be made. Nor is there any documented evidence to indicate by which sea route knitting arrived in Shetland.

Mundane garments such as stockings, gloves, and caps made for everyday use by common people, disintegrate with wear or perish with age, leaving little or no trace for the historian to examine. Scotland is fortunate in having in the Royal Museum of Scotland, Edinburgh, a rare set of knitted woollen garments from a late seventeenth or early eighteenth century, which was found in Shetland. In 1951, in a shallow grave near the Lerwick-Hillswick road leading to Gunnister, in the parish of Northmavine, the body of a fully clothed young man was found preserved in a peat bog. One of the Swedish coins found in the man's purse has been dated to 1690, thus fixing the date of the man's death at around 1700. Gunnister Man had two brown woollen caps. The one found on his head was heavily felted and knitted in stocking stitch on four needles; the second cap was found wrapped round a horn spoon in the man's pocket. This cap, also constructed in stocking stitch, was slightly larger than the one found on Gunnister man's head, and had a looped pile in the inside and a tiny knitted loop on the crown (Fig. 1.4). His gloves were worked in brown wool in stocking and garter stitch, with lines of decorative stitches down the back of the hand, had no seams and showed considerable skill in their finger and thumb construction (Fig. 1.5). The stockings, 23ins (58cm.) from thigh to heel, with a foot length of 11ins. (27.5cm.), were worked in

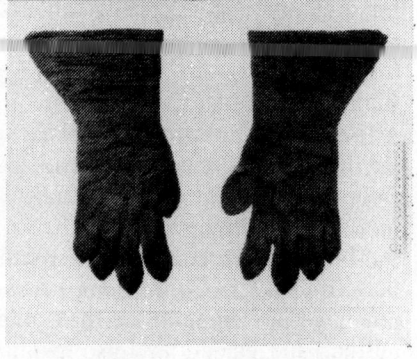

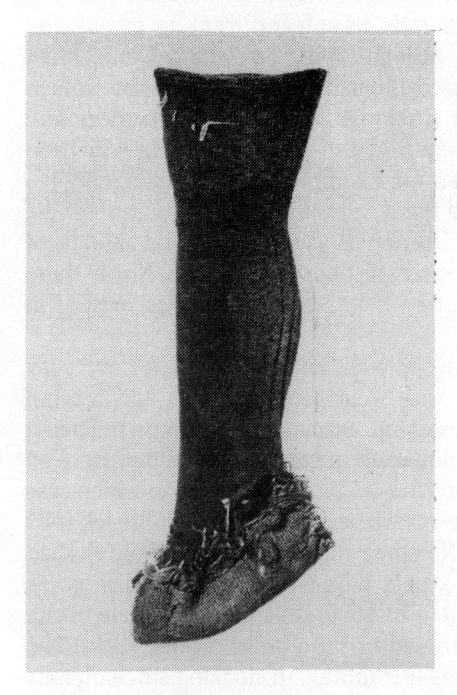

Above left, fig 1.4. Cap knitted with a looped pile on the inside, from Gunnister, late seventeenth century.
Above, fig 1.5 Gloves from the Gunnister burial.
Left, fig 1.6 Stocking from the Gunnister burial.
Below, fig 1.7 Purse from the Gunnister burial.
© *The Trustees of the National Museums of Scotland, 1994.*

garter and stocking stitch, except for the panels at the back and the clocks at the ankles, both knitted in moss stitch (Fig. 1.6). Gunnister Man's purse is multi-coloured and worked in the colour-stranded knitting now referred to as Fair Isle knitting (Fig. 1.7). The knitting is even and regular and obviously carried out by someone skilled in the understanding of the techniques of shaping, patterning and the construction of knitted woollen articles. It is not possible to tell if these garments were knitted in Shetland - the presence of foreign coins in the man's purse proves nothing about his origin but it does

INTRODUCTION

prove categorically that knitting had reached a high degree of sophistication and skill by the end of the seventeenth century and was seen in Shetland.

Early Traders

Although Gunnister Man's knitted garments cannot automatically be attributed to local knitters, it would seem most probable that this was the case, as a thriving stocking trade had been built up with visiting Hanseatic merchants and migrant Dutch and German fishermen. By the middle of June these fishing fleets had congregated in Bressay Sound, and a large fair was held on the 24th, St. John's Day, to which the local people would bring their goods to barter, the women having knitted in anticipation of this annual event. In exchange for fresh produce and knitted stockings and mitts, the Dutch would barter brandy, shoes, gin, tobacco and Dutch money. Likewise, the Hanseatic merchants set up their trading booths in advantageous locations rented from local land owners, and from which they traded with the local people. Martin Martin, writing c.1695 stated the importance of trade with visiting fishermen and merchants:

> The Hamburgers, Bremers, and others, come to this country about the middle of May, set up shops in several ports, and sell divers commodities, as linen, muslin and such things are most proper for the inhabitants, but more especially beer, brandy and bread, all of which they barter for fish, stockings, mutton, hens etc. and when the inhabitants ask money for their goods, they receive it immediately.[8]

Brand, who visited Shetland in 1700 as one of a commission of ministers sent by the General Assembly of the Church of Scotland to examine the state of the Church in the north, gave an interesting insight into the hand knitting industry and its place in the islands' economy at that time:

> The Hollanders also repair to these waters in June... for their herring fishing, but they cannot be said so properly to trade with the country, as to fish upon their coasts, and they use to bring all sorts of provisions necessary with them, save some fresh victuals as sheep, lambs, hens etc. which they buy on shore. Stockings also are brought by the country people from all quarters to Lerwick and sold to these fishers, for sometimes many thousands of them will be ashore at one time, and ordinary it is with them to buy stockings to themselves and some likewise to their wives and children; which is very beneficial to the inhabitants for so money is brought into the country, there is vent for the wool, and the poor are employed. Stockings also are brought from Orkney, and sold there, whereby some gain accrues to the retailers, who wait the coming of the Dutch Fleet for a market.[9]

Under the direction of the Hanseatic merchants Shetland enjoyed a relatively stable and prosperous economy. This period of Hanseatic trade domination lasted from c.1500 to the beginning of the eighteenth century, when two separate events severely disrupted the status quo and had a catastrophic effect on Shetland life and trade. These two events were, the burning of the Dutch Fleet in Shetland waters by the French in 1703 and, the introduction of a tax on foreign salt in 1712.

The burning of the Dutch Fleet in Shetland waters, regarded by Dr. Hance Smith (author of *Shetland Life and Trade 1550-1914*) as one of the most important contributory causes to the decline in the economy and the poverty of the lower classes in the 1700s, caused a temporary cessation in, but not the total extinction of, the lucrative visiting market created by the Dutch fishers. Thomas Gifford of Busta stated that:

> These Dutchmen used formerly to buy a considerable quantity of coarse stockings from the country people for ready money at tolerable good prices, by which means a good deal of foreign money was annually imported, which enabled the inhabitants to pay the land rent, and to purchase the necessaries of life; but for several years past that trade has failed, few or none of those busses coming, and those that come if they buy a few stockings, it is a very low price, whereby the country people are becoming exceedingly poor, and unable to pay the land rent.[10]

However, by 1774, the trade was obviously thriving again:

> The whole time the fleet lay the country people flocked to Lerwick with loads of coarse stockings, gloves, night caps, rugs and a very few articles of fresh provisions. Several thousand pounds are annually drawn for the first article, tho' a pair of stockings seldom sells for more than 6d. or 8d. I don't say but they make finer stockings than these, having been informed of a pair of stockings made in Lerwick and sold at 36sh. ster., but the most valuable for the country in general, and the most profitable, are the coarse ones, of one very thick thread, which consumes a great deal of wool, but requires not a great deal of labour. The country folks are very smart in their bargains with the Dutch; they are now paid in money for everything, no such thing as formerly trucking one commodity for another...[11]

Of even greater long term consequence was the introduction of the tax on foreign salt in 1712 which, backed up by the promise of a bounty on all fish cured with British salt and by British merchants, was designed to break the monopoly of foreigners fishing in British waters. Its effect was to reduce drastically the number of foreign fishermen and traders, and in Shetland, to force local landowners to fill the economic vacuum left by them. To this end many were forced not only to take over the role of fish curers but also to take over the role of these visiting merchants as exporters of the country's produce and importers of their needs.

Extensive details of this transition from landowner to merchant-laird, were given by Thomas Gifford in 1733:

> Commodities yearly exported are fat well-dried cod, ling, tusk and saith fish, some stock fish and salted herrings, butter, fish oil, stockings and worsted stuffs to foreign markets; and wool, horses, and skins coast-wise to Orkney and Scotland. For the exporting of fish, butter and oil which is the principal product of Zetland, there used formerly ten or twelve small ships to come here annually from Hamburg and Bremen, and these Hamburg and Bremen merchants had their booths in the most convenient places, where they received the fish, butter and oil from the country people ... These foreigners did yearly import hemp, lines, hooks, tar, linen-cloth, tobacco, spirits and beer, for the fishers, and foreign money wherewith they purchased their cargoes. But when the high duty was laid upon foreign salt, and custom house officers sent over, and a custom house settled at Lerwick, these foreigners could not enter, and so the inhabitants, and many of the heritors or landlords, were obliged to turn merchants and export the country product to foreign markets, and had in return for money and such other necessaries as the country could not subsist without.[12]

INTRODUCTION

By comparison to these Hanseatic merchants, the new merchant-landowners now directing Shetland trade were amateurs, with only a few, like Thomas Gifford of Busta and John Bruce of Symbister, meeting with success in their trading ventures. Initially it was possible for them to keep their land and fishing interests separate. However, as the combined adverse circumstances of famine, war, smallpox epidemics, coupled to their own lack of commercial expertise, took its toll, it became increasingly difficult to separate the two functions. And it was from this fusion of land and fishing interests that the fishing-tenures and truck system arose, which lasted until the end of the nineteenth century.

Fishing Tenures

During the eighteenth century Shetland suffered from many poor harvests both at sea and on the land, causing widespread hardship and destitution; a situation which led to an accumulation of unpaid rents and extended credits, and one which was undoubtedly aggravated by the absence of foreign buyers. As the landlord's returns from their land diminished, they turned to fishing, the cornerstone of the Shetland economy, to make good their losses. To this end, they contracted with their tenants to buy their catch and increased the number of their fishermen-tenants by encouraging early marriages by the offer of land, and to accommodate this increase in population, split crofts into outsets*. Even allowing for the introduction of the potato around 1750 which enabled the land to support a larger number of people than the traditional crops of bere, barley, oats, turnips and cabbage, crofts became so small that they could no longer adequately support their occupants. Fishermen-tenants fell heavily into their landlord's debt, so that this system, instead of benefiting the landlord, led to the social and economic bond between him and his tenant tightening. Unwittingly, both had become victims of this system, named by some commentators the 'Shetland Method'.

This increase in population did enlarge the laird's fishing crews, but it also put the islands' scant food resources under great strain; what benefit the laird may have gained from larger catches, was more than wiped out by the heavy burden of an increased number of near-destitute people looking to him for support. Ill feeling between the two arose as families fell deeper into debt. It was the laird who set the price paid for wet fish, but it was also the laird, through whose stores the fishermen were paid, who set the price of goods and provisions. The fisherman and his family had become trucked to his laird, with apparently no legitimate means of breaking free from this trap. One possible solution was the clandestine sale of fish to other merchants. This practice was much frowned on by lairds, who felt that their tenants had a moral obligation to sell their fish to the laird who provided them with credit in times of need and who supported the poor who were unable to pay him; "whereby," as Thomas Gifford forcibly pointed out, "a considerable part of my Stock is sunk".[13]

Prolonged periods of famine led to the balance between subsistence and destitution becoming more precarious. After the crop failures of 1782 and 1783, many landowners went bankrupt, whilst others turned to landless merchants, engaging them to manage their business affairs. By the 1770s, the landless merchants had begun to emerge as a new and separate class between the laird and his tenant.

Shetland Stocking Trade

Throughout this bleak period in Shetland's history there is no doubt that fish remained the dominant force in the islands' economy, as Customs Quarterly Returns for the Port of Lerwick and other sources show. It is difficult, if not impossible, to gauge the economic importance of the hosiery trade during this period. This is due to the total paucity of accurate records for hosiery exports and to the difficulties of assessing the quantity of hosiery sold casually to migrant fishermen and merchants. Hance Smith described the trade in hose before 1790 as very much incidental to that of fish, fish oil, butter and kelp, although Custom's Quarterly Returns show that from 1742 to 1790, between 11,000 and 23,000 pairs of woollen stockings were exported annually. Court of Session productions show that Shetland hose were being exported to Edinburgh, Hamburg, Spain, Lisbon, Madeira, Antigua, Barbados and Virginia. The earliest record of the export value of Shetland hosiery was made by Sir John Sinclair in 1767, when he estimated its value to be £1,650. His estimate of fish exports was £11,375, making hosiery equivalent to one seventh of the value of the fish exported. In the absence of data explaining how Sir John arrived at this estimate for hosiery exports, it is difficult to gauge its accuracy.

By the second half of the eighteenth century, there seems to have been a marked deterioration in the standard of knitted hose - many of the ministers' entries in the Old Statistical Account decry this manufacture as a miserable mis-spending of time and waste of wool. Standards had dropped so low that attempts were made by the Commissioners of Supply to introduce a branding system to improve the quality. Thomas Mouat of Unst, landowner and himself a Commissioner of Supply, was much involved in this scheme, in which he had a considerable vested interest, as in 1779 stockings were being accepted as currency for payment of rent and duties. This use of stockings as a medium for rent payment was undoubtedly forced upon the landlord in the absence of money which had in the past usually been obtained from the sale of stockings and fresh produce with visiting merchants and fishermen.

This deterioration in quality was felt to be so widespread, that an assessor was to be appointed by the Commissioner of Supply to ensure that regulations concerning stockings were published in every parish in Shetland. The following is an extract from the instructions which were sent to the Stamper of Woollen Stockings in the South Parish of Unst in 1779:

All stockings presented to you for stamping you are to compare in size and shape with

INTRODUCTION

the Wooden Patterns now delivered you, and all such as agree nearly either with the pattern for Men, Women, or Childrens stockings and are knit of one sort of wool, worsted or equal size, free from left loops, hanging hairs, bunt cuts or mended holes you are to stamp near the brow...[14]

Many other details were included in these instructions. It was an expensive scheme to set up and operate, and this alone may give some indication of the importance of knitted hose to the Shetland economy. Prior to this event, no attention had been given to the improvement of the woollen industry.

By the end of the eighteenth century, Lerwick had become the established centre of the Shetland stocking trade, the quality of knitted hose had deteriorated (although fine knitted stockings could still be obtained) and hand knitting was used for producing family clothes, supplementing the domestic-subsistence economy, as a form of currency for rent payment and as an export commodity both to foreign and British markets. It was from the importance of this stocking or hosiery industry that the term Shetland hosiery is derived. It is used in Shetland to cover all types of knitwear, not just knitted hose.

References - Chapter 1

1 Smith, P., *Wool Knowledge*, Winter 1958. 'Shetland sheep and Shetland's wool industries', part 1, p. 4.
2 Wheeler, *Geographical Field Group Regional Study, No. 11, Isle of Unst*, (1964), appendix to chapter 3.
3 Loch, David, *Essays on the trade, commerce, manufactures, and fisheries of Scotland*, (Edinburgh 1778), Vol. 1, p. 9.
4 Edmondston, A., *A View of the ancient and present state of the Zetland Islands*, (Edinburgh 1809), Vol. I, p. 222.
5 Bremner, D., *Industries of Scotland*, (Edinburgh 1869), p. 172.
6 Bodleian Library, Oxford. MS.43**, fol. 1 (v), entitled 'Fragments of a book of travels giving an account of Poland, the Shetland and Orkney Islands, Scotland, Greenland etc'.
7 Bremner, D., *Industries of Scotland*, (Edinburgh 1869), p. 173.
8 Martin, Martin, *A Description of the Western Islands of Scotland*, (1703), p. 385.
9 Brand, J., *A New Description of Orkney, Zetland, Pightland Firth and Caithness*, (Edinburgh 1703), p. 131.
10 Gifford, Thomas, *An Historical Description of the Zetland islands*, (London 1786), Thule Print 1976 edition, p. 6.
11 Low, G, *A Tour through Orkney and Schetland*, (Kirkwall, 1879), p. 67.
12 Gifford, Thomas, *An Historical Description of the Zetland Islands*, (London 1786), Thule Print 1976 edition, p. 28.
13 Reid Tait, E.S. (ed.), *The Hjaltland Miscellany*, iv (1947), p. 111-113.
14 O'Dell, A.C., *Historical Geography of the Shetland Islands*, (Lerwick 1939), p. 157.

Chapter 2

The Shetland Method 1790-1872

The Old Statistical Account (OSA), masterminded and compiled by Sir John Sinclair, and written by the parish ministers between the years 1791 and 1799, is an invaluable source of information on life in Scotland at that time. Even allowing for a possibly biased and intolerant outlook from the manse, it is possible to piece together a fairly accurate picture of the contemporary attitudes towards agricultural improvements and religious matters, the state of education, living conditions, as well as employment and trade openings, in Shetland during the last decades of the eighteenth century.

Although most ministers bemoaned the lack of manufacturing industries throughout the islands, they seem to have been more concerned with their congregations' spiritual rather than temporal well-being, as, for example, no attempts had been made by the Established Church to alleviate distress during the terrible starvation years of the early 1780s when "people lived mostly on whelks, limpets and such other shell-fish as the sea-shore afforded"[1] and government meal cargoes had to be sent to prevent mass starvation. In fact, the accounts, written within approximately 10 years of this period of destitution, are devoid of compassion, with few ministers seemingly even aware of the extent of human suffering in their midst, and indeed, one minister, the Rev. John Mill of Dunrossness, complaining of the unsuitability of being asked to oversee the distribution of charity meal in his parish. Unlike the Roman Catholic Church's policy in Ireland, neither the Established Church nor the Free Church - formed after the Disruption of 1843 and noted in many areas for its relief work - seem to have felt any responsibility to help innovate schemes to alleviate distress by creating employment.

This whole problem of destitution and lack of employment, was greatly aggravated by a 34% increase in the population from 15,210 in 1755 to 20,451 by 1790 - an increase considerably in excess of that in any other Highland county. This increase was generally regarded as being the result of the early marriages, and splitting of outsets favoured by landowners, and as the Rev. John Menzies pointed out :

> In most countries, the increase of population is reckoned an advantage, and justly. It is, however, the reverse in the present state of Shetland. Were manufacturers established here, to employ the people, and enable them to procure a comfortable subsistence, their increased numbers would be pleasing to every patriotic mind; but it is believed, that there is at present, in these islands, double the number of people they can properly maintain.[2]

The lack of manufacturing industries, mentioned in the OSA by all ministers, was of critical importance to Shetland at the turn of the century, with its escalating social and economic problems, caused by rising population, destitution, changing trading patterns and trade disruptions. The importance of the knitting industry was pointed out by the Rev. James Sands of Lerwick: "The only manufacture, carried on in the parish, is the knitting of woollen stockings, and in this almost all the women are more or less engaged".[3] Several ministers pointed out the stupidity of earlier attempts at establishing a linen industry, stating for example:

> A linen manufacture was surely improper as a first attempt to introduce manufactures into this country... The same sum expended in establishing a woollen manufacture would have employed many a hand which is now idle, or employed in destroying materials, which ought to be turned to a more profitable account.[4]

Following the creation of the Board of Manufactures - set up after the 1707 Treaty of Union - many schemes promoting the linen industry were to be found throughout Scotland, schemes which were regarded by David Loch, the ardent protagonist of the Scottish woollen industry, as "unnatural and absurd" compared to the "superior advantages of woollen manufacture over that of linen".[5]

The above reference to "destroying materials", whilst mentioned by several ministers, is unsubstantiated by others. However, it is clear from contemporary writers, that around this time, the standard of knitted stockings had deteriorated. Conflicting reports, make it difficult to assess the extent of this deterioration. For example, the ministers of Aithsting, Delting, and Yell were unanimous in decrying the quality of knitted stockings, whilst those from Tingwall and Unst, referred to them as a 'lucrative stocking trade'.[6] By the time the OSA was written, Tingwall stockings were of sufficiently high quality to be marketed in Edinburgh and this trade was attributed to "the patriotic and benevolent exertions of Sir John Sinclair".[7] If the volume of correspondence between Sir John and Thomas Mouat of Unst on wool matters can be taken as a guide, it would suggest that it was also Sir John who was responsible for introducing Unst stockings to the Edinburgh market. From this, it may be assumed that the quality of the coarse stockings manufactured by the less skilled had deteriorated as the number of Dutch fishers dwindled, whilst the more skilled knitter had turned her attention to the knitting of finer goods for coastwise exportation to the Scottish market.

This then was the picture painted by the OSA of Shetland life and trade at the end of the eighteenth century, with knitting and agricultural work presenting themselves as the main means of employment for women, both modes of employment being no more than subsistence activities.

Role of Women

Employment opportunities within Shetland for women throughout this period were limited. In 1802 a straw plaiting industry had been set up in Lerwick by a London company but had ceased to function some time in the

1820s. This company, initially employing 90 girls in Lerwick, opened another branch in Dunrossness. Straw was imported from Dunstable and workers paid on a piece rate basis of 1d. per yard of plaited straw. Another separate factory was started a few years later in Lerwick, so that by 1809 approximately 180 to 200 girls were being employed daily - a very small number compared to neighbouring Orkney where straw plaiting occupied upwards of 4,000 girls, women and old men. Like the linen spinning industry of the previous century, this too failed. The inherent weakness in both these industries lay in their dependence on the importation of the basic raw material, and their subsequent vulnerability to disruption, whether by stormy weather, wars or even smuggling.

However, unlike the straw plaiting industry, the kelp industry, established in Shetland c.1780, benefited considerably from the trade disruptions caused by the Napoleonic wars, as Spanish barilla, preferred by manufacturers to kelp, was cut off by wartime blockades. Kelp, the residue left after the burning of seaweed, was used as a source of alkali in the bleaching trade, and in the production of glass, iodine and soap. This dirty and tedious process employed many women and children in the cutting, gathering and burning of tangle weed. Production, and with it prices, continued to rise until the bottom fell out of the market with the re-introduction of Spanish barilla and pot ashes in the 1820s. Kelp burning continued to provide a limited amount of employment throughout this period, but never regained its former economic significance. Shetland landlords had never exploited or depended on their 'golden fringe' to the same extent as their counterparts in the Western Isles, as for example whilst the Hebrides were exporting between 15,000 to 20,000 tons of kelp annually at the beginning of the nineteenth century, Shetland kelp exports amounted only to 500 tons, and therefore the dwindling economic importance of the industry was less severely felt.

Domestic service was a possible source of employment for women, but in Shetland, with its dearth of well-to-do people, such opportunities were limited. Domestic employment in Shetland often involved working on the land as well as indoors, and like fishing, could therefore be seasonal; many unmarried women gained temporary employment in this manner during the summer months. Old women were employed to carry peat from the hills to Lerwick, combining this work with stocking knitting - see fig. 2.1. This phenomenon was often commented on by visitors, as for example, James Wilson, a wealthy amateur scientist, visiting Shetland in 1841, recorded in his diary, that when returning from Fort Charlotte in Lerwick, he passed:

...droves of women proceeding on their never-ceasing journey to the mosses in the hills for peats, with their cassies or straw baskets on their backs, and knitting eagerly with both their hands...[8]

Others, like 'Baabie' engaged by Hay & Co., made a scratch living acting as messengers, or by hawking or simply by begging. The entries in the Poor Roll of Lerwick in 1843 make it clear that many relied on regular charity from the better off. For example, a Mrs Greirson's name recurs as giving charity to at

Fig 2.1 – Women knit whilst carrying kishies of peat c.1900. Photo: Thomas Kent

least nine different people, whilst other entries state 'assisted by a lady in Edinburgh', by Mrs Hunter, Miss Irvine etc.

The fishing industry required women packers and gutters, working in teams of three, during the fishing season which ran from May to September, although unlike the fish wives of the Western Isles, Shetland women did not follow the fishing fleets to other parts of the country and were wholly Shetland based.

The comprehensive role of women in Shetland was summed up in the OSA by the Rev. William Jack of Northmavine:

> The women look after domestic concerns, bring up their children, cook the victuals, look after cattle, spin and knit stockings; they also assist, and are no less laborious than the men in manuring and labouring the grounds, reaping the harvest and manufacturing their crop.[9]

In any seafaring community, where the men were absent for long periods, whether at the fishing or whaling, or in the merchant or royal navy, women had to shoulder the responsibilities which normally fell to men, in addition to coping with their own homemaking and domestic roles, and their biological function, as bearers of the next generation. As in other seafaring communities, like Peterhead in the north east of Scotland or Staithes in the north east of England, Shetland men expected their women to undertake this multiplicity of tasks as a matter of course. Given their traditional role of head of the household and breadwinner, Shetland men enjoyed this superior status, regardless of the burdens which fell to women. For example, Sir Walter Scott, when visiting Shetland in 1814, noted in his diary that.

> The women are rather slavishly employed, however, and I saw more than one carrying home the heavy sea-chests of their husbands, brothers, or lovers, discharged from on board the Greenlanders.[10]

In Shetland, where the family was dependent on the produce of the croft for subsistence, these burdens were considerable, as they included the vital farm work normally done by men in inland crofting areas. It has often been noted that Shetland women were better workers than men, who whenever they returned from the sea, felt that their labours were over and did little to help in the home or on the land, even when they were idle during the winter months. These facts were noted in 'The Third Report on Highland Destitution' in 1849, which stated:

> ...the moment the boat touches the beach the fisherman considers himself a privileged being, exempt from the ordinary lot of humanity, and nearly the whole labour of cultivating the farms is devolved upon the women, who as one of the Sappers remarked, with regard to their efforts in road-making, "The women, Sir, are the best men in Shetland".[11]

It was also the custom for Shetland women, married or otherwise, to supply themselves with clothes from their own handiwork. Fig. 2.2 shows the typical dress of Shetland women and the knitted caps and surtouts of untanned hide worn by Shetland men - the woman is of course knitting.

The constant demands of the croft and family, meant that for married women or women with dependents, employment outwith the home was not feasible. Knitting fitted in with the rhythm of this way of life, particularly as it

Fig 2.2 – Costume of the Shetland fishermen and women c.1822.

complemented rather than interfered with croft work, and was therefore the obvious choice as a spare-time/part-time occupation. For example, the following statement taken from Edward Standen's short treatise on the Shetland Islands reinforces the compatibility of knitting and crofting:

> The Shetland woman knits from childhood: her ball of worsted and wires accompany her everywhere - into the fields, to be taken up at intervals of rest: even during hard work she plies her industrious fingers, for she may be met on the hill-side with a heavy burden on her shoulders, bending beneath the weight, but still knitting.[12]

Removed as they were from industrial centres offering steady full-time employment, pluralism of employment was essential and the norm for most people and as the Rev. Patrick Barclay of Unst, pointed out "nobody can earn 'bread' by any one occupation alone...except the minister".[13] Thus knitting, lending itself to be lifted and laid as time permitted, was ideally suited for married women, women with dependants, widows or spinsters, as a subsistence activity.

The Shetland Hand Knitting Industry

The Industrial Revolution of the late eighteenth century made little impact on the hand knitting industry in Shetland, which remained a home-based cottage industry whose workers knitted as individuals, or as part of a family unit, using their own home-grown yarn, and relied primarily on the annual visits of the Dutch and other migrant fishers for the marketing of their products. Apart from attempts to improve the quality of stockings knitted as part payment of rent, and despite the Highland Society's report on the Shetland woollen industry published in 1790, little attention had been given to the organisation and development of this industry by the Shetland merchant-laird or other entrepreneur, until about the 1830s, by which time the demand for stockings had fallen off considerably, with knitters still relying on visiting Dutch fishermen - greatly reduced in numbers - for their main transactions. This lack of organisation was in sharp contrast to Aberdeenshire, regarded as the most important centre of the stocking trade in the north east during the seventeenth and eighteenth centuries. Here agents travelled round the countryside, giving out yarn, specifying articles to be made, whilst at the same time, collecting completed orders. Unlike the Shetland hand knitting industry which used only locally produced wool, this trade was based on both local and imported wool. In 1757 the export value of the Aberdeen stocking trade was estimated to be £80,000 and had risen to £200,000 by 1784. However, this important industry went into decline c.1793, and never recovered from the trade disruptions caused by the Napoleonic Wars and the increasing competition from the stocking frame. Aberdeen changed over to the stocking frame, and thus became centred on the factory, and not the domestic putting-out system, taking the work out of the hands of many crofters and cottars, and denying them a small but valuable source of supplementary income. Interestingly, there is no documentation to suggest

THE SHETLAND METHOD 1790-1872

that stocking frames - invented in 1589 - ever reached the Shetland Islands then or later.

The earliest valuation of the Shetland hand knitting industry at £1,650 - this sum representing the export value of 50,000 pairs of stockings @ 6d. per pair, with rugs and fine stockings valued at £400 - was, however, a mere fraction of the export value of the Aberdeen stocking trade. Though the hand knitting industry had been described in the OSA as a miserable mispending of time, by 1797, the total annual production was estimated to be worth £17,000. Following this, the hosiery trade went through a prolonged period of recession, with its value falling to £5,000 by 1809. This was due to the interference to the Shetland trade with the Dutch and German fishermen caused by the Napoleonic wars; and to the great drop in demand for Shetland stockings all over Britain, which Edmondston (see below) attributed to the "uncommon degree of attention bestowed at present in these countries to increase the quality and improve the quantity of wool".[14] Unlike the Aberdeen stocking industry, the Shetland hand knitting industry survived by diversifying into new markets, so that by 1871, Cowie estimated its value to be between £10-12,000.

Very little detailed information on the hosiery industry is available from after the late 1790s to the 1830s, with only Dr. Arthur Edmondston's *A view of the ancient and present state of the Zetland Islands*, published in 1809, giving such scant information as the knitting of worsted stockings, caps and gloves being 'among the most ancient', and:

> Besides the sale to shipping, stockings are bartered to the shopkeepers, for such commodities as the people need; and like the wadmal of Iceland, form a principal article of exchange in the country,[15]

while Samuel Hibbert, writing in 1822, made only a brief reference to stockings ranging in price from 5d. or 6d. to half a guinea, the most common quality costing 3/- or 4/-. From around 1830 it is possible to discern the first signs of organisation in the industry and to trace its development and diversification to the present day. However, this dearth of information does not extend to other aspects of Shetland trade, aspects of trade which affected the hand knitting industry.

The changes in Shetland trade which took place around 1790 were much less clear-cut than those which had occurred as a result of the exodus of the Hanseatic merchants from 1712 onwards. Small, but significant, shifts in trade patterns began to occur as the new class of landless-merchant emerged, usurping the merchant-laird. Lerwick, founded as a trading post with the Dutch in the seventeenth century, was now firmly established as Shetland's main port, trade and distribution centre, and underwent considerable expansion between 1790 and the early 1800s. Timber, imported from Norway for boat building , was now also being used to build lodberries* and merchants' houses in Lerwick. This was also a time of great mercantile expansion with merchants acquiring ship owning interests or co-operating in chartering ships for the export of fish cargoes - the number of trading vessels registered at Lerwick increased sharply during this period. However, the key factor to these merchants' successful expansion lay in their agency work as import-export agents, that is, exporting fish and other commodities from the islands, and importing general commodities in conjunction with British merchant houses. In addition to this, agency work for the Greenland whaleship owners, proved a lucrative source of income for many merchants, enabling them to expand the retailing side of their business. As Hance Smith pointed out "The period from around 1790 until 1820 was the era of the individual merchant engaging in as many branches of trade as possible".[16] Thus, although the sale and movement of fish dominated and directed Shetland trading activities, hosiery, locally produced from native wool, was an item which increased trade openings could turn to some profit.

From c.1820, the number of small merchants dealing in more or less every item the community required rose both in Lerwick and in country districts. The extent of the general merchants' business can be gauged from a respondent giving evidence to the Poor Law Enquiry of 1843:

> Shetland business consists of everything a man can make profit by. The merchants here do not confine themselves to any particular branch of business.[17]

This is borne out by Duncan's 1854 *Zetland Trade Directory* listing no less than 141 merchants in the islands, with 52 of them centred in Lerwick. So that, whilst fish was still the main export throughout this period, other commodities such as hosiery, fish oil, kelp etc. were also being exported, with imports consisting of fishing materials, grain, woollen and linen goods, tea and spirits. For those of better station household stores were imported from Leith and Hamburg. As trade with Spain and other continental countries became disrupted by the Napoleonic Wars, it was superseded by coastwise trading, with Leith continuing to act as Shetland's main port of communication with Scotland.

This increase in coastwise trading gradually led to more regular and improved communications with Scotland and was a key factor in the development of the hand knitting industry. For example, Laurence Laurenson, the first to open an outfitter-cum-hosiery store in Lerwick, did so in 1818. He was followed by Robert Linklater in 1835, whose business dealings were so successful that he opened a second shop in Lerwick and a large retail establishment in Princes Street, Edinburgh. From 1832, when the first steamer arrived in Shetland, sailing ships began to be replaced by the more reliable and faster steam ships. By 1838 Shetland had a regular weekly service with Leith during the summer. This service also carried mails. In 1839 a regular service with the North Isles, that is Unst, Yell and Fetlar, was inaugurated, allowing them greater trading participation with Mainland Shetland and Britain. The following year the penny post was introduced throughout Britain - a service which allowed hosiery merchants to expand their markets in the south. By 1840 another large specialist hosiers - Robert

Sinclair & Co. - had opened in Lerwick, whilst many small general stores both in Lerwick and throughout the islands, were also dealing in hosiery. This increase in communications with the outside world, particularly the greater comfort of steamer travel, opened up the Highlands and Islands to tourists. Shetland, popularised by Sir Walter Scott's *Pirate*, was no exception, and enjoyed an influx of well-to-do, leisured visitors during the summer months who were anxious to return home with locally produced knitwear, particularly, the beautiful and prestigious Shetland lace shawls.

In 1842 the collapse of Hay & Ogilvy, Shetland's biggest company, and the Shetland Banking Co. - a provincial bank owned largely by the same firm - brought widespread unemployment, hardship and destitution. These bankruptcies, precipitated by three bad harvests between 1835 and 1839, successive poor fishing seasons, and a catastrophic gale in 1840 from which the fishing industry never fully recovered, led to widespread unemployment, destitution and hardship. Virtually the whole community was affected by the collapse of the islands' biggest single employer. The earlier collapse of the kelp industry exacerbated this situation; thousands found themselves out of work with no money. Fishing boats lay idle as men could not raise the cash to buy lines or gear. Many who could, joined the merchant navy, whilst young single men emigrated. The old, the infirm and unemployed were left to manage as best they could. This disastrous situation was further aggravated by Shetland's first clearances for sheep walks in Upper Weisdale, in the Parish of Delting. Knitting, the old standby, had become even more important to the domestic subsistence economy, with unemployed men relying increasingly on the earnings of their wives and daughters. The Poor Law Inquiry held in Shetland at this time, illustrated the extent to which women relied on knitting to eke out their pittance. For example, Agnes Coutts, a 71 year old widow, supplemented her monthly allowance of 1/6d. from the Poor Roll by knitting; Grizel Brown earned 4d. a week knitting stockings; whilst, Catherine Green, who supported her paralysed sister, did so by knitting and taking in lodgers, charging them 1d. per night. By 1861, when Shetland population figures peaked at 31,670, there were no less than 142.6 women to each 100 men recorded, which even allowing for the absence at sea of many men, still left a considerable surplus of women without a partner to help support them (see fig. 2.3). This surplus, called 'Shetland housewives', with little opportunity of gaining employment, had few resources but their own handiwork.

1790 to 1872 was arguably the most important period in the organisation and development of the Shetland hand knitting industry. During a period when other cottage industries, like the hand knitting industries of the Dales and Cumbria, were dying, the Shetland hand knitting industry expanded, with knitters successfully making the transition from coarse stockings to finer ones, and diversifying into knitted lace to meet fashion demands, whilst increasing their output of underwear, traditionally produced for home use, capitalising on "the notion gaining ground that woollen under-clothing is

KNITTING BY THE FIRESIDE

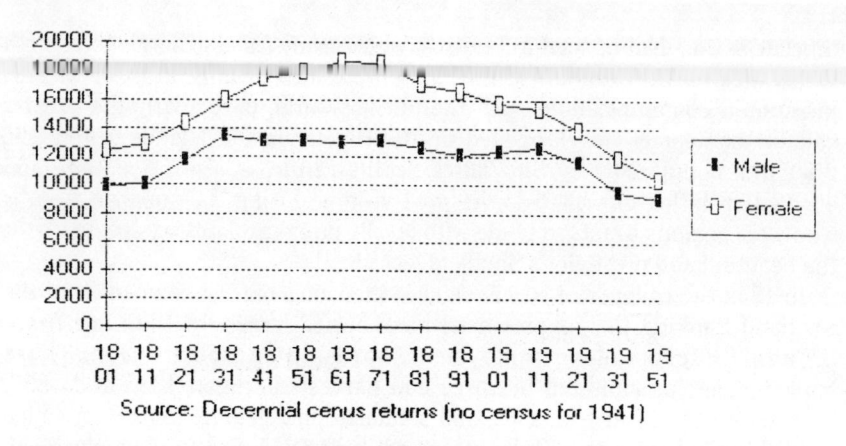

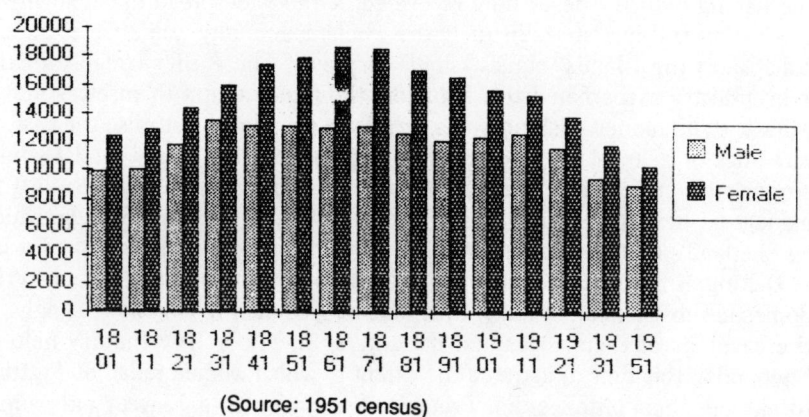

Fig 2.3 – Shetland population statistics from 1801-1951 showing the marked imbalance in the sexes.

more suited than any other for our variable climate".[18] The transition had been so successful that by the end of the period, each district had established its own speciality in the hosiery line, with Northmavine producing soft underclothing; Nesting, stockings; Walls and Sandsting, socks and haps; Whiteness and Weisdale, fancy coloured gloves; Lerwick and Unst, shawls, veils etc.

Organisation of Labour

Lack of documentation makes it impossible to ascribe the first attempts to organise the hosiery industry to any specific person or even date. However, as Laurenson & Co., was the first firm to set up in the hosiery business as "Shetland Warehousemen and Clothiers" in Lerwick in 1818, it would seem most likely that it was this firm which pioneered the organisation of the Shetland hand knitting industry. The flow chart - fig. 2.4 - shows the basic lines along which the industry had developed by c.1870, with the Lerwick hosiery merchants dominating the scene. Compared to the rigidly structured

THE SHETLAND METHOD 1790-1872

factory-based system of outworkers and agents operating, for example, with the Ayrshire tambourers* - where patterns, rates of pay and time allowed for the work were lithographed on to pieces of material and distributed from a central source by agents who also collected in the finished work - the organisation of the Shetland hand knitting industry was casual to the point of disorganisation, using neither patterns nor agents for their hosiery.

The Shetland hand knitting industry c.1872

Worsted from **wool dealers**.

wool from **crofters agents wool dealers**

Wool sent to **spinner** and returned as worsted.

SHETLAND HOSIERY MERCHANT

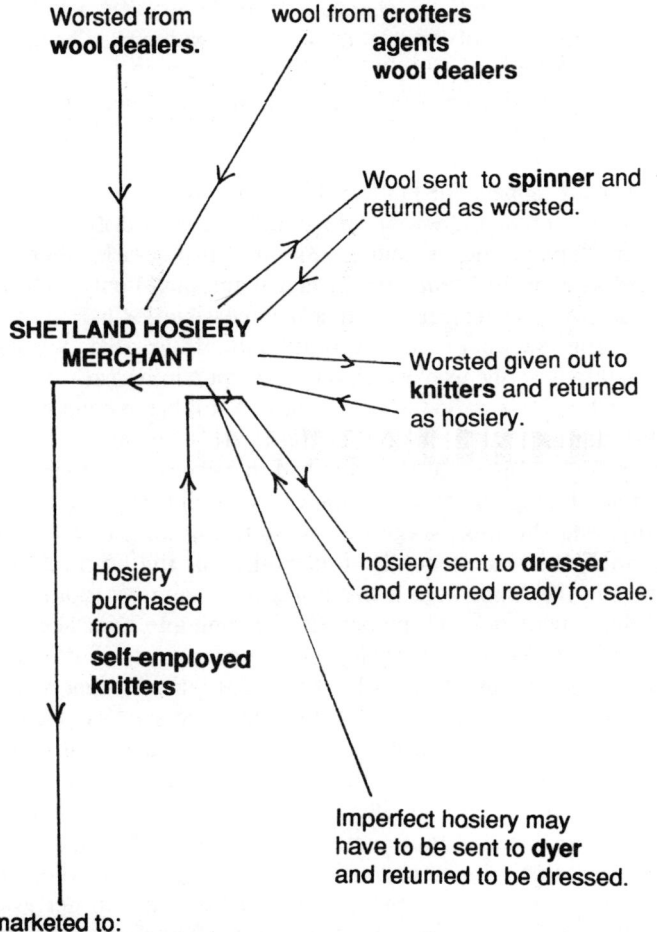

Worsted given out to **knitters** and returned as hosiery.

Hosiery purchased from **self-employed knitters**

hosiery sent to **dresser** and returned ready for sale.

Imperfect hosiery may have to be sent to **dyer** and returned to be dressed.

Hosiery marketed to:
   private people / tourists
   by consignment in the south

N.B. A small minority of knitters marketed their hosiery independent of Shetland merchants.

Fig 2.4 Structure of the Shetland hand knitting industry c.1872

Wool and Worsted

The first stage in the production of Shetland hosiery was to obtain the raw wool, the best and most plentiful supplies coming from the north isles. The crofter-knitter with her own sheep was in an advantageous position. For merchants and knitters without their own sheep, wool could be obtained direct from the crofter, from farmers, wool merchants, women who bought and slaughtered sheep, selling the wool and mutton separately, from country merchants in the north who did not deal in hosiery but bought wool for resale to knitters or to Lerwick merchants, or wool dealers who bought up wool on a large scale throughout the islands for resale within Shetland. In addition to these arrangements, the larger hosiery merchants in Lerwick had their own agents in the north isles buying up wool for them. These agents were usually small merchants running a general store in country districts. Because of its scarcity, Shetland wool was always in great demand and difficult to obtain without ready money. The knitter without her own wool, and no ready money, had problems obtaining wool or worsted. In country districts, she could work as a farm servant and be paid in wool, but in Lerwick, where worsted was regarded as a 'money item', that is, merchants would only sell it for cash, not exchange it for hosiery, it was almost impossible for her to obtain wool or worsted. The raw wool then had to be spun into worsted - worsted being the term used to describe wool which has been spun into yarn.

Throughout this period, native wool was still being hand carded and spun on the islands, that is, mainly in the north isles and in Lerwick. Before spinning could commence, the wool had to be sorted or graded, the fine wool being sold at a higher value, and the coarse wool being kept for domestic use. Carding was the next stage before spinning and, in a crofter-knitter's household, this was generally undertaken in the evening by the female members of the family unit. It was tiring, dirty work occasionally lightened by help from neighbours and the occasion turning into a social called 'a cardin'. Finally spinning, an exclusively female occupation, was usually undertaken by the older members of a family who, being less active, had more unbroken time to sit at it. Outwith the family unit, spinners were employed by private people and by merchants on a domestic, 'putting out' basis, and were paid in cash or in goods at wholesale prices. For example, Margaret Clunas, a native of Unst, was a self-employed spinner, who bought wool from her crofting neighbours, spun the wool and sold the worsted at 3d. a cut to Mr Jamieson, merchant in Unst, and was paid in 'money articles' - that is goods at wholesale prices or provisions not available normally to trucked workers. In her evidence given before the 1872 Truck Inquiry, Margaret Clunas stated that spinning paid better than knitting. Thus, although spinning was more fatiguing than knitting, because of the constant demand for their skills and the better pay, being paid in cash or goods at wholesale prices, spinners were in a superior position to knitters, and less likely to fall victims to the truck system.

The use of imported yarns such as alpaca, mohair, Pyrenees, Bradford and

Scotch by local merchants became increasingly common from around 1840. This departure from the exclusive use of local wool can be attributed to several factors - the expansion in the Shetland hosiery trade, the scarcity of native wool as a result of sheep scab, and the greater availability of alternative yarns because of the general expansion in trading with Scotland - made easier by the new regular steamer service - and the rise in advertising through trade journals such as Duncan's *Zetland Trade Directory*.

Hand Knitters

At the manufacturing centre of the whole industry lay the hand knitters. Hand knitting in Shetland has always been an almost exclusively female occupation; the very few males who did knit being regarded as "scornfully effeminate".[19] In his evidence to the 1871 Truck Commission held in Edinburgh, George Smith, Sheriff Clerk and Clerk of Supply in Shetland, estimated that four-fifths of the female population were engaged in this industry and suggested that the number of knitters listed in the census returns accounted only for those to whom knitting was their sole means of support. Census returns give unrealistically low figures; the 1861 census gave 1,454 knitters, which is far too low considering that Robert Sinclair and Robert Linklater alone were each employing in excess of 300 knitters. But it is likely that George Smith's estimate of four-fifths is too high, and included women who knitted for family use only. It was generally agreed that census figures represented the 'town knitters', that is the knitters in Lerwick and Scalloway whose sole occupation was knitting. Added to this, it must be remembered that knitting was seasonal, being pursued with great vigour during the long, dark winter months but neglected during the demands of the growing season. Allowing for the fact that the very young and very old would not be knitting, for the absence of alternative employment and the economic pressure of hard times, a more realistic estimate would be that approximately two-thirds of the female population was involved to varying extents in hand knitting as an industry.

It is clear from the 1872 Truck Inquiry (from which the bulk of the structural information on the knitting industry in this chapter is based) that in this home-based industry knitters fell into two categories; that is self-employed, or employed by a merchant to knit with his worsted. It would be an exaggeration to describe the latter category as employees, as this term implies some regularity of employment, formal contract, set rates of pay etc., none of which existed in the Shetland hand knitting industry until well into the twentieth century.

A self-employed knitter was at liberty to sell her hosiery as she chose, and was generally anxious for sales with visiting merchants, private people and summer visitors rather than local hosiery merchants, as she felt that she got a better return for her work, but more importantly, received ready money for her hosiery. The self-employed knitter was generally a superior knitter to one employed by local merchants, and preferred by them, as they were at liberty to accept or refuse hosiery offered for sale, there having been no previous outlay of worsted. Self-employed knitters were not under contract to sell their hosiery to any one merchant, although it was generally felt that it was wiser to stick to one merchant to ensure future sales. This was a very different situation from fishermen-tenants who were trucked to the one merchant.

Of the 51 knitters examined by Sheriff Guthrie, Chief Commissioner of the 1872 Truck Inquiry, 26 were usually self-employed and only resorted to knitting for merchants when they had no worsted of their own. In this barter economy, where hosiery was paid for in 'soft goods' - that is, tea and haberdashery such as calico and flannel - obtaining wool or worsted was a continual problem as both these commodities had to be paid for in ready money. As well as this initial outlay, money was required for dressing hosiery - that is, washing and finishing of hosiery - as no merchant would accept hosiery unless already dressed. This stale-mate situation made it difficult to become, and stay, self-employed without some other means of support. This was easier for knitters from the north isles than Lerwick-based knitters, as many had their own wool and used knitting as a part- or spare-time occupation to be fitted in with crofting work. These self-employed country knitters would sell their hosiery locally to merchants, to summer visitors or occasionally visit Lerwick to sell their knitwear to hosiery merchants. For example, Catherine Petrie of the island of Fetlar, came annually to Lerwick to sell the shawls which she had knitted during the winter. In Lerwick she lodged with Mrs Park of Charlotte Place, and had her shawls dressed by a Miss Robertson before selling them to Robert Sinclair & Co.

Catherine Petrie's situation was rather different from that of a self-employed knitter living in Lerwick. In the town wool was difficult to obtain, and unlike the north isles, where knitting was very much an extended family business with all the necessary processes being carried out within the family, in Lerwick wool generally had to be put out to the spinner, who in turn had to be paid in ready money. Dressing too, had to be paid for in ready money; so that unless the Lerwick self-employed knitter had some other means of support, she had great difficulty in remaining in business, particularly as there were other cash demands, such as rent, taxes, food etc. on her slender resources. Her best chance of obtaining ready money, and thereby staying in business, was by selling her hosiery to summer visitors, travelling merchants or through friends or relations in the south who were willing to sell her work for her.

Knitters Employed by Merchants

Throughout the archipelago, merchants employed knitters to knit for them. This custom of giving out worsted had started between 1840 and 1859 and, despite the fact that merchants tried to play down this side of their business at the 1872 Truck Inquiry for fear of infringements under the 1831 Truck Act, the system of employing knitters was still in full swing in 1872. In contrast to the factory based putting-out system in operation in the Borders around this time, Shetland knitters entered into no formal contract with their employer. There were not even any set 'factory days' for returning work or receiving new supplies, nor were any conditions or security of employment offered, although merchants stated that they tried to keep needy knitters in work even when there was little demand for hosiery. Employment was on a piece work basis, that is, payment was made on completion of each item or batch of items returned, with the price being set by the merchant. Prices fluctuated according to the time of year and state of the trade. Knitters were rarely paid in cash, although occasionally very small amounts of cash, for example 3d., were given in part payment, with the remainder paid in 'soft goods' or tea.

Dressers

The next stage in the manufacturing of Shetland hosiery was dressing. This was done by women who whitened, scoured, stretched and mended shawls, veils, underwear and other hosiery. These processes required considerable space and equipment. White or off-white hosiery was first whitened using rock sulphur. Old barrels with lids were used for sulphuring. Brimstone was sprinkled on to smouldering (but not burning) coals contained in a metal basket at the foot of the barrel, the hosiery carefully draped over a pole balanced across the top of the barrel and the lid replaced. The sulphur fumes whitened and disinfected the hosiery. Once whitened, hosiery was washed in a mild soap solution, rinsed in luke warm water, laced on to stretchers and left to dry out in the open. Fig. 2.5 shows shawls which had been dressed and

Fig 2.5 — Shawls dressed and pegged out on the grass to dry at Lower Brouster, Walls

pegged out on the grass to dry at Lower Brouster, in the Parish of Walls.

As with knitters, dressers could be independently employed or by a merchant and paid on a piece work basis. Interestingly, all five dressers interviewed by Sheriff Guthrie, were also self-employed knitters, using this secondary form of employment to fill in slack periods. Independent dressers were paid in cash by their clients per item on completion of dressing, the typical fee for a shawl being 6d. and for a veil 1½ d. Ann Arcus, who was extensively examined during the 1872 Truck Inquiry, dressed hosiery for Robert Sinclair & Co., as well as for private knitters. Her dealings with Robert Sinclair & Co., were confined to dressing, but when dressing for self-employed knitters, particularly country girls, she, and other dressers, also acted as agents, selling their client's hosiery to Robert Sinclair & Co. on a commission basis. This custom was adopted by some country knitters, partly because they did not have sufficient time to spend in Lerwick whilst their hosiery was being dressed and partly because some felt that the dresser could get a better bargain from a merchant. In these cases, dressers arranged the payment for the country knitter's hosiery. This was usually done in the form of a line (written credit note) which could be redeemed when the knitter next visited Lerwick; alternatively, the price due her would be marked in the merchant's book.

Employee dressers, like Mrs John Gifford, a Lerwick dresser engaged by Laurenson & Co., organised their work in the same manner as an independent dresser with, presumably the main difference being that they did not have the materials or space to work on a freelance basis.

Merchants

Whilst the knitters were at the heart of the hosiery production, it was the merchants who dominated it economically, as it was in their hands that the bulk of the marketing lay. Merchants ran their businesses on the store system, that is using truck shops to pay their workers. A reasonably clear picture of the "complicated, antiquated"[20] business dealings of the nineteenth century hosiery dealers can be gleaned from the comprehensive information given in the 1871 and 1872 Truck Inquiries, with confirmation from the many other primary and secondary sources available.

In Shetland the store system, based on the barter system used by the Hanseatic merchants, was the customary and accepted way in which knitters were paid. For fishermen this system disappeared in the mid 1880s, but trucking continued for knitters well into the twentieth century. Despite its many disadvantages, it was a system convenient for the domestic economy as, for example, in country districts, merchants both bought all that the district produced and sold virtually all that the district required:

> The merchant...buys all that leaves the country, from a whale to an egg, and sells everything that the country people want, from a boll of meal or a suit of clothes, to a darning needle.[21]

In the town, merchants confined their purchases largely to hosiery and wool, although some smaller Lerwick shops bought eggs and other home produce. These cumbersome business methods were indicative of the shortage of working capital experienced by merchants throughout the early days of their increased trade with Scotland and of the acute shortage of currency in Shetland - the legacy of barter trade with visiting foreigners and prolonged periods of destitution - coupled with the general risk involved in the hosiery trade. Few merchants were prepared to overextend themselves as Hay & Ogilvy had done. Shortage, or even downright lack, of capital forced most merchants, particularly country merchants like James Williamson of Mid Yell, to run their business from their domestic premises, thus cutting down overheads by combining living and working costs. Even Robert Linklater described as 'a leading draper and hosier' lived above his shop in Commercial Street, Lerwick for many years before moving to a separate dwelling. During this period of emergence into a modern economy, many merchants, like William Pole of Mossbank and Arthur Laurenson used judicious marriages - for themselves, their siblings or sons and daughters - to raise capital to extend their business interests.

Arthur Laurenson, Lerwick Hosiery Merchant

The following analysis is largely based on the evidence of Arthur Laurenson (Fig. 2.6) and paints a fairly representative picture of the workings of a large Shetland hosiery dealer around the middle of the nineteenth century. Arthur's father, Laurence Laurenson, set up in business in 1818 as 'Draper, Outfitter and Hosier', and was succeeded by his son, who went into partnership with his brother-in-law in 1867 to form Laurenson & Co. The following reminiscence by T. Manson, editor of *The Shetland News*, throws light on the extensive nature of Laurenson & Co.'s business dealings in Britain:

Fig 2.6 – Arthur Laurenson (1832-1890).

> A large connection was built up in the south, the firm enjoying the patronage of royalty, many of the nobility, and doing besides an extensive wholesale trade...Besides hosiery and drapery, millinery and dressmaking were branches of the business which won and maintained a high reputation.[22]

The buying and selling side of Laurenson & Co. business dealings involved up to twenty different stages, ranging from the initial acquisition of wool, to the purchasing of 'soft goods' with which to pay knitters, through to the final dispatch of hosiery for marketing. Once the wool had been purchased, it had to be put out to spinners, or alternatively, worsted either could be ordered from the north isles or imported from southern spinning mills. Next, hosiery orders were sent out to country merchants who acted as agents for the firm, or to knitters engaged locally. Knitters who were employed to knit for Laurenson & Co., involved the firm in a considerable amount of extra work, a point made by Arthur Laurenson in the 1872 Truck Inquiry:

> The raw material has to be ordered, and money paid for it pretty soon; and then it has to be given out, and these accounts kept, and the articles have to be dressed. In fact we have three or four times the trouble about articles of that description which we have with regard articles we buy in exchange.[23]

Arthur Laurenson does not state how many knitters he employed, other than to say that this practice of employing knitters, which had started in the mid forties, was in decline. On return of the completed work by the knitter to Laurenson & Co., Laurenson's shopmen reweighed the knitting to ensure that the firm had not been cheated of any worsted given out by them, and then gave out goods in exchange for the work. Arthur Laurenson fixed set rates of pay for standard items such as veils, gentlemen's drawers, and ladies' sleeves, the rates being based on the state of the hosiery trade and on what other local merchants were paying at that time. Unlike Robert Sinclair and Robert Linklater, Arthur Laurenson did not give out lines or pass books recording work received and goods given out in exchange. Such books, were much less common with knitters than with fishermen. Money payments, when given, were recorded in a separate 'cash book' and had to be authorised by one of the partners. If goods were not required, a note was made in the shop's 'work book' of the amount of goods due.

Knitting was also 'purchased' from self-employed knitters. Laurenson & Co. dealt extensively in country hosiery, that is ladies and gentlemen's underwear, and lace work. Where a self-employed knitter brought in an individual item, like an intricate shawl, one of the partners - not the shopman - would fix the price. The next stage was to have hosiery dressed and if need be, dyed. Work to be dyed or redyed had to be sent south. For instance, Robert Sinclair & Co. used P. & P. Campbell of Cockburn Street, Edinburgh. After dressing, hosiery was sorted, priced, ticketed, invoiced and packaged ready for posting south. A 'letter book' was kept recording invoices and correspondence with other merchants and wholesalers. Finally on the buying side, freighting had to be arranged and markets found either through agents or by direct contacts with merchant houses in the south, or even in the case of sub-standard hosiery, arrangements made to auction it in job lots.

The different transactions listed above necessitated the merchants employing clerks, book keepers and shopmen/women. These employees held permanent positions and were paid on a weekly rate, unlike the merchants' own dressers and knitters, who were merely paid per item. It was the book keeper's responsibility to deal with and keep records of orders and invoices of both hosiery and soft goods, the clerk's duty to keep the day to day entries of accounts, lines, pass books etc. in the various day books, letter books, womens' books, the shopman/woman's job to serve at the counter, weighing and giving out yarn to knitters, reweigh it on return and exchange it for goods, settle with self-employed knitters and issue lines, as well as helping with the sorting and packing of hosiery; whilst it was the partner's responsibility to authorise any cash payments, price any exclusive items individually, ticket hosiery for export, as well as finding the best markets for his goods.

This whole time consuming business was aggravated by the lack of uniformity in the Shetland hand knitting industry.

> There is great difficulty ...owing to the want of uniformity in the articles, and the great variety of them. You can never get two shawls alike; you cannot even get a dozen pair of half-stockings alike. If you were to get an order for twenty dozen socks of particular colour, size, and price, you would not be able to get that number of socks alike in Shetland.[24]

This lack of uniformity limited demand for Shetland hosiery, particularly when mass production, based on knitting machines, in areas like, for example, Leicester, could guarantee uniformity of colour, size, shape. Therefore, it was only warehouses in the south familiar with these peculiarities who dealt with Shetland merchants. Not surprisingly in the face of this type of competition from machines, Shetland hosiery merchants constantly had difficulty in marketing all but the best of their hosiery - items which were not reproducible by machine - and only did so on the strength of the profit they made on their 'soft goods'.

In addition to Laurenson & Co., Robert Linklater & Co., and Robert Sinclair & Co., the three largest hosiery dealers in Lerwick, James Tulloch and William Johnson, both ran smaller hosiery businesses along the same lines, whilst Thomas Nicholson and Hugh Linklater, stated that they were drapers, obliged to accept hosiery in order to carry on their business.

William Johnson's advertisement (fig. 2.7) gives an interesting insight into the running of his business on the store system principle. This combination of general merchant, draper, clothier, hatter and manufacturer of every

---

WILLIAM JOHNSON
GENERAL MERCHANT

(Agent for Young's Paraffine Oil Lamps and Oils — has always on hand every variety)

DRAPER, CLOTHIER AND HATTER;

Manufacturer of every description of Shetland Hosiery,

Lace Shawls, Veils, &c. &c.

W. J. visits the Markets twice a-year, and always has on hand a good Stock of the Newest and most Fashionable Goods, at very low prices.

119 Commercial Street, LERWICK

Fig 2.7 – William Johnson's advertisement.

description of Shetland hosiery, lace shawls, veils etc. was typical of all but a few of the larger shop keepers at that time. His reference to visiting the market twice a year, refers to the southern market, most likely Edinburgh, where presumably he arranged the marketing of consignments of his hosiery, whilst purchasing 'soft goods' to exchange with his knitters.

Country Merchants

In country districts not one of the merchants examined by Sheriff Guthrie dealt exclusively in hosiery - although Spence and Co. of Unst, dealt extensively in it. However, acting as fish curers or running a general store, most country merchants like those in Lerwick, found that in the absence of money and in order to do business, they had to accept hosiery as a form of currency, exchanging it for goods. For example, Hay & Co.'s Uyeasound shop records show many entries of hosiery, despite the fact that William Hay, when giving evidence before the 1871 Truck Inquiry in Edinburgh, stated that his firm did not deal in hosiery. Ready money was in such short supply and times so hard for everyone, that most merchants had to resort to the old barter system of payment in kind in order to obtain sales, with hosiery as a principal article of exchange.

Hay & Co., Uyeasound, Unst

An examination of this shop's ledgers and day books gives a fascinating insight into the running of a country store in the late 1850s. In 1856 Hay & Co. obtained the lease of the premises at Uyeasound and Newgord from the Garth estate, with the intention of developing the herring and white fish industry, running their shop at Uyeasound on the store system to provide their fishermen with gear and provisions. In addition, Hay & Co. acted as wholesalers to many other country shops, supplying them with goods imported from the south - see fig. 2.8. The shop manager also had instructions to buy eggs, butter, feathers and other home produce as well as fish. A separate folio was kept for each commodity purchased. Provisions, clothing, ironmongery and much more were all dealt with by country merchants. Hay & Co. bought locally spun worsted and sold the bulk of their hosiery to Robert Leisk & Son. Robert Leisk bought mainly veils, shawls, and fine stockings, and was allowed a discount of approximately 2½% on hosiery purchased from Hay & Co., who also supplied Robert Leisk & Son with imported mohair - black, white, brown and 'super silky black mohair'. Times were not easy and ledgers show unsold hosiery lying at Hay & Co.'s Lerwick depot from 1 February 1861 and then being shipped to New Zealand for sale 18 months later. This shop was not a success, largely because of inept management, and was closed in 1868 and the stock handed over to the new firm of Spence & Co., who took over the tenancy early in 1868, and dealt extensively in hosiery. This failure undoubtedly explains why William Hay denied dealing in hosiery.

THE SHETLAND METHOD 1790-1872

SHETLAND ISLANDS
Hay & Co.'s wholesale dealings from 1844.
Hay & Co. supplied the retailers marked on the map

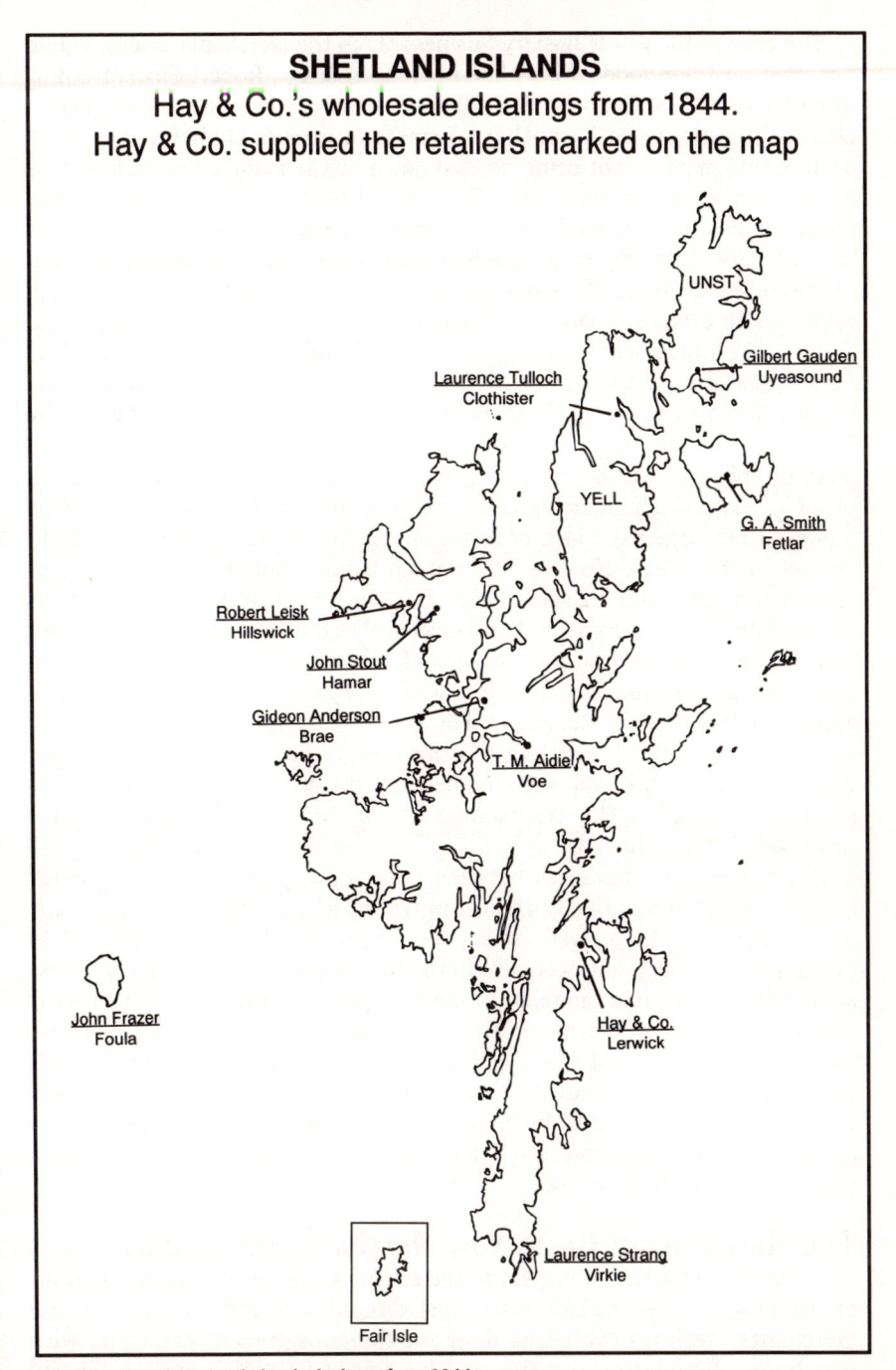

Fig 2.8 – Hay & Co.'s wholesale dealings from 1844.

The crux of the whole hosiery business lay in the merchants' ability to find a market for their goods. Firms like Laurenson & Co., Robert Sinclair & Co., Robert Linklater & Co., who dealt almost exclusively in hosiery, were able to establish contacts with southern firms and pursue their business in a professional manner, not being bogged down by the many different functions carried out by country merchants. This specialisation of dealing in one or two commodities obviously paid off, as for example, Spence & Co. who took over at Uyeasound from Hay & Co., dealt successfully in fish and hosiery well into the twentieth century. Mr Sandison, partner in Spence & Co., travelled south each year to establish market contacts. In May 1868 he travelled to England and later in August went to Glasgow and Edinburgh, looking for new markets for fish cured by the firm, but at the same time managing to establish new markets for his hosiery in Glasgow and London. Giving evidence before the 1872 Truck Inquiry, Alex Sandison stated: "my object in dealing in hosiery is more to oblige my customers than because it is an article on which I make a profit".[25] Like all the merchants examined in the 1872 Truck Inquiry, Alex Sandison bemoaned the lack of profit on hosiery because it was difficult to market in the south. However, he was an astute enough business man to realise that in order to sell in his shops he must accept hosiery. Less successful country merchants had considerable difficulty in marketing their hosiery. Sandison sold hosiery to Lerwick merchants, or sent it south when suitable trade openings arose. Shetland country merchants also acted as agents for the Lerwick merchants. For example, Arthur Laurenson regularly sent orders to country merchants "... for hosiery just the same as we order goods from the south, and the merchants in the country make them up...we pay them in cash".[26] This last method was doubtless preferable as payment was faster and guaranteed.

The two major differences between the country stores and the Lerwick hosiery stores were, firstly that country merchants stocked provisions, ironmongery, boots, as well as 'soft goods', which they were prepared to exchange for hosiery; and secondly, in the true tradition of running a business on the store principle, merchants were prepared to extend credit to their knitters by allowing them to run up accounts, which in 1872, Lerwick merchants professed not to do, although interestingly, Commissary Records show that at the time of Arthur Laurenson's death in 1890, Laurenson & Co. were owed a total of £1,668-6/2d., much of it made up of small debts run up by knitters. Thus the country knitter was in a much more advantageous position than the town knitter.

The Marketing of Hosiery by Merchants and Agents

Obtaining a market for hosiery in the south - generally in London, Glasgow or Edinburgh - was probably the most difficult and protracted of all the merchants' dealings. This was done on the consignment principle, with merchants shouldering the risk and burden of freighting and of delayed payment - often up to 18 months - plus the cost of paying a sales agent in the south on a percentage basis and a 5% discount for cash, even when payments were greatly delayed. With the exception of Robert Linklater who had his own retail shop in Edinburgh, neither Robert Sinclair nor Arthur Laurenson or any of the smaller hosiery merchants, were working as part of a consortium, feeding large wholesalers.

Commissary Records, show that Shetland hosiers dealt with a large number of retail and wholesale hosiers in the south. The large wholesale hosiery dealers in the south, like Mr Mackenzie, Shetland Warehousman, Princes St., Edinburgh, and Mr Thomas Peace of Kirkwall, Orkney, visited Shetland annually to purchase hosiery at wholesale prices from both knitters and Shetland merchants; whilst, for example, Mr John White, Frederick Street, Edinburgh employed local agents - in this case, Miss Mary Hutchison of Lerwick - to complete orders for him. On receiving a hosiery order from him, Miss Hutchison would purchase wool or worsted, give it out to selected knitters with oral instructions as to what was to be produced. Miss Hutchison then arranged for the dressing and freighting of these items, and in due course received a post office order or bank cheque from Mr White. Her knitters were not trucked but paid in cash, and it was this payment in cash which ensured that she was never at a loss for willing knitters and had the pick of the best from which to choose. Mr White also employed a number of skilled knitters, like Andrina Anderson, who sent work to him independent of an agent. Agents were also employed by Lerwick merchants, as for example, Joan Ogilvy from Unst, acted as an agent for Peter Edward Petrie, a hosiery dealer in Lerwick. Peter Petrie would supply Joan Ogilvy with goods from his shop, with which she paid local Unst girls, whilst herself working on a commission basis. Edward Standen, an Oxford merchant of great Christian charity, bought knitting direct from knitters which he sold on the London market.

The Marketing of Hosiery by Self-employed Knitters

Hosiery could also be marketed through benevolent private people, thus by-passing merchants, and obtaining both a better price and payment in cash. The 1872 Truck Inquiry mentions Mr Garriock of Reawick, Dr Hamilton of Bressay, Dr Cowie's lady, the Rev. Mr John Walker's lady and Miss Jessie Ogilvy as people buying hosiery from needy people on a charitable basis and not on a business footing. These people would obtain orders from friends from the south and buy hosiery from needy people who had no means of earning their livelihood other than by knitting. Such transactions were invaluable to knitters, as they were paid in ready money, and could therefore buy food, pay their rent, etc. After the introduction of a regular steamer service and the subsequent rise in the number of summer visitors, knitters sold their knitting direct to them by either going to local lodging houses, or by accosting visitors in the street. In the country "A great loss arises to the poor cottars, from travelling pedlars, who tempt them with worthless trumpery, and carry off the produce of their industry at very low prices".[27] Merchants too, were on the look out for sales to private persons, but were still very dependent on marketing the bulk of their hosiery outwith Shetland.

Profit on Hosiery

The poor returns and lack of profit from hosiery, were complaints constantly aired by merchants, knitters, philanthropists, and Commissioners of Supply alike. In fact, it was probably the only point on which everyone connected with the hosiery industry could agree. It is extremely difficult to work out realistic figures of profit and loss, particularly in the absence of shop books and invoices.

Fall handled by Robert Sinclair of Sinclair & Co.,(p. 55).

Worsted	=	6d.
knitting	=	1/-
dyeing & freight	=	1½d.
dressing	=	1d.
	=	1/8½d.

Sold at 2/- therefore profit = 3½d. a profit of 17%

Shetland Shawl handled by Robert Sinclair (p. 58).

Worsted - 36 cuts @ 4d. a cut	=	12/-
knitting	=	14/-
dressing	=	6d.
	=	26/6 total cost to produce

Sold at 30/- therefore profit = 3/6 a profit of 13.2%

Shawl handled by Robert Linklater of Linklater & Co. (p. 60).

Worsted-36 cuts @ 4d. a cut	=	12/-
knitting	=	13/-
dressing	=	6d.
	=	25/6 total cost to produce

Sold at 30/- therefore profit = 4/6 a profit of 17.6%

Fig. 2.9

Profit on Fine hosiery

Fig. 2.9 has been compiled from information taken from the 1872 Truck Inquiry, and shows the profit made on fine knitted articles. Even this can not be taken as more than a guide as it is often difficult to decide from the evidence if the price stated referred to the price paid in wages or the price at which merchants sold these items. In addition, few merchants were prepared to divulge their business dealings in detail in an open court in front of their rivals and employees, and were prone to evading questions or giving misleading or confusing answers. For example, Arthur Laurenson, regarded as an honest, upright and reliable witness, was not prepared to give the profit made on a black shawl costing 15/- to produce, whose worsted cost 4/6d., with 10/- being paid to the knitter and 6d. to the dresser. It must be remembered that the curse of the Shetland hand knitting industry was the risk involved in marketing it. This was primarily caused by poor quality work depressing hosiery prices and, because in the absence of machinery and mass production, each item produced by hand knitters was unique, a one-off. This was in contrast to, say the Borders, where retailers could place large orders, stating exact quantities, specifications and delivery dates. The very nature of hand knitting was against this type of uniformity and organisation. Recommendations had been put forward suggesting that merchants set up workrooms in Lerwick, give out patterns and set knitters to work on a factory system. Shetland workers were not used to such rigid working conditions, and these proposals were not adopted. Hand knitters continued in their old independent way, of knitting what they chose to, so that merchants were often left with an ill-wrought assortment of unsaleable goods, and adopted a policy of lowering the prices paid for hosiery to guard against loss from these, whilst still ensuring an overall profit by allowing a 25% profit margin on drapery, that is 10% above the normal profit margin charged in the south.

By the time of the 1872 Truck Inquiry, Shetland had an excess of 5,402 females to males, an imbalance which left many women without the support of a spouse. For these spinsters knitting and agricultural work, with the addition of seasonal kelp and fish work, were the only modes of employment open to women. At knitting it was estimated that veil knitters could make, if very industrious, 6/- a week and at stocking and underclothing, an average of 4/- to 5/- a week. However, as these sums were of course paid in 'soft goods' or truck credit, it meant that the true value of the goods was reduced by 25%, which coupled with the lack of ready money, caused considerable hardship for many knitters. And it was the hardship experienced by these knitters and by Shetland fishermen, which led to the 1872 Truck Inquiry (Shetland).

References - Chapter 2

1   OSA, p. 422.
2   OSA, p. 396.
3   OSA, p. 444.
4   OSA, p. 421.
5   Loch, D., *Essays on the trade, commerce, manufactures and fisheries of Scotland*, (Edinburgh 1778), Vol. I, section II, p. 2b.
6   OSA p. 491 and 507.

7 OSA p. 491.
8 Wilson, J., *A voyage round the coasts of Scotland and the Isles*, (Edinburgh 1842).
9 OSA, p. 464.
10 Grierson, H.J.C., (ed.) *Letters of Sir Walter Scott*, (Edinburgh 1932).
   In 1814 Sir Walter Scott accompanied Robert Stevenson, Commissioner of the Northern Lights on his annual tour of inspection. It was from information gathered on this trip that Scott wrote *The Pirate*.
11 'A Scotsman', *A Trip to Shetland*, (1872), p. 28.
12 Standen, E., *The Shetland Islands*, (Oxford 1845), p. 30 and 31.
13 OSA, p. 387.
14 Edmondston, A., *View of the Ancient and Present state of the Zetland Islands*, (Edinburgh 1809), Vol. I, p. 224.
15 Op. cit., Vol. II, p. 1 and 2.
16 Smith, H., *Shetland Life and Trade 1550 - 1914*, (Edinburgh 1984), p. 128.
17 Minutes of Evidence taken before the Poor Law Enquiry Commission for Scotland, 17-20 July, 1843.
18 Standen, E., *The Shetland Islands*, (Oxford 1845), p. 32.
19 Edmondston, E., *Sketches and Tales of Shetland*, (Edinburgh 1856), p. 171.
20 PP, Cd., 555-1, 1872 Truck Inquiry, p. 43, q., 2183.
21 PP, Cd., 555, 1872 Truck Inquiry, (Thule Print edition 1978), p. vi.
22 Manson, T., *Lerwick During the Last Half Century*, (revised edition, Lerwick 1991), p. 54.
23 PP, Cd., 555-1, 1872 Truck Inquiry, p46, q.2271.
24 Op. cit., p. 43, q. 2194.
25 Op. cit., p. 248, q. 10203.
26 Op. cit., p. 48, q. 2345 & 2346.
27 Edmondston, E., *Sketches and Tales of the Shetland Islands*, (Edinburgh 1856), p. 176.

Chapter 3

Truck and the Shetland Hand Knitting Industry 1790-1950

With a snow-white hap on her head,
and rivlins tied on her feet,
A fair-haired, rosy-cheeked Shetland maid
Trudged with a kishie of peat.
Trudge, trudge, trudge,
She trudged the scathold along,
And still as she went, with her body bent,
She sang this sorrowful song:

From the morning till late at night
My knitting wires seldom are still;
I can clip & roo, & card, & spin too
And knit whatever you will.
Knit, knit, knit
A shawl that the Queen could wear,
A stocking or sock, or a sailor's frock,
To keep out the Greenland air.

But my labour is all in vain
Somebody has stolen my luck
For all that I make to the shop I must take
And hand it over to Truck.
For calico, sugar and tea;
No money I get for the wares I knit,
Or it would be better for me.

My father he goes to the haaf,
In a boat that floats like a duck,
But the cod and the ling to the man he must bring
Who keeps the station for Truck.
Truck, truck, truck,
For the meal we got last year;
Since he worked when a boy in the trucker's employ
He has lived in hunger and fear.

My brothers Magnus and Tom
Made a trip to Davy's Straits,
But all that they earned when they returned
Was kept for my father's debts.
Truck, truck, truck -
Oh! shame on the Kingdom and Crown
And fie on the laws that dally & pause
In putting the truck-rig down.

With a snow white hap on her head
And rivlins tied on her feet,
A blue-eyed, rosy-cheeked Shetland maid
Trudged with a kishie of peat.
Trudge, trudge, trudge.
She trudged the scathold along,
And still as she went bent with her body
She sang that sorrowful song.

(From *"King James Wedding and Other Poems"* by J. Sands)

KNITTING BY THE FIRESIDE

Strictly speaking, truck was the system whereby wages were paid in kind rather than in 'the coin of the realm'. However, in Shetland by the time of the 1872 Truck Inquiry, the term had been extended to include the exchange over the shop counter of local produce for shop goods or services. This extension of trucking is usually referred to as 'barter-truck' and had become the norm in Shetland's close-knit internal trade dealings.

Trucking in Shetland was a legacy from the days of the barter trade with the Hanseatic merchants and their merchant-laird successors; from bartering with Dutch and other fishermen; and from the payment (or part-payment) of rents and teinds in local produce, customary in Shetland up to the end of the eighteenth century. From this legacy, developed the 'Shetland Method', whereby the fisherman was tied by a system of barter and debt-bondage to his local merchant-laird or merchant-tacksman*, who bought his fish and his family's produce and upon whom he and his family depended for their croft, and for everything not gained directly from the land or sea. And it was this bond between the land and sea which lay at the heart of the whole truck system in Shetland. In essence, by the middle of the nineteenth century, the land could not support its vastly increased population - which had risen by approximately 50% from 20,451 in 1790 to 30,670 by 1861 – without the importation of meal and other foodstuffs. The fishing industry had to produce a commercial surplus to foot the bill for such imports. However, poor fishing seasons and/or harvests necessitated the extension of credit, offered by the store system, without which widespread starvation or mass emigration would have been rife.

In Shetland the victims of truck, as opposed to barter-truck (that is, people who exchanged their produce whether hosiery or home produce with merchants in return for provisions) were the fishermen, fish handlers, fish curers, and kelp gatherers who worked for their landlord-merchant, and the knitters who knitted for the merchant using his worsted. The most vulnerable of this group was the fisherman-tenant and his family, as failure to fish to his landlord could lead to forty days notice and eviction, which was a daunting prospect in Shetland, with its oversaturated population struggling to scratch a subsistence living, and alternative employment opportunities almost non-existent.

> Eviction to a Shetlander is a serious matter... A new farm is always difficult to get. In the south ... a man can shift from town to town and get employment; but here, if he leaves his house and farm, he has no place to go except Lerwick, and there is no room to be got there, either for love or money.[1]

It was to Lerwick that many of the people thrown out of work by the collapse of Hay and Ogilvy, made homeless by clearances or simply destitute from the harvest failures in the 1830s and 1840s, went to in the hope of finding refuge. According to one contemporary commentator, Lerwick and Scalloway had become the Poor House of Shetland. The Truck System, an indicator of poverty, destitution and oppression, became even more widespread, and as the Truck Commissioners pointed out in 1871, large families, ill health, bad times, accidental misfortunes, swell the population, making the unfortunate still more so. However in Shetland it was not just the poor but the whole society, regardless of class or profession, that was caught up in the truck system. By 1872, trucking was so enmeshed in the Shetland way of life that despite the inherently faulty principles on which it had been founded, it had become the accepted norm. This is illustrated by the following statement made by Mr. Bruce, younger, of Sumburgh before the 1872 Truck Inquiry:

> There are no doubt many things in the Shetland system of trade which might be improved, but the system is of long growth, and is so ingrained in the minds of the people, than any change must be very gradual: a sudden and sweeping change to complete free-trade principles and ready money payments would not suit the people, but would produce endless confusion, hardship and increased pauperism.[2]

Whilst it was the fishing-tenures which lay at the heart of the truck system, using truck in its legal sense, it was the barter-truck system which was responsible for perpetuating trucking in the hand knitting industry and in almost all internal trade dealings.

Truck was by no means a new phenomenon or one peculiar to Shetland. It was in fact a national, rather than a local, issue. At the time of the Union with England in 1707 Scotland was a relatively backward country economically, exporting - with the exception of linen cloth - primary products such as cattle, coal, wool, hides, fish and salt. The many new entrepreneurs who emerged and flourished in the period of trade expansion and industrial growth following the Union, often did so at the expense of their work force, so that by 1790, truck was enmeshed in the everyday dealings of many working class people. In Scotland it was most widespread and insidious in industrial areas like Motherwell and Hamilton and in mining districts in Ayrshire. In these areas, wages were paid by the employer into the company store, and it was through this store that rent was paid and other necessities purchased, being debited against the worker's account. The worker was truly thirled to his employer as he received no ready money to spend how or where he pleased. He was also the victim of exploitation as prices in truck stores were notoriously high. This type of trucking led to apathy and despair, and offered workers little opportunity of breaking free from the poverty trap.

Generally speaking, trucking in Shetland, was run on more benevolent lines than in the larger industrial areas. For poorer people the credit afforded by the truck system was a real form of 'social security', with fishcurers and merchants virtually running their own welfare system - the more benevolent of whom inevitably went under with their clients or died penniless. For example, James Williamson of Mid Yell when he died in 1872 had been in business for more than forty years as a general merchant selling all manner of provisions, as well as nails, cotton, shirting, India rubber shoes etc. and at the same time purchasing from his customers fish, livestock, birds' eggs and hosiery. He also

KNITTING BY THE FIRESIDE

ran the sloop *Matilda*, and farmed a croft. He died worth £2. A kindly merchant like James Williamson, soon found that in hard times he was bearing the burden of extended credit for many of his poorer customers. His papers contain many letters from local men who had gone off to sea or to the gold mines of Australia and California, asking him to provide for their mothers or wives in their absence. Other types of credit transactions included lending money, handing out provisions to people on the Parochial Board, paying rent, providing mort cloths and so on. Willingly or otherwise, James found himself in the role of a welfare officer which was to cost him dearly. An accumulation of bad debts and his own misadventures in business, left his widow virtually penniless.

The 1831 Truck Act, which replaced a long series of measures passed during the eighteenth and early nineteenth century, primarily dealt with the prohibition of payment of wages in kind and had little or no effect on stamping out truck in Shetland or elsewhere. And as a result of the many complaints about the widespread practice of wages being paid in kind, Parliament appointed the Truck Commission under the Truck Commission Act of 1870 to look into these problems, and to examine the degree to which the act of 1831 was being contravened. During the course of 1870 and 1871 the Commission held sittings in Glasgow, Edinburgh, Cardiff, Gloucester, Prescot, Birmingham, Nottingham and London. The case of Shetland was brought to the notice of the Commissioners by four influential people connected with Shetland: Mr George Smith, solicitor, who in his eight years residence in Shetland, had held many public offices like sheriff clerk, clerk of supply etc.; Mr A. J. Hay, merchant and fish curer and member of the firm of Hay & Co.; Mr John Walker, sheep farmer and factor for one tenth of the islands; and Dr. T. Edmondston, landowner and medical doctor in the island of Unst. A. J. Hay and John Walker gave evidence at the sittings in London and Edinburgh and it was this that led to the decision to hold a separate inquiry for Shetland - the Second Report of the Commissioners appointed to inquire into the Truck System (Shetland) in 1872.

The chief commissioner of this inquiry was William Guthrie, a Glasgow sheriff of enormous energy, immense patience and incorruptibility. On receiving his warrant as a commissioner under the Truck Commission Act of 1870, he proceeded to Shetland and started his inquiries immediately on arriving there on 1st January 1872. Hearings were held in Lerwick, Brae, Hillswick, Mid Yell, Baltasound, Uyeasound, Scalloway, Boddam, Kirkwall and Edinburgh (Fig. 3.1). Although the majority of Guthrie's time was spent in Lerwick, many 'country' people from outlying districts and islands were also interviewed. Citations were sent to people whose names had been put forward by local officials and dignitaries, but it was also made clear that anyone wishing to make a statement would be free to come forward and do so. Thus, it is not unreasonable to assume that Sheriff Guthrie interviewed a fair cross section of the inhabitants. The 1872 Truck Inquiry was largely concerned with

TRUCK AND THE SHETLAND HAND KNITTING INDUSTRY 1790-1950

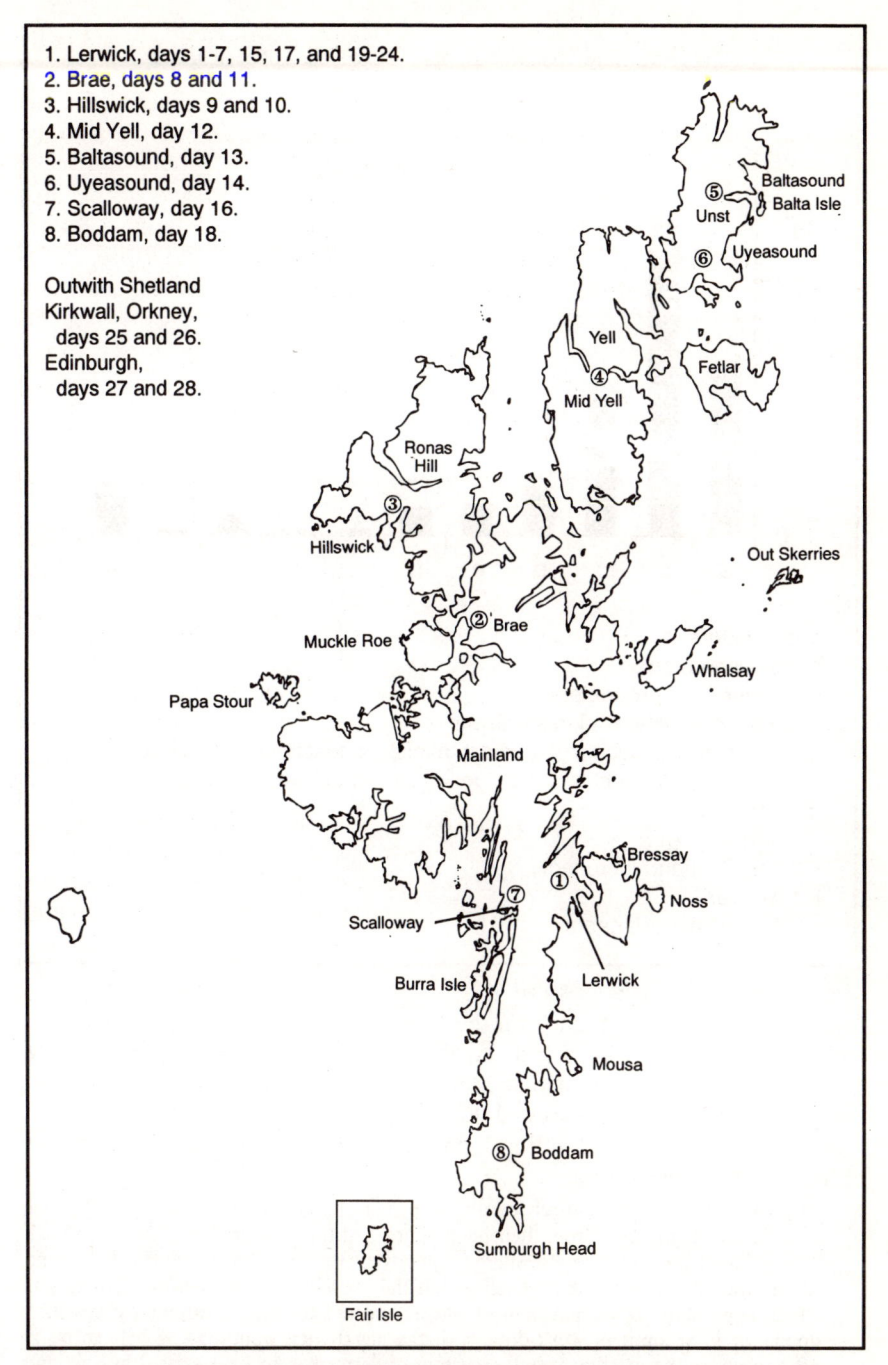

1. Lerwick, days 1-7, 15, 17, and 19-24.
2. Brae, days 8 and 11.
3. Hillswick, days 9 and 10.
4. Mid Yell, day 12.
5. Baltasound, day 13.
6. Uyeasound, day 14.
7. Scalloway, day 16.
8. Boddam, day 18.

Outwith Shetland
Kirkwall, Orkney,
  days 25 and 26.
Edinburgh,
  days 27 and 28.

Fig 3.1 – Map of the Shetland Islands showing where the 1872 Truck Commission held sittings.

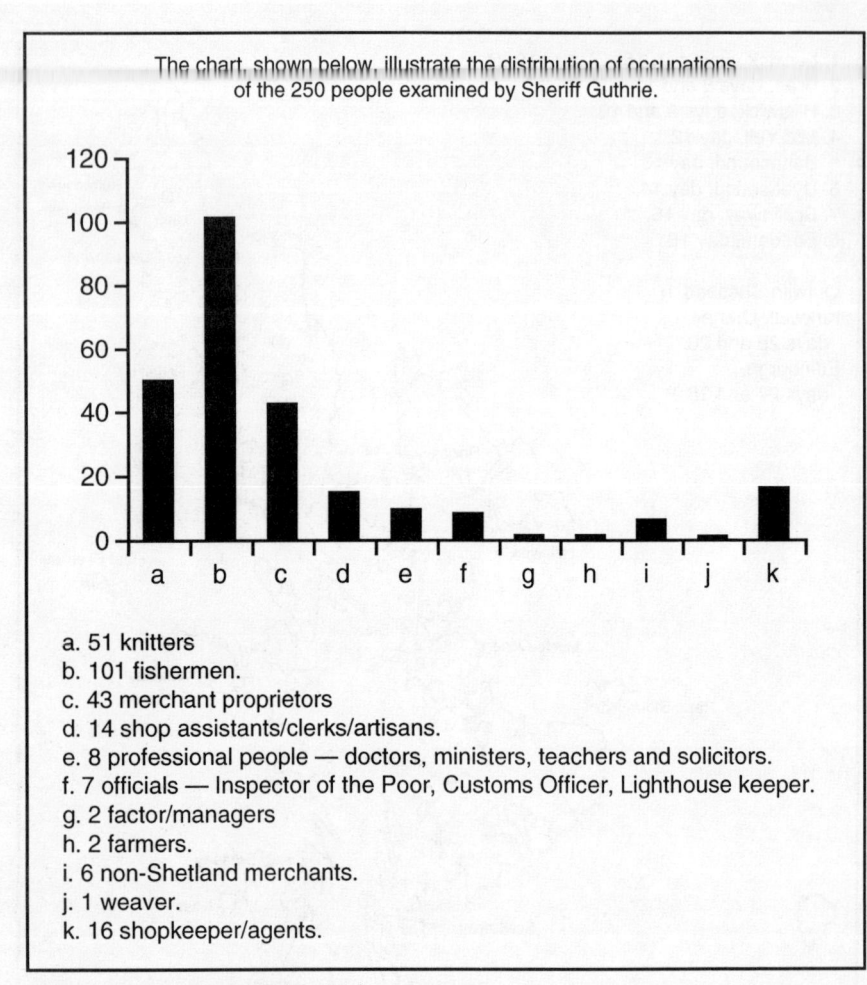

The chart, shown below, illustrate the distribution of occupations of the 250 people examined by Sheriff Guthrie.

a. 51 knitters
b. 101 fishermen.
c. 43 merchant proprietors
d. 14 shop assistants/clerks/artisans.
e. 8 professional people — doctors, ministers, teachers and solicitors.
f. 7 officials — Inspector of the Poor, Customs Officer, Lighthouse keeper.
g. 2 factor/managers
h. 2 farmers.
i. 6 non-Shetland merchants.
j. 1 weaver.
k. 16 shopkeeper/agents.

Fig 3.2 – 1872 Truck inquiry (Shetland).

examining the effect of truck on the fishing and hand knitting industries. In all 17,070 questions were asked and along with their answers, recorded in two volumes. As well as fishermen and knitters, local doctors, ministers, inspectors of the poor etc., were interviewed (Fig. 3.2).

As regards the hand knitting industry, in his summing up of the inquiry Sheriff Guthrie noted that :

> Originally the trade was entirely carried on by persons knitting the wool grown by their own flocks, or procured from their neighbours; and they bartered the articles so made to merchants in Lerwick or elsewhere for goods of every kind. Transactions of this kind, which are still common, do not fall within the provisions of the existing Truck Acts, which apply only to the payment of wages, and not to sales... Although payment in goods, or in account of work done with the merchants' wool may be held to be an offence under the existing law, the custom of barter has so long existed in Shetland,

TRUCK AND THE SHETLAND HAND KNITTING INDUSTRY 1790-1950

and is so thoroughly interwoven with the habits of the people, that the question has never been raised in the local courts, and it does not even appear to have occurred to merchants that they might be held to infringe the law. In regard to both branches of the trade, the sale or barter of the knitted articles, and the employment of women to knit them, evidence has been freely given by the merchants themselves.[3]

It was only since around the mid 1840s that the merchants had started giving out worsted - this date significantly coinciding with the collapse of Hay & Co. and the Shetland Banking Company in the 'hungry forties' - that hosiery merchants had become liable to prosecution under the 1831 Truck Act.

This then was the situation which had been developed over the years, with the exchange of hosiery for goods - rather than ready money - as the norm. An effort had been made by Arthur Laurenson, principal partner in Laurenson & Co. and Robert Sinclair of Robert Sinclair & Co., to show that they did give out small amounts of cash for specific purposes such as rent payment. However, Sheriff Guthrie was quick to realise that these payments were so small and so infrequently made as to be negligible, and that cash payments were confined to highly skilled knitters like Catherine Brown formerly of Lerwick, or Joan Ogilvy from Unst, whose work was always in demand and much sought after by all the merchants. Interestingly, Margaret Jamieson of Quarff, who knitted for Robert Sinclair, related how, having persuaded Robert Sinclair to give her 9d. in cash, he was unable to do so as there was no money in the shop, and he had to borrow the cash from one of his serving-men! A recurring phrase from the evidence of knitters, was that they never asked for money for their hosiery as 'it was not the custom' or that 'merchants never gave it'.[4] In the early days of trucking, groceries were available for hosiery, but by the time of the 1872 Truck Inquiry, in Lerwick nothing but 'soft goods' or 'lines' (credit notes) were available for hosiery. The smaller mark up on groceries and their perishable nature made them less profitable than 'soft goods' with their almost limitless shelf life; oatmeal and hosiery did not mix well, as meal was found to attract moths which damaged hosiery stocks. Lines were issued if the knitter did not want goods that day, or in the case of Robert Sinclair, if the shop was very busy.

This custom of payment in 'soft goods' particularly told against the town knitters dependent on knitting as their sole means of livelihood. Charlotte Sutherland who pointed out that "Knitting does very well in Lerwick for those that have friends to live with and keep them, but not for me when I had to look after myself",[5] had to leave Lerwick and go to Orkney where she could get cash for her hosiery. This custom of payment in goods led to a whole infrastructure of ancillary sales and to a network of middlemen. For example, these knitters frequently sold their 'soft goods' or bartered them with neighbours for provisions. Mary Coutts from Scalloway stated that she exchanged tea which she had received for hosiery with farmers for potatoes and meal but had sometimes had to get her aunt to go as far as Walls and Sandness to make such exchanges. Guthrie noted that:

tea especially is a sort of currency with which knitters obtain supplies of provisions... in one account, more than a half of the total amount consists of ¼lb. packages of tea.[6]

The excessive consumption of tea was frowned on by many moralists as a misuse of time and effort. For instance, Edward Standen who was responsible for introducing fine Shetland hosiery to the London market c.1840, decried this widespread addiction in Shetland:

> The fondness for tea is carried to an excess by the Shetland wife; for the sake of it she knits at all opportunities, spending sometimes in this way the whole of the wool and labour of the season, when a part of it ought to be applied to her husband's comfort, in giving him warm clothing for his exposure on the sea. Thus he suffers by his wife's intemperance, not in spirits but in tea.[7]

Lines also acted as a form of currency and were sold at a reduced rate to their face value. There is also a mention of lines being bought by charitable persons to help knitters. In Lerwick, such sales were necessary to raise ready money not only for rent payments but also for food, doctor's bills and many of the other necessities of life. Another means by which money could be obtained, was by employing a hawker on a commission basis to sell the 'soft goods' received in payment of hosiery. Hawkers, such as Betty Morrison and Jean Yates, went round the country districts selling or exchanging these 'soft goods'. In the 1872 Truck Inquiry, Dr R. Cowie referred to sumptuously dressed knitters, starving through want of ready money with which to buy food. This extravagance in dress - locally referred to as 'bedizened' - was noted by many writers, and represented truck in Shetland at its most pernicious. This custom of paying knitters in soft goods also had the hidden effect of creating an unnaturally high demand for drapery, to the extent that hosiery exchanges were propping up many merchants' drapery trade. Surprisingly, this acute shortage of ready money does not seem to have led to prostitution, Shetland having the second lowest illegitimacy rate of any Scottish county. Only one of the knitters interviewed, a Margaret Tulloch spinster from Lerwick, sounded as if she might have been augmenting her meagre income in this manner, as she described how men would come to her house to buy tea which she would make for them. However, prostitution among knitters, euphemistically referred to as 'evil courses' by Sheriff Guthrie, remained a moot point, as when questioned on this issue, Mrs Anderson, one of the older witnesses from Lerwick, evaded this question, rather to Sheriff Guthrie's annoyance.

The obvious and over-riding disadvantages of truck, were the limitations it placed on its recipient's freedom of choice. The same Mrs Anderson felt that if knitters received money for their work they could save a good deal by spending less on clothes or put money in the missionary box. However, the church, never slow to pass by an opportunity to make money, did so by raising funds in kind. The United Free Missionary Magazine related how some twenty Fetlar girls met once a week at the manse, and by donating their own wool, time and skill, raised £14-7/3d. for foreign missions. A rather sad case of a victim of truck was noted by Sophia Cracroft, Lady Jane Franklin's niece.

TRUCK AND THE SHETLAND HAND KNITTING INDUSTRY 1790-1950

Lady Franklin and her niece, travelled to Shetland in 1849, in the hope of learning news of the whereabouts of her husband, Sir John Franklin the explorer, from the returning Greenland whalers. At the same time, she was involved in a scheme to promote emigration to Australia for young Shetland women. However, although the passages offered were assisted, interested parties had to tender a £1 deposit. This proved a major stumbling block as few knitters could raise such cash. Sophia Cracroft recorded how one eminently suitable candidate asked Lady Franklin if she might give one of her finest knitted shawls as her deposit as she had no money. The diary does not state if this request was granted. Interestingly, Dr. A. Edmondston, writing in 1809, noted that many of the girls employed in the straw plaiting industry earlier established in Shetland, used their cash earnings to leave Shetland and emigrate to Edinburgh and take up domestic employment there.

Trucking in the country districts was less pernicious and caused less hardship than in the town, as other forms of work, like fish or field work, were more readily available. Most people had their own produce or were able to earn it by outdoor work, although even there, lack of cash still had its problems as Charlotte Johnston's case study illustrates. Charlotte Johnston lived at Collafirth, near Ollaberry, and knitted and dressed hosiery for Mr Morgan Laurenson, merchant at Hillswick. Mr Laurenson allowed Charlotte Johnston to run up an account on credit, and in order to settle these debts, had continued to send her hosiery to dress, although she no longer wished to work for him. It appears that she got into debt through having a house built; unable to pay the workmen in cash she paid them in tea and other provisions, taking out a great deal more provisions from Mr Laurenson's store than she needed for her own use. This was by no means a unique case. Workers seem to have accepted that it was often not possible to be paid in cash, as for instance, the girl who helped Catherine Borthwick, a Lerwick knitter, with her peats, was quite happy to accept a petticoat as payment.

One of the peculiarities of the hosiery trade, as described in the evidence given by merchants, was the lack of profit they realized on hosiery sales. Merchants stated that they invoiced hosiery to wholesalers and retailers in the south at the same price which they had paid for it in goods, or so little higher as to cover only the risk and loss upon damaged articles and job lots. The only exception to this was fine lacework, often bought for cash, and on which they were assured a profit. From the evidence presented to him, Sheriff Guthrie tended to feel that merchants, when invoicing their goods to trade purchasers in Edinburgh, London and elsewhere, did so at prices sufficient to free them from any loss, allowing only a very small profit amounting to no more than a small commission for the trouble of disposing of hosiery. This was not the case when dealing with private purchasers - a smaller but still considerable trade - in which they realized a substantial profit. In the absence of cash, hosiery was taking the place of money as a form of currency among knitters and merchants. Initially, Shetland merchants who dealt in hosiery were drapers and clothiers or general merchants who sold their wares in exchange for hosiery rather than money, and in order to make allowances for this inconvenience, raised the profit on their shop goods beyond the normal retail level; southern merchants allowed a 15% mark up on their drapery, whilst Shetland merchants took a 25% profit. Therefore, although merchants denied that there was a profit in any but fine lace hosiery, merchants obtained a profit on their hosiery - this profit amounting to a hidden or double profit on their shop goods. For example, if a merchant bought tea at a wholesale price of 1/6d. per lb. and sold it in his 'cash shop' for 2/- he would make a 33.3% profit. However, if he sold the same tea in his 'truck shop' for 2/6d. per lb., he would then be making 66.6% profit. As Sheriff Guthrie pointed out:

> But while the merchants assert that they have no direct profit upon their sales of knitted goods, or at least none but the smallest, they do not deny that, in order to repay themselves for the trouble and risk involved in the two transactions upon which this profit is realized, they charge considerably more for their tea and drapery goods than the ordinary retail price in other districts. In other words, although there is nominally no profit upon the knitted goods there is a double profit, or a very large profit, on the drapery goods, tea, etc., bartered for it.[8]

In addition, Sheriff Guthrie noted that in some places there were two prices for goods according to whether they were paid for with hosiery or with money. For example, Robert Sinclair who kept two drapers shops in Lerwick, a 'truck shop' and one which dealt purely in cash sales, admitted grudgingly that there was 'a very small shade of difference' between the price of goods in the two different shops. This two-price system also prevailed in rural districts and from it arose two anachronisms. Firstly, the system of 'money items' and secondly, the practice of giving less money for hosiery than its value in goods -usually 20% or more. 'Money items', such as Shetland worsted, were not available through truck exchanges and could only be purchased for cash. When cash was given to knitters in payment for their work, a discount of 20 - 25% was deducted by merchants for this concession; therefore, a knitter who would have received 1/- in truck goods, would receive only 9d. in cash.

At the heart of the whole matter lay the profit margin merchants allowed on the goods they exchanged for hosiery. It is difficult to assess the extent to which merchants exploited knitters in this issue of prices. On the one hand the minister of Northmavine, the Rev. James Sutherland, stated that he bought in his provisions from the south as he could not afford to buy at the local store and Mr. Newlands, a factory inspector, stated having seen flannel which sold in Glasgow at $3\frac{1}{2}$d. a yard, being sold at 1/- in Shetland. This was probably an extreme case and not a particularly valid comparison, as freight and handling charges upped the price of all goods imported to Shetland. For the same reasons, Shetland country merchants had to charge higher prices than in Lerwick. On the other hand, a knitter who relied on her merchant to take her possibly poor quality, and therefore difficult to resell, hosiery, and to extend her interest-free credit in times of need, was fortunate to be accommodated by him. On the whole, Sheriff Guthrie felt that:

TRUCK AND THE SHETLAND HAND KNITTING INDUSTRY 1790-1950

> In Lerwick...competition and the greater facility of communication with other places, have kept the prices of the necessaries of life to a moderate figure. No complaints were made as to prices there.[9]

However, he goes on to point out that:

> It is a fact of some significance, that few persons above the condition of peasants purchase supplies for family use from the shops in Shetland. Provisions, groceries, as well as clothing, are to a large extent imported by private individuals from Aberdeen, Leith and Edinburgh.[10]

It is also difficult to separate the extent of truck from barter-truck, particularly as most local transactions were based on the latter. However, unlike the fishermen, knitters were not directly trucked through land tenure - there is only one instance mentioned in the 1872 Truck Inquiry of a knitter's hosiery merchant also being her landlord - nor were they generally thirled to the one merchant. In country districts, the distances between shops usually meant that knitters dealt with the same local merchant, but some did save up their hosiery and travel to Lerwick occasionally, whilst in Lerwick, knitters dealt with the merchant from whom they felt they got the best bargain.

Looking at the truck system in Shetland as it stood at the time of the 1872 Truck Inquiry, it is easy to make judgements based on twentieth century standards. It is particularly easy to condemn the merchants and to label them as oppressive tyrants living off the 'fat of the land' at their clients' expense. In reality, there was little or no 'fat' and those merchants, marketing their goods as they did on the consignment system, had much of their capital tied up in hosiery, and in addition, were shouldering all the risks inherent therein. Hosiery merchants were suffering the effects of prolonged periods of extended credit, capital scarcity, and a fall off in demand for hosiery, all aggravated by the quantity of poor quality hosiery foisted upon them, whilst isolation, acute poverty, evictions and wool shortages, had severely disadvantaged the knitters' position; all of which added up to an inevitable extension of trucking. For example, when Arthur Laurenson, principal partner in Laurenson & Co., died in 1890, a memorial was erected to his memory by the people of Lerwick, in recognition of services to the community. He founded the Shetland Literary and Scientific Society, was a town councillor, member of the School and Parochial Boards, director of the Anderson's (Shetland Fishermen's) Widows' Fund, had organised the destitution appeal for Foula in 1885, and the travelling and accommodation arrangements of the Fair Isle girls attending the Shetland stall at the Edinburgh International Exhibition in 1886. Commissary Records show Arthur Laurenson's net personal estate to be only £1,346-15/6d., not a large sum for a leading merchant. It is interesting that Laurenson's biographer, Catherine Spence, does not mention his partnership in Laurenson & Co. and makes no allusion to his hosiery business. Arthur Laurenson seems to have been more interested in his literary and public works rather than in business pursuits. For example, he travelled to Norway, Sweden and America for literary and linguistic studies, and became a voluntary teacher in the Lerwick Instruction Society.

KNITTING BY THE FIRESIDE

Despite the pains taken by Sheriff Guthrie to investigate fully the true state of truck in Shetland, the 1872 Truck Inquiry, lasting almost four months, did virtually nothing to change the truck system in Shetland. It had no agitational value and was followed by no legislation until 1887. It did, however, leave a lasting record of Shetland life in Victorian times, both in the actual report and in the contemporary press - little compensation for contemporary Shetlanders! Brian Smith pin-points the inherent weakness in the 1872 Truck Inquiry as Sheriff Guthrie's failure to link the tenurial system with the truck system. In Guthrie's own words: "I have not felt myself at liberty to enter upon the land question in Shetland..."[11] And it was this omission which rendered the report as good as useless in bringing the truck system to an end. Shetland had to wait for more than another decade before change came.

Possibly the greatest evil of trucking in the hand knitting industry in Shetland, was that the system inadvertently propped up the poor quality knitter and her inferior articles. Many merchants for charitable reasons, or through force of habit, continued to buy poor quality hosiery. Naturally this led to an overall lowering of prices to compensate for the risk with this type of work, but more significantly, it acted markedly against the hand knitting industry as a whole, lowering its reputation in a time of increased competition from machine made goods. That trucking continued for so long in the Shetland hand knitting industry, was undoubtedly due to the presence of this poor quality hosiery, carelessly and hastily produced, to the isolation and generally low standard of living, and to a continuing high excess of females to males, coupled with lack of alternative employment for women. As Lord Napier, the chairman of the royal commission set up in 1883 to 'inquire into the condition of the Crofters and Cottars in the Highlands and Islands of Scotland', astutely pointed out - for crofters with their lack of tenure:

> ...conditions of life for a family in the island of Heisker in the outer Hebrides, or Foula in the Shetland Islands, are almost as different from those of a family in Midlothian or Middlesex, as if they lived in another hemisphere.[12]

He concluded, rather prematurely in the case of knitters:

> ...we remain under the impression that abuses incidental to the isolation of the country, the ignorance and poverty of the people, and the power of monopoly or combination among employers, are gradually melting away, and have to a large extent disappeared before the forces of increasing intelligence, public opinion and commercial competition; that the interest of the employer and employed are being harmonized by natural causes; and that legislative interference ought not to be hastily attempted...[13]

The Crofters Holdings (Scotland) Act followed in 1886. Based on Lord Napier's investigations, although rejecting his recommendations, the Act gave crofters security of tenure, fixed fair rents, compensation for improvements, and the facility to increase holdings, and finally freed the Shetland fisherman-crofter from the evils of truck, so that when anti-truck legislation did come in 1887, it was unnecessary in practical terms for all but the hand knitters. Knitting, a subsistence activity inextricably linked with barter-truck, lagged behind the fishing industry and experienced a very protracted transition from a barter to cash economy. For fishermen this period of transition from truck to free trade was much shorter. In addition to the security of tenure granted by the Crofters Holdings (Scotland) Act, the boom in the herring industry in the 1880s and the increase in modern communications, acted to help fishermen market their fish independently of their merchant-landlord. Unlike the knitters, who worked in isolation or in family units, fishermen formed co-operatives buying shares in boats and/or companies. For example, the Shetland Fishing Company, registered in 1872, was set up with the specific aim of prosecuting fishing free of truck. This type of unity helped strengthen a concerted effort to break away from truck. It took knitters another seventy years before they too united to form their own protective and marketing organisation.

Giving evidence before the Napier Commission in 1883, William Garriock, merchant from Reawick, pointed out that "In every insular locality the merchants must to accommodate the people both buy and sell and give credit".[14] Thus, although money payments were felt to be preferable, for many knitters the truck system continued to provide an invaluable safety net against destitution. In country districts, knitters still depended on their local merchant to buy their hosiery, eggs and other produce and when need be, advance them meal or other necessities against work to come. The trucking of hosiery had done much to keep the poor alive, supplying them with both food and raiment, and many knitters, especially those who knitted inferior articles, felt deeply indebted to their local merchant. An illustration of this is found in a letter to *The Shetland Times* dated 9th April, 1887. It is written in dialect and simply signed 'a knitter':

Ales! ales! Dey rin doon what dey caa "truck", and rin doon da merchants, but if it wisna fur baith some o' wis wid be waur off.[15]

It was generally recognised that it was the risk associated with the poor quality knitwear that led to the merchants setting such high profit margins. In effect, the poor knitters were benefiting at the expense of the superior ones, with the old system being best for the former.

Fifteen years after the 1872 Truck Inquiry, the Truck Amendment Act was passed on the 17th September 1887. Section 10, which dealt with home-workers clearly stated:

Where articles are made by a person at his own home, or otherwise, without the employment of any person under him except a member of his own family, the provisions of this Act shall apply as if he were a workman, and the shopkeeper, dealer, trader, or other person buying these articles in the way of trade were his employer, and the provisions of this Act with respect to the payment of wages shall apply as if the price of an article were wages earned ...[16]

In essence, this Act set out to plug the loop-hole regarding the payment of home workers in cottage industries, but although section 10 was almost tailor-made to suit Shetland hand knitters, trucking continued unchecked. Unfortunately, the Truck Amendment Act coincided with a depression in the hosiery trade and it was feared that the new act, rather than helping knitters would bring the country to a standstill and close down stores. The newspapers warned dealers in country districts that it was part of the Procurator Fiscal's official duty to investigate and prosecute offences under the act. Dealers started to refuse to buy hosiery unless it would meet the requirements of orders received from the south for hosiery. The price paid by merchants to knitters for hosiery fell drastically. For example, ladies' spencers which had formerly been bought for 1/4d., were now only fetching 8d., whilst knickerbockers went down in price from 2/- to 1/4d. The hand knitting industry was in turmoil, with truck being as warmly defended as it was hotly denounced. Leonard Lyell, M.P., addressing a meeting of constituents in Lerwick Town Hall in 1888, defended the Act, feeling that it would ultimately benefit both knitters and merchants, by leading to the production of better quality hosiery, thus enabling merchants to find "a more ready and remunerative market".[17] Many knitters felt themselves worse off than before the passing of this Act, and the opinion of Margaret Johnston from the island of Muckle Roe, was commonly held among the knitters: "Our only complaint against the cash system is that the prices of the goods remain the same, and we get less for our hosiery".[18]

This state of affairs led to the knitters and makers of claith (home spun cloth) in the Parish of Delting, sending a petition to Queen Victoria asking her to suspend section 10 of the Truck Amendment Act. The Queen referred this petition to a committee of the Lords of the Council for consideration, which resulted in the Sheriff-Substitute of Shetland, David MacKenzie, being asked to hold an inquiry. This inquiry, known as the Delting Truck Inquiry, was conducted on far less formal lines than the 1872 Truck Inquiry, with no official citings or hearings taking place. The hand written report - it was never officially printed - is lodged in the SRO at West Register House, Edinburgh.

At the 1881 census, Delting had a population of 1,654 people, being a decrease of 205 from that of 1871 - a decrease in line with other Shetland parishes. Out of this number, the names of no less than 500 knitters and makers of home spun cloth were to be found on the petition. However, many of these names were given in people's absence - for example, girls at school - and were written in by Peter Blance, the man responsible for going round the parish with the petition. In short, not all the names on the petition were added with the owner's permission, although, it was averred that no pressure had been used. However, Sheriff MacKenzie felt that the main complaint of the petition, namely the loss occasioned to the knitter by the low prices given by the merchants for hosiery in cash, was one which was felt by all, whether signatories of the petition or not. The petition was drawn up, not by knitters, but by the following merchants: Mr. Pole, of Pole, Hoseason & Co., Mossbank, Mr Inkster of Brae, Mr Sinclair of Graven, all of whom were aggrieved by the new system of cash payments. In effect these merchants were using the knitters to agitate for a return to the old, and to them, more profitable system, and having discussed the complaints made to them by the knitters as to the operation of the new Act, drew up the Petition as embodying these complaints, and as a means by which the knitters might give expression to their alleged grievances. Mr Pole's son, helped by Mr Woods the Firth Public School teacher, wrote out the Petition. The Petition, was then given to Peter Blance, a seaman, for the purpose of laying it before the knitters, prior to being forwarded to Mr. Leonard Lyell, MP.

Sheriff MacKenzie began his inquiry by travelling to the Parish of Delting on the 20th June, 1888. The following day, he visited Voe and its neighbourhood "calling upon the cottagers and conversing with them. In this manner I traversed the districts of Voe, Kirkhouse, Flett, Susetter, Dale etc." (Fig. 3.3). Sheriff MacKenzie found the knitters intelligent and industrious

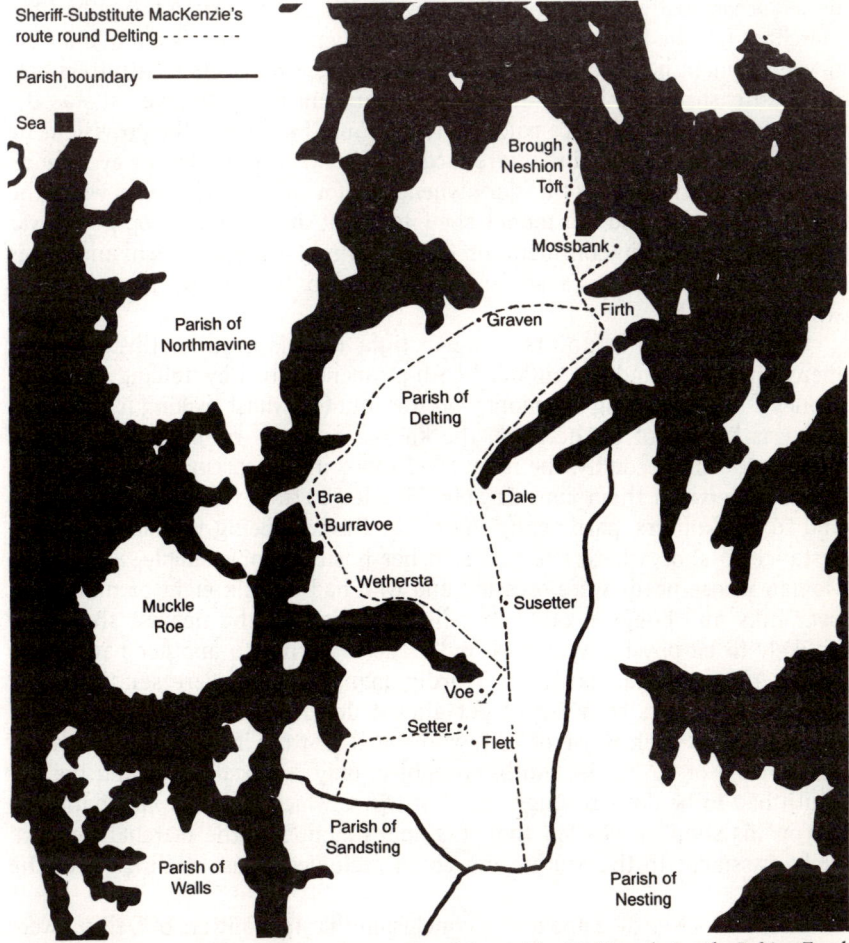

Fig 3.3 — Sheriff-Substitute MacKenzie's route round the parish of Delting, during the Delting Truck Inquiry, 1888.

"knitting by the fireside and on the hillside", and felt that they gave their evidence in a frank and unbiased manner and:

> ...while making the complaints which are noted in this Report they as a rule spoke in a tone of friendship and kindliness towards the merchants with whom they dealt, often expressing their obligations under which they stood for what the merchant had done for them in hours of need. This in my opinion was done without servility...[19]

As was the custom throughout Shetland prior to the Truck Amendment Act of 1887, knitting had been exchanged for goods, the merchants fixing the price of both. In Delting, unlike Lerwick, these goods were not confined to drapery but embraced every article of domestic consumption, and where knitters did not use their own wool, but got it first of all from the merchant, the exchange took the form of advances upon the credit of the work to be done. Occasionally small sums of money were paid for hosiery but only if the merchant felt the knitters needs were extremely necessitous. Section 10 of the new enactment had changed the character of these transactions. Knitters now received cash, but only the amount the merchant chose to give - it was the merchant who set the price paid for hosiery and the price of the provisions he sold. The inquiry showed that a reduction of between 10 to 30% or even more, was made on the price of hosiery when paid for in cash. However, when the knitter came to spend this money she found that the price for shop goods was in no way lowered in consideration of her paying for them in cash, and it was this double loss, which caused so much hardship, that was at the nub of the whole inquiry.

Other interesting points came to light in this inquiry. Firstly, some merchants got round the enforced cash payment system by 'tabling down the money',[20] that is laying the money on the counter, whilst making it clear that if it was taken out of the shop, the knitter need not return in future with hosiery to sell. Secondly, the number of shops in the parish was few and the distance between them considerable. This led to an absence of competition and to the knitters, particularly the old and infirm, being virtually forced by distance to shop where she had sold her hosiery. For example, a poor old woman whose needs were pressing and who had to walk eight or nine miles over hilly and boggy ground to sell her hosiery at the nearest shop, was unlikely to be physically able to undertake a journey to another part of the parish to spend her earnings. Thirdly, many knitters were sending their hosiery south, as they could get almost double for it that way, as was illustrated by Sarah Boyle of Toft, who stated that the little shawls which she sold for 5/- or 6/- in the south, brought in only 3/- locally. Sending hosiery south had to be done through the Post Office which the local merchant also ran in his shop. It was felt that this dual function of the merchant caused embarrassment to the knitter and could prejudice future dealings with the merchant.

Sheriff MacKenzie came to the conclusion that the knitters of Delting were not complaining of the recent Act, but of the merchants' action in lowering the price for hosiery without a corresponding lowering of the price of goods

TRUCK AND THE SHETLAND HAND KNITTING INDUSTRY 1790-1950

which had been adopted in consequence of the passing of the Act, and felt that:

> Whether this is a necessary and permanent consequence of the Statute, or merely an experimental and temporary cause of action, time alone can... show.[21]

He felt that, as the Act had only had a trial of twelve months, it would be premature to pass judgement until a longer time had elapsed. Sheriff George Thoms, the Procurator Fiscal of Shetland and ardent adversary of truck, was very much against any suspension of section 10. The Scottish Secretary, commended MacKenzie on the thorough and tactful way in which he had managed the investigation, but felt that "...the only remedy to the evils complained of seems to be private enterprise instituting competition" and suggested that the Post Office might be asked to look into the possibility of establishing post offices other than in the merchants' shops.[22]

Section 10 of the Truck Amendment Act was not suspended nor was any action taken. Surprisingly little space was given to this inquiry in *The Shetland Times*. More interest seems to have been centred on Peter Blance's unaccountable part in the petition and the number of false signatures, than anything else. From the knitters' stand point, the generally accepted point of view was voiced by Ellen Clark, a knitter from the Livinister and Firth district, who stated "I don't care what system it is, if I could only get a fair price for the article".[23]

This was the state of affairs in 1888, with barter-truck as extensive as ever, as the following extract from *The Shetland Times* illustrated:

> At present the system of barter is so general all over the islands that the doctor has to keep a yard on purpose of receiving his fees, which take the form of fowl, fish and all manner of useful articles.[24]

However, this was not a static situation. With the help of the increased communications with the south, particularly the parcel post, and the interest of both philanthropists and the anti-truck league, many of the more skilled knitters like the Shetland lace knitters, were by-passing local merchants and marketing their hosiery outwith the islands. As will be seen in the chapter on Shetland lace, the amount of patronage Shetland knitters received was small compared with, say, the Harris Tweed Industry. However, from 1872 onwards there was an increasing awareness by the well-to-do of the destitute state of many Shetlanders and, in keeping with the Victorian work ethic, many individuals and organisations strove to render some assistance. For example, the Shetland Knitters Repository was set up in Edinburgh in 1884 with the specific aim of selling Shetland hosiery free of truck. The Countess of Aberdeen, the Repository's patron, did much good work by arranging drawing room sales and opening exhibitions of Shetland hosiery. She was an informed speaker and dedicated worker in the fight against truck. The Shetland stand - called the Jaw Bone Stand because of the arch over it formed by a whale's jaw bone - at the Edinburgh International Exhibition in 1886 was also highly successful in bringing the evils of truck to the notice of the public (fig. 3.4).

KNITTING BY THE FIRESIDE

Fig 3.4 – The Jaw Bone Stand, Edinburgh International Exhibition, 1886.

TRUCK AND THE SHETLAND HAND KNITTING INDUSTRY 1790-1950

The Shetland stand was organised by Sheriff Thoms, resident of Shetland and ardent campaigner against the evils of truck, who believed that by bringing the knitter and purchaser closer together, it would help to bring the truck system to an end. Relays of six girls, three from Fair Isle and three from the rest of Shetland, were sent down to Edinburgh.

Individual names also crop up in anti-truck propaganda. For example, an article written in *Womanhood* in 1899 credits Margaret Currie (nee Colvin), a native Shetlander, with alerting the 1872 Truck Commissioners to the plight of the knitters, the result being:

> ... a Bill was passed which made the whole system illegal, and it was at once and for ever abolished, while each woman was for the future able to command a fair price in cash for her work.[25]

This article is so farcically inaccurate as to render its contents of little worth, but other sources suggest that Margaret Colvin did sell Shetland hosiery to the nobility and royalty, sending the cash back to the knitters. She is reported to have taken pity on a 'poor creature' who had been offered such a miserably low sum of money by the local merchant for her fine lacework, that she offered to give her some money, taking the shawl to try and sell herself. This she did by sending it to her late husband's hosier in Edinburgh, who paid a good price for it and ordered more. She established contacts with wholesalers in London and sold the fashionable lace work through the drawing room parties held by the aristocracy, undoubtedly using her energies in the fight against truck to further her own social standing:

> My work prospered, and being on a visit to Edinburgh...to Lady Emma MacNeill, only sister of the Duke of Argyll, I made the acquaintance of the Princess Louise...They were most kind, not only by making purchases themselves, but in introducing the industry of the Shetlanders to Her Majesty the Queen, and to members of the aristocracy.[26]

As a result of her crusade, she opened a truck-free hosiery shop - Schoor & Co., Esplanade, Lerwick, which was run by her sisters, Mrs. Schoor and Mrs.

---

158   Mansons' Shetland Almanac Advertiser.   **1893**

Personally Patronised by Her Majesty the Queen and Princess of Wales. Edinburgh International Exhibitions, 1886 & '90, rewarded with Gold Medal. By Special Appointment to H.R.H. Princess Louise, Marchioness of Lorne. A Diploma of Honour, (Highest Award given), at East End Exhibition, Glasgow, 1891

SCHOOR & CO.,
SHETLAND AND FAIR ISLE HOSIERS,
ESPLANADE, LERWICK, SHETLAND, N.B.

KNITTING OF ALL KINDS IN SILK AND SHETLAND WOOL.
ORDERS PER POST PROMPTLY ATTENDED TO.
Telegrams—SCHOOR, LERWICK.   KNITTERS PAID IN CASH.

Fig 3.5 — Advert taken from Manson's Shetland Almanac Advertiser in 1893.

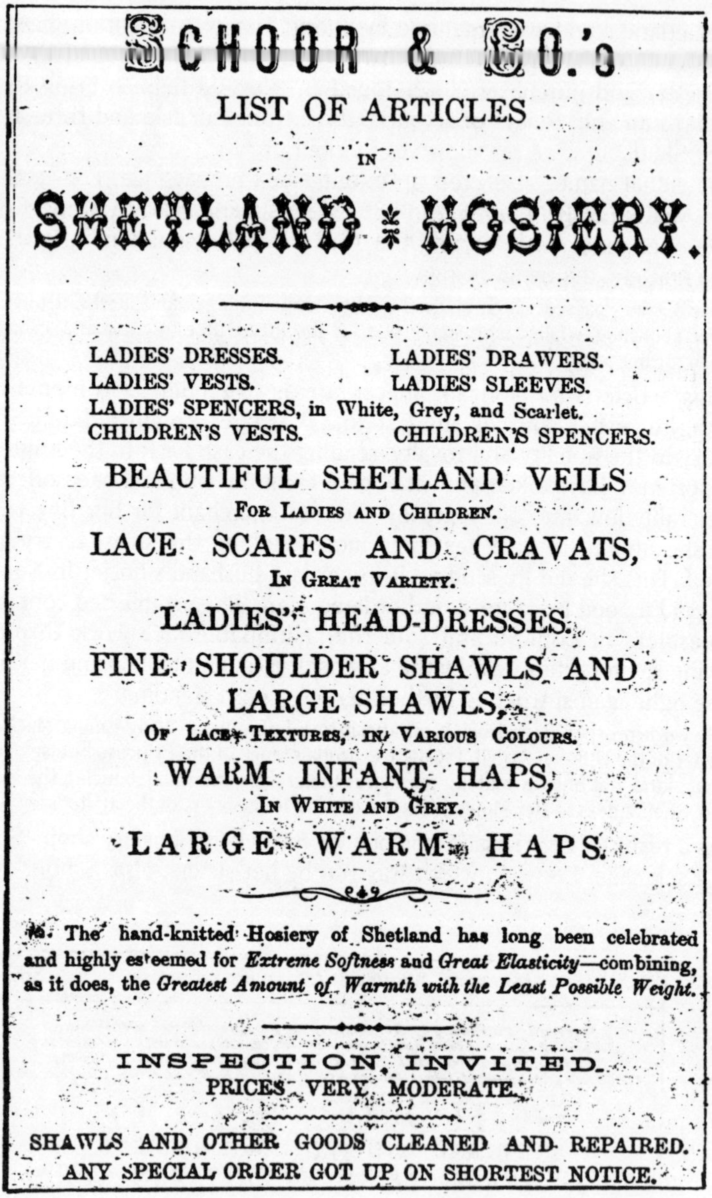

Schoor & Co.'s
LIST OF ARTICLES
IN
SHETLAND HOSIERY.

LADIES' DRESSES.   LADIES' DRAWERS.
LADIES' VESTS.   LADIES' SLEEVES.
LADIES' SPENCERS, in White, Grey, and Scarlet.
CHILDREN'S VESTS. CHILDREN'S SPENCERS.

BEAUTIFUL SHETLAND VEILS
FOR LADIES AND CHILDREN.

LACE SCARFS AND CRAVATS,
IN GREAT VARIETY.

LADIES' HEAD-DRESSES.
FINE SHOULDER SHAWLS AND LARGE SHAWLS,
OF LACE TEXTURES, IN VARIOUS COLOURS.

WARM INFANT HAPS,
IN WHITE AND GREY.

LARGE WARM HAPS.

The hand-knitted Hosiery of Shetland has long been celebrated and highly esteemed for *Extreme Softness* and *Great Elasticity*—combining, as it does, the *Greatest Amount of Warmth with the Least Possible Weight*.

INSPECTION INVITED.
PRICES VERY MODERATE.

SHAWLS AND OTHER GOODS CLEANED AND REPAIRED.
ANY SPECIAL ORDER GOT UP ON SHORTEST NOTICE.

Fig 3.6 – Advert for Schoor & Co.

Muir, and which paid knitters in cash. Figs. 3.5 and 3.6 show Schoor & Co. advertising as Shetland and Fair Isle Hosiers paying their knitters in cash. Schoor & Co. sold direct to the public, and judging from their prestigious patronage and awards, obviously had a high reputation for quality. This would

TRUCK AND THE SHETLAND HAND KNITTING INDUSTRY 1790-1950

have been a natural consequence of dealing in cash, as they would have had the pick of the knitters' work. In addition to shop sales, this company ran a mail order business and took advantage of the telegraph system installed in 1870. An interesting statement from the 1908 Truck Inquiry, referred to a Lerwick shop which paid its knitters in cash - undoubtedly Schoor & Co. - having to delay payments for several weeks due to lack of funds. Although, Schoor & Co. lacked working capital, many knitters were still happy to be out of pocket for a short time when money was required, rather than go to truck shops. There is no evidence to show that other merchants followed suit. Schoor & Co. remained in business for at least 25 years.

Truck in the hosiery industry, continued largely unchecked by the legislature well into the 1900s. Between 1887 and the 1908 Truck Inquiry there were only eight prosecutions in Shetland under the 1887 Truck Amendment Act, with far from punitive fines ranging from £1 to £2-10/- being imposed (fig. 3.7).

Date	Name	Amount fined
10/12/1887	Gilbert Irvine	£2-2/-
10/12/1887	Robert Fraser	£2-2/-
10/12/1887	Thomas Anderson	£2-2/-
30/1/1888	Peter Linklater	£2-2/-
2/5/1892	John Spence	£2-10/-
2/5/1892	Daniel Fraser	£1-10/-
1/2/1899	C.McLaughlin	£2-2/-
28/8/1902	William Pole	£1-0/-
15/5/1908	C.G.Williamson	?
29/10/1908	Pole Hoseason	£10-0/-
26/6/1909	John Kennedy	?
March 1910	Robert Leask	£2-0/-
March 1910	James Leask	£2-0/-
March 1910	C.G.Williamson	£6-0/-

Fig 3.7. Truck Prosecutions

In no way did these prosecutions benefit the knitters' lot. The most noticeable effect of both the 1872 Truck Inquiry and the Truck Amendment Act of 1887, had been to bring the hosiery trade to a standstill periodically. Wary of possible prosecution, merchants steered clear of giving out work every time it looked as if the Truck Amendment Act might be enforced.

Following the prosecution of a Shetland hosiery merchant in 1902, there was felt to be a temporary improvement in the situation, however, it seems to have been short lived as Parliament found it necessary to hold another truck inquiry in 1908. In *The Scotsman's* 1908 annual review of Shetland, Fordyce

KNITTING BY THE FIRESIDE

Clark, journalist and native Shetlander, pointed out that :

> The Truck Act since it came into force has been more noticed in the breach than in the observance ... undesirable conditions which called it into existence do not now obtain to anything like the same extent.[27]

The 1908 Truck Inquiry, chaired by the Lord Advocate, the Rt. Hon. Thomas Shaw, devoted considerable time to trucking in the Shetland hand knitting industry. Evidence concerning Shetland was given by Millicent, Duchess of Sutherland, in her role as President of the Scottish Home Industries Association (SHIA), by Miss Mary Paterson, inspector of factories, Mr Archibald Newlands, factory inspector in whose territory Shetland lay, Mr James Kirkland Galloway, Procurator Fiscal of Shetland, and Mr Gifford Gray, Superintendent of the Shetland County Police. Although this inquiry was not confined to Shetland, it amply highlighted how little trucking in the Shetland hand knitting industry had changed since 1887, or even 1872. For example, the following statement made by Miss Paterson showed that goods were still being exchanged for hosiery:

> In Lerwick the hosiery people who have shops for the tourists and so on all keep tea, simply for the purpose of paying the hosiery knitters, who do not buy hosiery...[28]

whilst it was clear from statements made by Mr Newlands, that a reduction was still made if cash was given in exchange for hosiery:

> What is known as the two price system is practiced. A cash buyer can buy for considerably less than a knitter can get in truck transactions. That varies as much as 10 to 25% on the price of the goods.[29]

Rather embarrassingly for the Duchess of Sutherland and the Scottish Home Industries Association, the inquiry brought to light that the SHIA was extensively involved in truck, mainly in the Western Isles where the largest purchaser of Harris Tweed was found to be a Glasgow tea merchant, but also in Shetland. The lace shawls bought by the SHIA were not bought direct from knitters but through the hosiery merchants - a severe affront to the Shetland knitters as the SHIA had been set up as a marketing organisation for home workers, whose policy it was to buy directly for them, paying a fair price. However, the inquiry also exposed what had been blatantly obvious since the passing of the new Act, that the Shetland Constabulary stood by whilst trucking went on under its very nose. Hasty and rather thin explanations were proffered by Gifford Gray, as to the difficulties of a shortage of manpower and the problems posed by the police having to wear their uniform on duty. The Lord Advocate was irritated and unrelenting. Action was to be taken. From the knitters' standpoints, few were prepared to come forward and report their truck merchant for fear of reprisals. This point was noted by Miss J. Cochrane of Edinburgh, who described herself as "a humble fellow worker against the dread evils of the Truck system" and who, since 1900, had been visiting Shetland, buying up hosiery which she mainly sold through the Scottish Home Industries, 132 George St., Edinburgh. In a letter to Mrs Tennant, one of the commissioners of the 1908 Truck Inquiry, she averred:

TRUCK AND THE SHETLAND HAND KNITTING INDUSTRY 1790-1950

> Unluckily it [Truck Amendment Act] gets enforced in Shetland occasionally for a short time and then it is dropped. Each time that happens it is a great misfortune. Some women support it and they are marked and can sell no more knitting. All around observe the consequences. Hence it is nearly impossible for the authorities to find cases to prosecute...If only the women could be assured that the Truck Act has at last come to stay numbers would flock to assist the authorities. It is the uncertainty that is the ruin... I assure you it is the uncertainty of the powers that be continuing to act that paralyses all.[30]

The outcome of the 1908 Truck Inquiry was a predictable lowering of prices and reduction in hosiery sales, a few token prosecutions with some half dozen merchants being fined derisory sums, but in reality it was business as usual, and it really did seem as if the Shetland hand knitting industry would never rid itself of truck. However, as *The Scotsman* pointed out:

> If the Truck Act is to be stringently enforced, it will be a sorry thing for Shetland, and the sooner the knitters realise this the better. It is futile to force the hands of the merchants in this way. It is unreasonable to expect them to accumulate piles of unsaleable hosiery goods and pay ready cash for same...[31]

The survival of truck in the Shetland hand knitting industry continued because of this unmarketable poor quality hosiery. Improved communications meant that the knitters of good quality hosiery, particularly Shetland lace, were by-passing increasingly local truck shops for their sales; poor quality work was perpetuating the system and giving Shetland hosiery a bad reputation. Free trade principles enjoyed by Shetland fishermen, were being unnaturally and unhealthily suppressed in the hosiery industry. But for the increasing competition from machine knitted imitations (dealt with in Chapter five) which was undercutting Shetland hosiery and threatening to exterminate the Shetland hand knitting industry, truck might well have lingered into the ultra-modern Oil Age of the 1970s. Understandably, knitters resented the low prices being paid for hosiery, but they seemed incapable of seeing that complaining would not halt the march of progress and that it was only by raising standards and producing well designed, evenly shaped and perfectly knitted articles, they could compete favourably with machine produced ones. By knitting exclusively for the luxury market, where top prices demanded top quality, truck could have been eliminated and the future of the hand knitting industry secured.

The hosiery merchants were well aware that if they were to survive, they would need to replace truck with cash payments. However, chronic shortage of capital meant that much of their wholesale trade was done by barter, whilst extended credits of up to 18 months and the general uncertainty of the trade, made it almost impossible to run their businesses on modern lines. For example, Miss Paterson, in her evidence to the 1908 Truck Inquiry, stated that:

> One merchant in particular said to me that the system was much more extensive than I knew of; that as a matter of fact he could hardly stop it unless it were stopped at the same time on a big scale; that his transactions with the people who supplied him with goods were carried on in the same way with the Glasgow merchant and so on - that he paid them in Shetland goods also.[32]

Cash payments and short credits were deemed by most to be preferable to the old system, but thwarted by lack of capital, this system presented difficulties of implementation, and as the Duchess of Sutherland, in her capacity as President of the SHIA, pointed out to the Lord Advocate, Thomas Shaw, "Our desire is not to have truck...when we make advances to the people we do so to keep them from starvation..."[33] This policy had been adopted and sanctioned by the Government during the destitution years of the 1840s, when islanders were paid in meal for labouring on the 'meal roads' and the elderly and infirm set to work earning their allowance by knitting.

Just before the outbreak of the First World War, the Highland and Islands Home Industries Report, compiled by Professor W. R. Scott, of St. Andrews University, was published. Considerable space was devoted to the Shetland hand knitting industry, but very little to the vexed question of eradicating truck. In fact, Professor Scott seemed more taken up with the "complete absence of the rush and strain of factory work..."[34] and other rather nebulous advantages of home workers, than he did with help for trucked knitters. He noted that knitters felt "the view is prevalent that the enforcement of the Truck Act has been prejudicial to them".[35] As with the aftermath of the Truck Amendment Act when the Delting knitters had suffered from a considerable lowering in the price paid for hosiery, it was reported in *The Scotsman* "There is a strong feeling amongst the knitters that Government should be petitioned to repeal the Truck Act".[36] Nothing came of this, but the six prosecutions (see fig. 3.7) under the Truck Amendment Act which had taken place between 1908 and 1910, had led to a nervousness amongst merchants about giving out hosiery. This move, coupled with the depression in the hand knitting trade brought about by, not only machine made goods, but also by the great rise in the number of Shetland imitations flooding the market, led to prices having fallen more than in proportion; that is, the conversion of 'soft goods' into cash was not in line with their monetary value. Failing to grasp the extent or true nature of trucking and the Shetland hand knitting industry, Scott concluded "...in the summer of 1912, several merchants had decided to abandon this side of the business".[37] In reality this was not the situation and amounted to little more than the usual tactics employed by merchants to evade prosecution.

Arguably, the First World War, did more to eradicate truck than past legislation. War time shortages, trade disruptions, and the cash payments received for hosiery sold to servicemen billeted locally, helped even the poorer knitter to turn her work to cash. For example, the Board of Agriculture, working in conjunction with the Army Authorities, suggested that wool be supplied to Shetland knitters to knit socks for the Army. The Board recognised that such a scheme could best be organised by one of the Associations or Committees interested in the furtherance of home industries who were familiar with local conditions, and asked the Co-operative Council of the Highland Home Industries to undertake this scheme, promising a grant of £100 towards the administrative costs. Through its success, Shetland hand knitters received £2,300 paid in small sums to individual workers. In addition to this scheme, the pre-war supply of cheap imported underwear from the Continent, which had been entirely cut off by the War, led to an increase in demand for Shetland hosiery, and to a rise in prices. The benefits of the War on the Shetland hosiery had given the trade an additional boost. By 1918, it was reported that demand was much greater than supply. And it was this shift from foisting unwanted articles on to local merchants, to knitting to order for money, which allowed Shetland hand knitters to participate temporarily in a fully developed, modern, albeit artificial, market and to break free of truck.

However, a post-war slump in the hosiery industry was severely felt in the autumn of 1920 when cheaply produced machine made goods reappeared on the southern markets, and the Shetland hand knitting industry was in a state of stagnation. Shocked by their sudden loss of earnings, knitters, desperate to 'sell' their hosiery, inevitably resorted to trucking with their local merchants again. Scottish Office records show that in 1924 truck was still an issue in the Shetland hand knitting industry. The Board of Agriculture for Scotland's 1924 report on "The social and economic conditions in the Highlands and Islands", suggested that co-operative credit might help overcome this problem and felt that a home industry might be regarded as an agricultural purpose within the meaning of the Agriculture Credit Act of 1923. This scheme was not pursued and trucking continued unchecked until the Second World War.

The presence of many thousands of servicemen stationed on the islands during the Second World War, had the enormously beneficial effect of allowing the knitter to cut out the middleman-merchant by dealing directly with this new local market. And it was this unique position of strength which encouraged knitters to band together and set up their own knitters' co-operative, the Shetland Hand Knitters Association (SHKA). This association was regarded by many as one of the main factors which put an end to any remnants of the barter system, by establishing set rates for prices of knitwear, although contemporary Scottish Office files suggest that this statement may have been over-optimistic:

> The barter system, resulting in the exchange of knitted goods for the necessities of life through a local merchant is still practiced and cannot be defended as being a sound system in the interest of the industry. It is detrimental to the maintenance of a high standard in design and craftsmanship, and it is said to result in the knitting of a large quantity of goods which are of inferior quality.[38]

Despite the lingering existence of small amounts of trucking, it can be said that the Second World War was to the hand knitter what the Crofters Holding (Scotland) Act of 1886 had been to the fisherman.

The Shetland hand knitting industry had survived into the twentieth century because of the cheap and flexible supply of its labour force; its workers' pressing economic needs meant that knitters were prepared to accept payment in goods, and a pittance at that. The introduction of the non-contributory Old Age Pension in 1908, increased communications, the slow but steady rise in the general standard of living, increase in the local circulation of cash and alternative employment opportunities, all eroded this archaic time warp. Thus, hosiery which had been the only means by which many Shetlanders had been able to purchase goods, was replaced by cash and with it barter-trucking, at last came to an end. Nevertheless, it must be recognised that whilst truck in the Shetland hand knitting industry had been responsible for perpetuating inferior work, thereby threatening the hand knitting industry's existence, it had done much to prevent widespread destitution and hardship, rural depopulation, and emigration. By present day standards, life for many was at a grim subsistence level, but for the many cottars and 'Shetland housewives' with no land and little means of support, knitting offered an alternative to the Poor House for the old and emigration for the young.

References - Chapter 3

1. PP, Cd. 326, (1871), Report by the Commissioners appointed by the Truck Commission Act 1870..., p. 10.
2. PP, Cd. 555, 1872 Truck Inquiry, (Thule Print edition 1978), p.11.
3. Op. cit., p. 45
4. Ibid.
5. PP, Cd. 555-1, 1872 Truck Inquiry, p. 426, q. 16,660.
6. PP, Cd. 555, 1872 Truck Inquiry, (Thule Print edition 1978), p. 48.
7. Standen, E., *The Shetland Islands*, (Oxford 1845), p. 17.
8. PP, Cd. 555, 1872 Truck Inquiry, (Thule Print edition), p. 49.
9. Op. cit., p. 31.
10. Op. cit., p. 32.
11. Op. cit., p. 56.
12. PP, Cd. 3980, (1884), Crofters and Cottars, Highlands and Islands of Scotland, p. 44 and 67.
13. Op. cit., p. 47 & 48.
14. Op. cit., p. 243.
15. *The Shetland Times*, 9th April, 1887.
16. PP, Cd. 4443, (1908), Minutes of evidence taken before the Truck Committee, p. 142.
17. *The Shetland Times*, 1st September, 1888.
18. SRO (WRH), Delting Truck Inquiry, HH1/848. Evidence of Margaret Johnston.
19. Op. cit., Sheriff-substitute MacKenzie's Report.
20. Op. cit., Evidence of Peter Blance.
21. Op. cit., This extract is taken from Sheriff Substitute MacKenzie's summing up of the inquiry.
22. Op. cit., Comments of Scottish Secretary (unnamed) in accompanying Scottish Office papers, dated 12th December, 1888.
23. Op. cit., Evidence of Ellen Clark, knitter.
24. *The Shetland Times*, 26th May, 1888.
25. *Womanhood*, Vol. 4, March 1899, p. 288.
26. Ibid..
27. *The Scotsman*, 20th January, 1909.
28. PP, Cd. 4443, (1908), Minutes of Evidence taken before the Truck Committee, Vol. II, p. 118.
29. Op. cit., p. 135.

TRUCK AND THE SHETLAND HAND KNITTING INDUSTRY 1790-1950

30 SRO (WRH), HH1/848. Letter from Miss J. Cochrane to Mrs. Tennant, dated 6th January, 1909.
31 *The Scotsman*, 20th January, 1909.
32 PP, Cd. 4443, (1908), Minutes of Evidence taken before the Truck Committee, p.118.
33 Op. cit., p. 168.
34 PP, Cd. 7564, (1914), Report to the Board of Agriculture for Scotland on Home Industries in the Highlands and Islands, p. 91.
35 Ibid.
36 *The Scotsman*, 20th January, 1909.
37 PP, Cd. 7564, (1914), Report to the Board of Agriculture for Scotland on the Home Industries in the Highlands and Islands, p. 92.
38 SRO (WRH), SEP12/30, "Some impressions on the Shetland Woollen Industry", prepared by Major the Hon. Robert Bruce of the Crofter Woollen Industries Committee of the Scottish Council on Industry - October 1944.

Chapter 4
The Origin and Development of Shetland Lace

The earliest example of Shetland lace knitting in the Shetland Museum's Collection is shown in fig. 4.1. This three-cornered shawl is reputed to have been worn by John Bruce of Sumburgh at his christening on 4th June 1837. It was knitted from extremely fine hand-spun native wool and, although less

Fig 4.1 — This three-cornered shawl was reputed to have been worn by John Bruce of Sumburgh at his christening on 4th June, 1837.

intricate than those of a later date, is a representative example of nineteenth century Shetland lace knitting. Strictly speaking, the term Shetland lace is a misnomer; a more correct term would be Shetland open-work. However, the beauty, delicacy, and artistry of Shetland lace, surely justifies the use of the word lace. The story of the origin and development of Shetland lace knitting in the mid 1830s is a fascinating combination of evolution, events and people.

The failure of Shetland's long established stocking trade at the beginning of the nineteenth century led to widespread hardship, exacerbated by poor harvests at sea and on land, so that by the time the Poor Law Commissioners visited Shetland in 1843, many people were found to be destitute. And it was during this prolonged period of extreme want and lack of alternative employment for knitters that Shetland lace emerged. This emergence was due to benevolently minded individuals who sought to help knitters fill the economic vacuum left by the stagnation in the stocking trade, by encouraging them to adapt their skills to produce this highly fashionable open work.

Origin

Many writers have attempted to pin-point the origin of Shetland lace knitting; most accounts have been incomplete, whilst others have been inaccurate or improbable. For example, James Norbury (1904-72), a television lecturer and pioneer in travelling to discover local knitting traditions, stated authoritatively in his book *Traditional Knitting Patterns*:

> In the early years of the nineteenth century a Mrs Jessie Scanlon visited Shetland, taking with her a collection of hand-made laces she had acquired during the Grand Tour. The Hunter family of Unst, who were very excited about these laces, developed a technique for copying them in hand knitting. The work of the family became famous, and one of the earliest lace shawls they knitted was presented to Queen Victoria in the early years of her reign.[1]

This account may be true but it is unsubstantiated by source material and James Norbury, an enthusiastic but untrained researcher, had a reputation for "drawing broad conclusions from slender evidence".[2] Mrs Jessie Scanlon's name fails to crop up in any of the more reliable accounts of the origin of Shetland lace written in the nineteenth century, whether by Shetlanders or outsiders. However, in fairness to Norbury, there was a Hunter family living in Unst who became well known for their lace knitting and Queen Victoria was presented with gifts of fine knitting in 1837. It seems most likely that the secondary source on which James Norbury based his assumption that it was the Hunter family who had created Shetland lace, was taken from *A Treasury of Knitting Patterns:*

> The Mrs Hunter who originated this pattern was a member of the famous Hunter family of the Isle of Unst, the most northerly of the Shetland Islands. The Hunters began and developed the art of Shetland lace knitting and have created lace shawls for the British Royal Family from the time of Queen Victoria to the present.[3]

Insufficient evidence makes it difficult to assess the extent of this family's contribution to the origin of Shetland lace. Lack of primary evidence would suggest that Norbury resorted to some convenient guess work to paint a romantic picture for his viewers and readers. Unfortunately, for lack of research into the origin of Shetland lace, his work is still referred to, and so the 'Jessie Scanlon myth' is perpetuated.

Undoubtedly the most reliable, semi-contemporary account of the origin of Shetland lace, is to be found in Dr Robert Cowie's *Shetland*, first published in 1871. This account is somewhat of a conundrum, but unravelled, basically tells the following story: Samuel Laing, parliamentary candidate for Orkney and Shetland, whilst visiting Shetland in 1833, stayed in Lerwick as the guest

The First Shetland Shawl

I stood on a cliff, while the Eastern beam
Shot forth o'er the sea its liquid gold stream;
I watched as the shadows awoke from their dream,
And fled from the glance of the water's bright gleam,
Silence reigned o'er the deep – the Storm-wave slept,
While Ripples alone had their vigils kept;
And now in the gold of the morning they dip't
Their feet, while along the dark rocks they trip't.
In vain did I listen for Ocean's old Hymn,
There seemed a brief pause in that Psalm of time;
Yet Ripples kept chanting a silvery chime
That awoke infant echoes in dark sublime.

Yet a strain of sweeter flow
On my ear is falling now –
'Tis the Mermaid's voice, I know,
Singing matins soft and low.
See her sit wild cliffs between,
Image of an Ocean Queen, –
Brow of pearl and locks of green,
Radiant in the morning sheen.
See her take her finest ball
Spun in deep-sea *Coral-Hall*.
And with pearly fingers small
Knitting the *First Shetland Shawl*.
Knitting "Wave," and "Pearl" and "Shell"
(Long she'd known these patterns well),
While her song, "The Ocean Swell",
Held my ear with magic spell.
Swift these pearly fingers play,
Weaving threads from morning's ray,

Dyed in colours fresh and gay
From the rainbows of the spray.
Swiftly now, and swifter still,
In the richest patterns fill –
With the "Wave", the "Pearl" and "Shell",
Weave the "Diamond," "Branch" and "Bell".
Now, in Robe of pearly hue,
On the rock she stood to view,
Near, the wondering fishes drew,
And on wing the sea-birds flew,
Yielding each the homage due.

But a Sea Nymph rode on a gilded cloud
To meet the sun as he rose from the flood,
And, envious, she the Mermaid viewed
As Queen of the Sea in her Robe so proud!
And downward she flew, and upward she drew
From Mermaid's shoulders the mantle new.
The Mermaid then raised a dolorous cry;
The Nymph, unheeding and bounding high,
Did over the crags and the mountains fly,
The Mermaid then blew her *Enchantress' Shell*,
And followed the Nymph with her deadliest spell.
Paralysis seizing her, down she fell,
And drop't her robe on a healthery spell.

A Thulean maiden, with surprise,
Saw the bright thing descend the skies;
And as she gazed with wonder eyes,
She flew to seize the matchless prize.

P.S. – Thule's daughters, great and small,
Thank your stars for this windfall;
But you should acknowledge all,
Mermaid knitted the *First Shawl.*

LERWICK, *August, 1868.*   R.S.

Fig 4.2. "The First Shetland shawl".

of Mr Charles Ogilvy, partner in Hay and Ogilvy. Mr Laing's daughter later sent Mr Ogilvy's infant son a christening cap which she had knitted in openwork in fine Lille thread. This christening cap was much admired and subsequently copied by a lady related to the family, who also knitted a pair of mitts in a similar style. This same lady in 1837, made a fine invalid cap for Mr Frederick Dundas, then M.P. for the county. Mr Dundas, when in Shetland, is reputed to have shown this cap to his Lerwick landlady and encouraged her to get the younger knitters to imitate the fine work in knitted shawls. This however met with no success. The story continues that Mr Edward Standen, a merchant from Oxford, whilst travelling in the islands in 1839, saw a shawl being knitted by 'the abovementioned lady' and on his return to Lerwick, mentioned it to the person he was lodging with and encouraged her to get other knitters to follow suit, thus "giving a fresh impetus to the fine-knitting of Shetland".[4]

Fig 4.3 — This christening cap dates the probable starting point of lace knitting in the Shetland Isles at 1833.

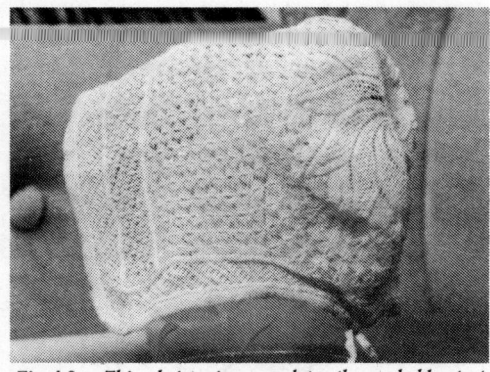

And it was from this point that Shetland lace knitting became recognised in its own right. This account, albeit rather confusing, is undoubtedly more plausible than credit being given to an unknown Mrs Scanlon, or even to a mermaid as the poem *The First Shetland Shawl* (fig. 4.2.) suggests! Furthermore, contemporary writers like Rampini and others, and twentieth century Scottish Office files, refer to Dr Cowie's account of the origin of Shetland lace and presumably would not have done so unless they felt it was of a trustworthy nature. What is particularly exciting about this account is that the lace cap referred to above, along with a silver christening cup engraved with the Ogilvy crest, has survived to the present day. The woollen christening cap is in perfect condition, although yellowed with age (fig. 4.3), and is the property of Charles Ogilvy's great great grand-daughter, Mrs Mary Downham, who lives in South Africa. Mrs Downham was left these articles by her father, Frederick John Ogilvy, who in turn had been left them in the 1920s by his 99-year old aunt Miss Ginny or Jenny Ogilvy. This cap therefore dates the probable starting point of the development of lace knitting in the Shetland Islands at around 1833.

Mrs Eliza Edmondston (1784-1869) of Buness, Unst, has been credited with having taught local women the art of Shetland lace knitting which she is thought to have copied from the lace in her trousseau. This explanation seems unlikely, when in *The Home of a Naturalist*, Mrs Edmondston's daughter, Mrs Jessie Saxby, mentioned that her mother's trunk, containing all her wedding garments, had gone to the bottom of the sea in a storm in Lerwick harbour. In a letter dated 21st April, 1928 to a Mrs. L.D. Henry, Jessie Saxby claimed that Shetland lace knitting began in 1832 when "My mother – at the suggestion of a gentleman friend - began the lace work and taught it to the women".[5] However, Mrs Eliza Edmondston, or in the Shetland tradition of keeping one's maiden name, Mrs Eliza MacBrair, in her book *Sketches and Tales of Shetland*, makes no such claim and herself gives a very plausible explanation as to how Shetland lace evolved:

> ...the open work knitting now so attractive to the poor artists, as to the public, is an invention for which the Shetland females themselves deserve all credit. From the simplest beginnings, led on and encouraged by some ladies as a pastime, it has progressed from one thing to another, till it has attained its present celebrity, without the aid either of pattern book, or of other instruction than the diligence and taste of the natives themselves.[6]

Nor is there any reference to Mrs MacBrair having taught local girls to knit fine lace in either Lady Jane Franklin's or her niece Sophia Cracroft's, journals written during their visit to Shetland in 1849. These chatty journals are full of domestic issues - Sarah Cracroft's containing a wealth of information on Shetland knitting. It would seem most probable that Mrs Eliza MacBrair, with whom Lady Franklin and her niece stayed in Unst, would have mentioned her connection with lace knitting, especially as she produced fine open-work to show Lady Franklin and gave her some "very pretty mittens etc. for sale to benefit a few".[7]

Whilst it would appear that Mrs Eliza MacBrair cannot be credited with having 'invented' Shetland lace knitting, she deserves much credit, as her daughter stated in her small book *Shetland Knitting*, for "being influential in encouraging and instructing knitters in fine lace work",[8] for her work in publicising the plight of Shetland knitters, and for making the public aware of the beautiful knitted products of these islands. This she did through her pen, hoping that it "... may enlist some kindly heart and generous hand in the patronage of the most northerly of the British Isles".[9] Her two main works were, *Sketches and Tales of Shetland* and *The Poor Knitters of Shetland*; the former published in 1856 and the latter in 1861 under the name 'A Lady Resident'. In *The Poor Knitters of Shetland* reference is made to a visitor coming to the islands in 1838, who suggested that shawls and handkerchiefs, with a few open work stitches as a variety would likely be marketable and remunerative:

> The idea was eagerly embraced and some ladies leading the way, one pattern after another was tried and adopted, long before pattern books ever reached this latitude, till gradually the combination of stitches and patterns reached its present perfection.[10]

The visitor may have been the Oxford merchant, Edward Standen or Frederick Dundas MP.

The gradual emergence of Shetland lace with "some ladies leading the way", rather than its origin being attributed solely to a single person or date, seems likely, as throughout Scotland in the nineteenth century, it was customary for fine knitting to be undertaken as a pastime by the female members of the leisured classes. Shetland was no exception. A hand written journal by an unknown author, written in the year 1832, and entitled *An excursion to the Shetland Islands* referred to the fine stockings knitted in Shetland:

> The finest fabrics are generally the handiwork of daughters of the ministers, or people in a respectable station, who having nothing wherewith to occupy their spare time...not infrequently employ it in this way; and woollen work of the finest kind is equal in texture and smoothness of appearance to silk.[11]

It was around 1835 that this pastime became a fashionable craze among English and Scottish ladies. This popularity was reflected in the introduction of the first written knitting patterns or 'recipes' to appear on the market. In Scotland, Jane Gaugain of George Street, Edinburgh, was the first to have printed privately in 1836, three knitting recipes for friends. Next came her *Small work on fancy work*, published in 1837, which was followed by several other new recipes and numerous reprints. These attractive hard backed books with a few colour prints and illustrations, were published by "I.J. Gaugain - Foreign and British depot of Berlin patterns and materials for ladies fancy work, 63 George Street, Edinburgh and Ackermann & Co., London".[12] A recipe for "A handsome Shetland square knit shawl", complete with laundry instructions, was included in her 1842 *A Lady's Assistant for executing useful and fancy designs in knitting, netting and crochet work*. Whilst Shetland knitters did not follow written knitting patterns, but knitted their patterns from memory, with their highly developed skills in fine knitting, it would have been relatively easy for the ladies of the upper classes to copy stitch patterns from the work of their Edinburgh friends. Shetland's close ties with Edinburgh were further strengthened by the custom of the better-off sending their children, including daughters, to school in Edinburgh. In addition, some Edinburgh families, like Mrs A. Traill who summered in Fetlar for health reasons, migrated from the city to summer in Shetland.

It is disappointing that there is no mention of lace knitting in the *New Statistical Account* or the 1843 Poor Law Inquiry - although the latter contains many references to knitting - as this would throw further light on the development of Shetland lace. However, the following extract taken from *The Poor Knitters of Shetland* is of interest:

> Until within the last 15 or 20 years, knitting for sale in these islands was confined to stockings and seamen's coarse frocks; the remainder of the wool was home-made into blankets and stuffs for common wear. It is now found more profitable to purchase Manchester and Leeds made cloths, and manufacture for sale the native wool into all sorts of delicate fabrics suited to the invalid - the noble - the lovely - and the wealthy benevolent.[13]

In 1851, William Baillie Mackenzie, hosiery merchant and importer of Shetland lace, at 126 Princes Street, Edinburgh, stated in his entry in the *Great Exhibition Catalogue:*

> Knitting is the chief employment of the female inhabitants of these isles in their own

homes. Stockings have been made there from a very ancient period; but the fanciful knitting comprising shawls, etc. is of a recent introduction.[14]

This dating of around 1840 for the emergence of Shetland lace knitting can be verified finally from evidence given by Arthur Laurenson, chief partner in Laurenson & Co., before the 1872 Truck Inquiry: "It was about 1840 or 1841 that the making of shawls began to get very common here".[15] It was shawls which were knitted initially in Shetland lace.

Edward Standen

Edward Standen - mentioned in Dr. Cowie's account of the origin of Shetland lace - made a brief but vital contribution to the story of Shetland lace knitting. Like many of the stories surrounding the origin of Shetland lace, his is rather involved, nor is it without a few queries. The bulk of reliable information on Edward Standen is to be found in his small treatise on the Shetland Islands, published posthumously in 1845. The introduction to this work, written by a friend of the family, referred to Edward Standen's keen interest in helping Shetland knitters. When visiting the islands in 1844, he had been the only survivor in a boating accident, which had however, left him weak. The following year, feeling it his Christian duty to return to Shetland, as God had spared him from drowning, he caught pneumonia and died at Sandlodge. The front piece of Edward Standen's published treatise is entitled *A Paper on the Shetland Islands, read at the opening of the Devonport Mechanics Institute, when an exhibition was made of choice specimens of Shetland knitting.* In his text, Edward Standen referred to the home spun yarn used in these examples as competing with, and surpassing, that spun by the finest machines and to the knitwear as "...showing so great a variety of patterns in fancy work, and such exquisite knitting in plain work".[16]

The queries in the Edward Standen story are as follows: Firstly, was he a hosiery merchant when he first visited the islands in 1839, or a dealer in Shetland ponies as *The New Shetlander* stated, or as a friend of Arthur Anderson, who was involved in the Shetland Fishery Company at Vaila, was he in some way connected with the fish trade? Secondly, whatever his reasons for visiting Shetland, why was he presenting a paper and exhibiting hand knitted Shetland articles at a Mechanics Institute? Presumably he held the work of these remotest of all islanders in high esteem and was using their example to encourage other unfortunates to greater things. Thirdly, was the Standen & Co., which exhibited fine Shetland lace at the Great Exhibition in 1851, his company? It seems highly likely that it was. Unfortunately there is a dearth of documented evidence to provide answers to these questions. Fig. 4.4 shows his widow advertising as trading at 28, High Street, Oxford, but does not mention a warehouse at Jermyn Street, London. However, an article in *The Shetland Times*, dated 16th October, 1909, referred to Joseph H. Standen - one of Standen's eight sons - having visited Shetland, and went on to describe him, as in business at the time of his father's death (1845) in the

MRS. EDWARD STANDEN,
No. 28, HIGH STREET,
OXFORD,

Desires to acknowledge with gratitude, the kind support which her Establishment has received since the decease of her late husband. She begs to remind her Friends, that the

SHIRT-MAKING

branch of her business is under the superintendence of Mr T. Nicholls, late of the firm of W. & T. Nicholls, St. James' Street, London. From his great experience in this department and in the

GENTLEMEN'S MERCERY

trade in general, she can with much confidence undertake, that in quality of make and material, combined with moderate prices, the greatest satisfaction will be afforded to her customers.

SHETLAND
KNITTED GOODS

Of every description, wholesale and retail. Shawls, Scarfs, Stockings, Socks, Mittens, Under-clothing for Ladies' and Gentlemen's use, and all other Goods of this Manufacture, so successfully introduced by the late MR. STANDEN.

Fig 4.4 – Advertisement placed by the widow of Edward Standen.

firm of 'Standen & Co.' Edward Standen's friendship with Arthur Anderson, may provide many of the clues in filling in these missing links. In 1837 Arthur Anderson suggested to a few Shetland knitters that they made some hosiery to be presented to the newly crowned Queen Victoria. This suggestion was followed up and Arthur Anderson personally presented both the Queen and the Duchess of Kent with some very fine hosiery. Queen Victoria responded handsomely by placing an order for one dozen pairs of stockings and requested that she be billed for them. Possibly, as a result of encouragement from Arthur Anderson, Edward Standen started importing hosiery from Shetland.

THE ORIGIN AND DEVELOPMENT OF SHETLAND LACE

It is apparent from his treatise that he was a deeply religious man, and therefore it may have been that, whilst travelling through the Shetland Islands on whatever business, he became aware of both the plight of the knitters in the hard times of the 1830s and 40s, and of the commercial viability of their handiwork, and felt it his Christian duty to help these people by marketing their work in the south. It was this introduction to the London market which was responsible for spreading the fame of Shetland lace and in creating a demand for this fine lace work:

> ...and by introducing the goods into the London market, was the means of converting what had been for a few years previously followed as a pastime, by a few amateurs, into an important branch of industry, affording employment to a large proportion of the female population of the islands.[17]

Standen's contribution to the story of Shetland lace was admirably summed up in the introduction to his book:

> It is, indeed, to his enterprise and energy that the public are indebted for the introduction into England of a comparatively unknown article of manufacture; whilst the inhabitants of Shetland owe to his sound judgement and honourable liberality, the development of resources with which they had been hither to unacquainted, but which have already proved of incalculable benefit to them...[18]

Thus the origin of Shetland lace can be attributed to an evolutionary development accelerated by two MPs and fostered by benevolently-minded Shetland ladies, who wishing to alleviate the distress of destitute knitters in the hard times of the 1830s, helped them to adapt their skills, turning this subsistence activity into a highly marketable product; whilst, the emergence of Shetland lace c.1840 on the southern market, can be attributed to the happy coincidence of Edward Standen's visits to Shetland. Without Edward Standen's contribution, Shetland lace is unlikely to have ever reached such fame, but more importantly, such constant demand for Shetland lace on the southern markets, acted as a stabilising force helping to stave off destitution, unemployment and rural depopulation.

The Origin of Shetland Lace Patterns

Many of the stitch patterns used in Shetland lace knitting like, Madeira stitch, Madeira cascade (also called old Spanish lace pattern) and others, are of Spanish origin and it is tempting to assume that there may have been some connection with Spain and Portugal, particularly, as Spain was regarded as the home of the finest white knitting in the world. As Shetland travellers and merchants sailing to America would have made their last stop at Madeira before picking up the trade winds necessary for the voyage across the Atlantic, it is tempting to draw some connection. However, there is no evidence to verify this supposition. Mrs MacBrair, in fact tried to make this connection herself, but without success. She mentioned having looked into this channel for possible connections with Madeira, Germany, and Malta but asserted:

We are, indeed, aware, that in Madeira, Germany, Malta, etc., very fine specimens of knitting in cotton and silk thread are produced; but after making every possible enquiry, we cannot make out, that they were in advance of the Shetlanders in the invention of the art.[19]

It is interesting that there may be a link with Russia. Jessie Saxby mentions having seen a Russian shawl exactly like Shetland lace in the Edinburgh Museum and interestingly states, "No doubt the work was known in England but not in our Isles before 1832".[20] A shawl offered for sale in a Moscow market in 1988 (fig. 4.5) is knitted in a very similar style and design to a Shetland lace shawl - the Russians also have the same tradition of passing the shawl through a wedding ring. The origin of this type of knitting in Russia, is thought to have come from the Volga-Deutsch in the eighteenth century. Furthermore, in *The Complete Book of Traditional Knitting Patterns* Rae Compton refers to a beautiful lace shawl, exhibited in the Victoria and Albert Museum, and knitted in the Shetland style but which is attributed to Russian origin and is extremely similar to a shawl shown in Bishop Rutt's *A History of Hand Knitting* knitted in vegetable fibre from the Azores. This similarity adds to the difficulty of trying to pin-point the origin of a particular type of knitting, and the cases of duplication from different parts of the world, shows the wary approach which must be taken when tracing the spread of knitting.

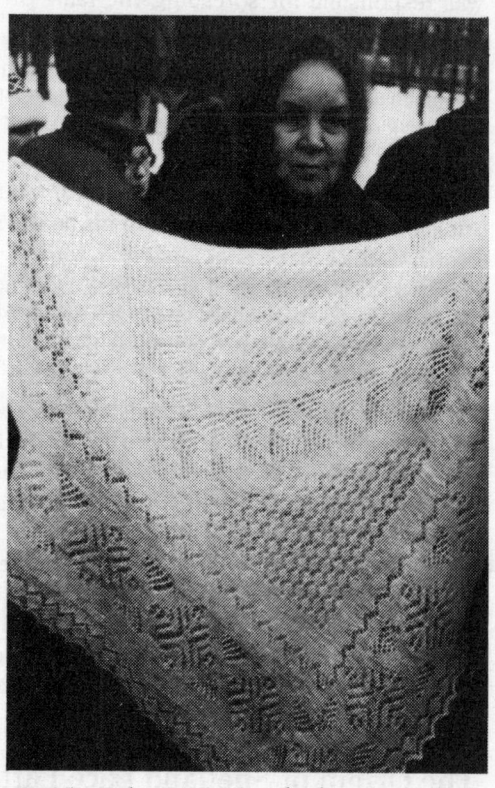

Fig 4.5 – Modern Russian lace shawl.

Several references have already been made to the fact that Shetland knitters never wrote down their patterns. Their work was frequently referred to as 'growing under their hands'. Dr. Robert Cowie, remarked that many of the peasant girls displayed great artistic talent in the invention and arrangement of patterns, which were formed "out of their own heads",[21] with the knitter often having no preconceived idea as to the stitch patterns to be used in the finished article. In her journal, Sophia Cracroft mentioned being told by a Mrs. Williamson of Hillswick, that:

THE ORIGIN AND DEVELOPMENT OF SHETLAND LACE

the women follow the most intricate patterns by recollection merely, and without any written directions. Some of them invent designs of which there are immense variety.[22]

Inevitably, when meeting together knitters would 'swap' patterns. Not only did Shetland knitters use no pattern books, but they knitted with great speed.

Their fingers move, with a rapidity their eye can scarcely follow, over the most complicated patterns, with no rule but memory and minute attention.[23]

Girls learned to knit from an early age and would go through an unstructured and totally informal type of apprenticeship, picking up their skills from the older female members of the family. Patterns were handed down from mother to daughter, with possibly a little individuality added each time. Daughters would progress from plain to lace knitting. Mrs Joan Mouat of the Heritage Centre, Unst, and lace knitting gold medallist at the Royal Highland Show, related how girls would learn to knit lace by knitting the plain rows between the patterned ones and thus intuitively picking up this skill.

Looking at old examples of fine lace shawls it is still somewhat of an enigma as to how the artistry of the design and the arithmetical computations necessary to achieve this, were married together with such perfection. Throughout the nineteenth century, all but the very small number of women belonging to the professional and upper classes, lived in overcrowded, smoke-filled, inadequately lit hovels, without proper washing facilities or even a suitable place to store their delicate white lace work. Although many knitters had two pieces of knitting on the go at the one time - coarse socks which they worked at between times, and lace knitting which was done in the evenings - it is difficult to imagine how Shetland women, with the constant demands on their time and whose labours perpetually soiled and roughened their hands, managed to produce these works of art. This point was mentioned in a lecture on Shetland Lace given by Mrs L.D. Henry in March 1931:

> ... if you could see the primitive houses in which these people live, the little buts and bens dotted here and there on scraps of cultivated land and clinging to the folds of the barren wind-swept mossland, you also would wonder how it was possible that such delicate wool as you see here to-day could have had its origin in such surroundings.[24]

Shetland lace has a wealth of stitch patterns with names such as

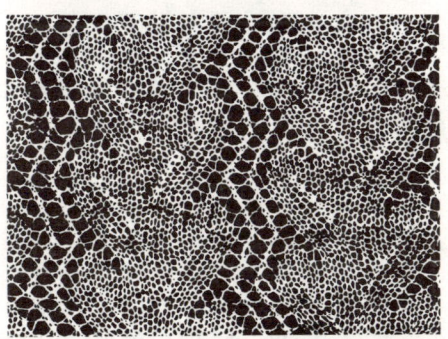

Fig 4.6 — Two traditional Shetland lace knitting patterns

'Old Shale'

KNITTING BY THE FIRESIDE

Fig 4.7 – Bestway knitting pattern leaflet.

peerie flea, cat's paw, acre, leaf, the puzzle, and many, many more. Tradition has it that these patterns were inspired from nature, as for example, 'old shale' being formed by the motion of the waves on the sand, and 'print o' waves', by the turbulence of the sea (fig. 4.6). Many of these patterns have now been put into written pattern form by firms like Bestway (fig. 4.7) and Patons & Baldwins, to make them available to the general knitting public,

THE ORIGIN AND DEVELOPMENT OF SHETLAND LACE

Fig 4.8 — Knitted shawl based on a traditional Shetland pattern designed by Mrs A. Hunter, Unst.

although patterns are rarely used by Shetlanders themselves. The Hunter family, mentioned earlier in connection with James Norbury, worked in association with Patons & Baldwins, and were the first to write down Shetland lace patterns in a commercial form. Fig. 4.8 shows extracts from an old printed pattern by the Hunters. Other names well known in connection with top quality lace spinning and knitting are the Sutherland family, the Jamieson sisters, and Mrs. Johnston, all of Unst.

Location

Unst, the most northerly inhabited island in the Shetland archipelago, was the home of the very best lace knitting, as this was where the very best wool was grown, whilst Lerwick, was the Shetland Mainland centre for lace work. Lerwick knitters however, never attained the same reputation for excellence as those of Unst. Sophia Cracroft noted this difference whilst staying in Unst with the Edmondstons:

> We talked of the Shetland knitting which is said to be more beautiful in Unst than in any other part and some stuffs of exceeding beauty were shown to us and some bought by my Aunt. We now regret having spent so much money on shawls etc. in Lerwick where they are not so fine made as those made here.[25]

Unst spinners were famed throughout Shetland for their superior skills. The connection between Lerwick and Unst as the homes of the finest lacework, probably stems from several factors: The finest wool was grown and the finest lace worsted spun on Unst, whilst Lerwick was the marketing centre for lacework; migration from the north isles, meant that many homeless people came to Lerwick, where there being no alternative employment, they were forced to take up knitting, using their skills and wool connections with the north; and possibly because in the summer time, the more well-to-do families moved out of Lerwick and took up residence in the country, particularly Unst, which was regarded as the "Bath or Brighton of Shetland",[26] taking their knitting skills with them.

Lace Yarn

Shetland lace is knitted on two knitting needles or wires - Shetland lace knitters never used circular needles. Imported wires rather than home made wooden pins, were used for knitting Shetland lace. Wires had been used by Shetland knitters from at least the early 1800s, when Edmondston, referring to the manufactures in Shetland, wrote in 1809 "the knitting of worsted stockings, caps and gloves, on wires, by the women, is amongst the most ancient".[27] By the time of Lady Franklin's visit to Shetland in 1849, some knitters were using brass wires as unlike steel wires, they did not rust. Only the finest wool was used for lace worsted. It was plucked from around the neck and breast and from behind the ears of the sheep. This wool, which has a very soft, silky feel and short staple, was sometimes combed rather than carded to separate the fibres before spinning, as it was felt that carding was too rough and would damage the delicate fibres. Before carding or combing, the wool was teased or lightly plucked to loosen the fibres. Both combing and carding were laborious, tiring and dirty operations. If carded, a pair of wooden wool cards* was used. The wool was lightly oiled, placed between the wool cards which were then gently drawn apart in opposite directions, thus separating the fibres. To avoid breaking the fine ends of the yarn, it was necessary to draw the hands well apart; this was one of the most exhausting parts of the whole process of preparing the wool for spinning. Using the backs of the wool cards, the wool was then made into small rolls. This prepared wool was now ready for spinning.

Spinning, described in *Scottish Home Industries*, as "pretty, graceful work, but very tiring...the poor old women, who are the principal spinners, complain very much of aching backs and sides after a spell of it",[28] was carried out on old lint wheels or the upright Scotch or Norwegian-type spinning wheel. For fine lace yarn, two pirns* were filled, and these yarns twined together into lace worsted, reeled into hanks on a niddy-noddy* or upright wool winder, ready for knitting. Fine lace worsted was measured in cuts of 100 threads, rather than by weight - a thread being one turn of the niddy-noddy and approximately one yard long. Writing in 1861, Mrs Edmondston noted that only a few people could spin from one ounce of raw wool, three thousand yards of thread, which being three-fold (that is made up of three plies), made nine thousand yards in all. The spinning of very fine lace yarn - sometimes referred to as gossamer or cobweb yarn because of its fragility and delicacy - required great skill and patience and only a few could spin to such a high standard. At the time of the 1872 Truck Inquiry, Shetland wool was still being spun on the islands, but the number of spinners left who could spin fine worsted was dwindling and imported Scotch (also called Pyrenees) worsted, silk and black mohair were regularly being imported and used for lace knitting. *The Old-Lore Miscellany of Orkney, Shetland, Caithness and Sutherland* of 1907 described cottage spinning as a lost art, and stated that spinning wheels had become no more than curiosities. Hunter's of Brora Wool Spinners and Weavers, Sutherland, started up in 1901 and along with Pringle of Inverness, dealt with the vast bulk of the Shetland clip. Of the two, Hunters of Brora remains as the only spinner of Shetland wool. However, no machine has ever been able to card or spin fine Shetland wool to the same standard as an expert hand spinner, although these firms did produce a lace weight yarn.

Knitted Articles in Shetland Lace

Shetland lace knitting is most famous for its beautiful shawls. These varied in size, style, colour and construction, from very large square ones, which would be used folded over to form a double triangle, to smaller three cornered ones, with white, grey or scarlet for general use, and black for mourning. Figs. 4.9-4.11 show a variety of Shetland shawls. On average, it took approximately 6,000 threads of fine home spun worsted, weighing 2oz., to make a good sized fine lace shawl - often called 'wedding ring 'shawls, as they were so fine that they could be drawn through a wedding ring - whilst, a medium weight shawl required 4 - 5oz. of yarn. These shawls were measured in scores, 23 score being a fairly large size. A score referred to the number of stitches and therefore a 23 score shawl would have 460 stitches on each side. Fig. 4.12 shows the ingenious technique used to create a seam-free square shawl. The knitter started with the lace edging. Approximately 10 stitches were cast on, and the lace edging knitted to the same length as the perimeter of the finished shawl. Once completed this edging was divided into quarters, and stitches picked up from each quarter to knit up the borders, which in turn formed the sides of the centre. The centre was then knitted in as shown in Fig. 4.12. By casting on only a very small number of stitches to start the lace edging, no harsh lines or seams were used which would have detracted from the shawls cobwebby perfection.

Crepe shawls have lace edges and borders but are knitted with a plain centre (fig. 4.10). Expert knitters felt that crepe shawls were as demanding on the knitter's skill as a fully patterned lace shawl, as considerable dexterity was required to knit the garter stitch centre in the perfect, even tension necessary to avoid irregularities. Hap shawls were generally knitted in two or three ply worsted, and traditionally had lace edgings, coloured borders and plain self-

Fig 4.9 – Fine lace shawl.

Fig 4.10 – Crepe shawl.

coloured centres (fig. 4.11). Although plainer than the one ply ring shawls, great skill was required in grading the natural colours used for the borders. Alice Grierson, in her report to the Scottish Home Industries Association c.1895, described the care and patience required to select, weigh out the wool in ounces, half-ounces, and quarter-ounces, before carding and spinning each shade separately, prior to knitting. Hap shawls, incidentally, were the only type of lace work worn by local women, and even then their shawls would have been coarser than the ones knitted for export. As well as shawls, veils or clouds, neckties, falls, stoles, cloaks, opera cloaks or burnouses, wedding veils, trains for court dresses, ladies lace sleeves and stockings, and handkerchiefs were all knitted in Shetland lace. Veils, which

Fig 4.11 – Hap Shawl.

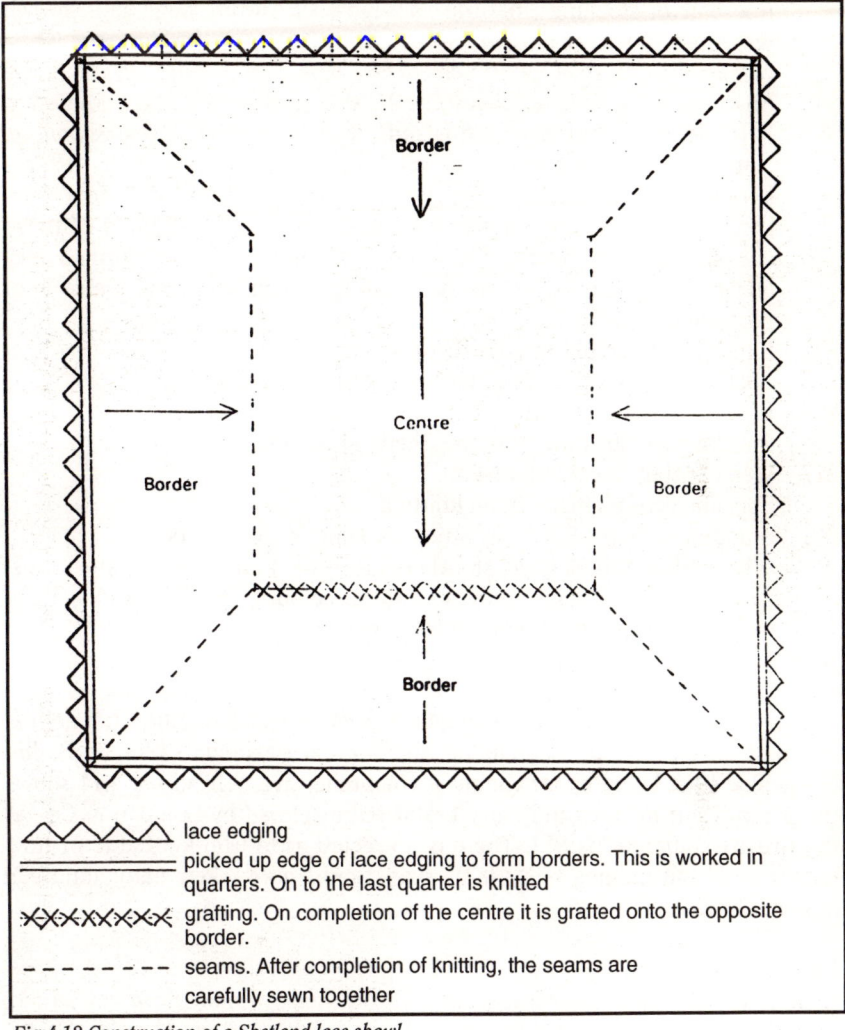

△△△△△ lace edging
───── picked up edge of lace edging to form borders. This is worked in quarters. On to the last quarter is knitted
✗✗✗✗✗✗✗ grafting. On completion of the centre it is grafted onto the opposite border.
─ ─ ─ ─ ─ seams. After completion of knitting, the seams are carefully sewn together

Fig 4.12 Construction of a Shetland lace shawl.

to some extent superseded shawl's after 1850, took approximately 1/2oz. of wool to knit.

Extracts from the 1851 Great Exhibition Catalogue

142 Mackenzie, William Baillie, 126 Princes Street, Edinburgh - Proprietor. Articles knitted by the hand in the Shetland Islands, from the wool of their sheep. Shawls; handkerchief; child's frock; veils of the natural-coloured wool; white and coloured gloves; ladies' white and coloured mitts; ladies' brown and white stockings, very fine wool; an extremely

fine pair of stockings; natural-coloured socks; white knee caps; brown leggings, natural colour; sleeves; ladies caps, nightcaps, wigs; comforters and shirt. Specimens of Shetland yarn, handspun; and of the Shetland wool, as it is taken from the sheep. Articles that are knitted in Fair Isle, one of the Shetland Islands - Fair Isle socks, gloves, vest piece, comforter and cap. Shawls and veils, knitted by hand in Shetland from a thread spun by machinery, composed of wool and silk together. [Knitting is the chief employment of the female inhabitants of these isles in their own homes. Stockings have been made there from a very ancient period; but the fanciful knitting, comprising shawls etc., is of recent introduction]

174   Linklater - Shetland Islands - Proprietor.
      Specimens of knitting peculiar to the Shetland Islands.
213A Lerwick Local Committee, Scotland - Producers.
      Specimens of knitting from the Shetland Islands.
217   Westminster, the Marchioness.
      Specimens of Shetland hand knitting.
281   Standen & Co., 112 Jermyn Street, St James's - Importers.
      White Shetland knitted shawl. Bridal veil. Pair of white stockings. Brown, grey and white gloves - natural colours. The Shetland wool of which these specimens consist is hand-spun.

Fig. 4.13

Fig. 4.13 is made up of the extracts from the Great Exhibition Catalogue, and lists all entries which included Shetland lace exhibits - William Baillie Mackenzie's list being by far the most comprehensive. Whilst, fig. 4.14 shows the magnificent madder and ivory bridal veil displayed by Standen & Co., at the Great Exhibition in 1851. There is no record as to who knitted it, or how long it took, but judging by its large size, it must have taken many hundreds of hours to knit.

Earnings

Despite the exquisite workmanship and the many, many hours of labour required to produce top quality Shetland lace, few knitters could make a living from knitting alone. For example, information given in the 1872 Truck Inquiry, shows weekly earnings ranging from 2/3d. to 5/7d., making the average amount earned weekly by knitting 3/9d. It must be stressed that due to lack of specific and detailed information, these figures can be no more than a rough approximation of the average weekly earnings of a lace knitter. These figures do however, tally reasonably well with contemporary estimates: *The Scotsman* reported in 1871 that "at veil knitting and shawl knitting the females, if very industrious, will make 6/- a week; and at hosiery and underclothing 4/- to 5/-".[29] As earnings were generally paid in goods throughout most of the nineteenth century, and the merchants' profit on

Fig 4.14 The madder and ivory bridal veil which was exhibited at the 1851 Great Exhibition.

these goods was abnormally high, the real value of these earning would be reduced by approximately 25%. Because of the small return in real terms which knitters obtained for their labours, most skilled knitters endeavoured to by-pass their local merchants, selling their lacework, when the opportunity arose, through alternative channels, such as merchants from Edinburgh, Orkney, agents in Shetland, or to private persons visiting the islands or to those "who desire to do the poor Shetlanders a kindness",[30] ordered direct from the knitters. At the same time, the Arts and Crafts Movement was gaining momentum and the public attitude to cottage industries changing.

Patronage

In the Machine Age of the nineteenth century, many concerned people were beginning to realise that the craftsman had become usurped by machines; worse still, that man had become a mere cog in the whole process of industrialisation. With the introduction of piece and shift work, few workers had the satisfaction of being responsible for the creation and completion of a factory produced article. Idealists, like Thomas Carlyle, John Ruskin, and William Morris, deplored this loss of creative individuality, and spoke out against its deleterious effect both on the morale of the worker and on the artistic value of his manufacture and tried to halt the march of progress by encouraging the revival of rural craft industries. And it was on these ideals that the Arts and Crafts Movement emerged around the 1870s.

The Arts and Crafts Movement (c.1870-1914), said to have its origins in a middle class crisis of conscience, was welcomed and supported enthusiastically by many middle and upper class women, whose position in society precluded them from gainful employment, but whose belief in the 'work ethic' made them abhor their enforced idleness. They threw themselves into reviving and supporting cottage industries, organising instruction for workers and arranging the marketing of their goods, often through exhibitions and drawing room sales. It was usually the middle class women who did most of the work, whilst the upper classes and aristocracy lent support through the prestige of names, possibly opening exhibitions or arranging drawing room sales for their wealthy friends to attend. The ailing hand-made lace industry, which enjoyed royal patronage and whose products carried the mark of wealth and prestige, was particularly popular with this type of philanthropist who gave it whole hearted support. Lace associations, like the Diss Lace Association in Norfolk, sprang up all over Britain. In Scotland, lace industries were started in Orkney, New Pitsligo and Tarbet, as cottage industries to create employment.

The increase in cruise steamers opened up the remote Scottish islands and coastal highland districts to an energetic, ever increasing and aspiring middle class which had made its money in industry or trade, and to whose Christian charity, many crofters had reason to be thankful for help in times of destitution. For this newly moneyed class, with its superiority and self-righteousness, travel to these remote places was very much in vogue. The poor destitute crofter, was to them not much more than a museum piece and an object of pity. In Shetland these visitors were welcomed as cash buyers of hosiery, but in the more destitute and remote islands, like for example, Hirta in the St. Kilda group, they unwittingly upset the fragile balance between subsistence and destitution.

THE ORIGIN AND DEVELOPMENT OF SHETLAND LACE

From this wave of philanthropy and interest in rural crafts, which swept Britain in the second half of the nineteenth century, the Shetland lace industry enjoyed a beneficial spin-off. It must be remembered, however, that the Shetland lace industry was not a dying one which was being revived, but one which had grown from the need to adapt to changes in fashion, one whose workers could not easily be supplanted by machinery, one which had rarely enjoyed sustained patronage, and one which was still dominated by the truck system - the latter being a subject dear to the hearts of many righteous Victorians. The 1871 and 1872 Truck Inquiries, extensively covered by the national 'dailies', had for many, put Shetland on the map, and much indignation had been aroused by the merchants' treatment of the knitters. It was this oppression by man, not by machine, which led to sporadic bouts of patronage; the Shetland lace industry never enjoyed the undivided support of

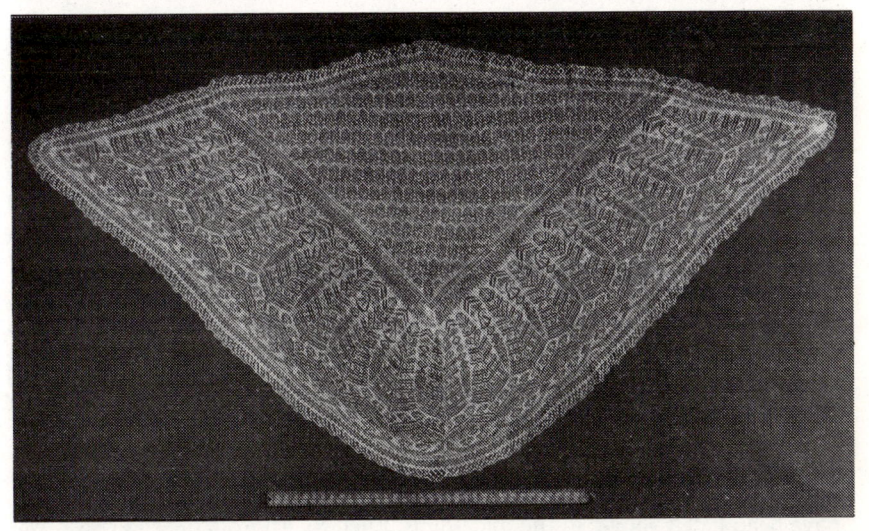

Fig 4.15 – Duplicate of the shawl presented to Princess Alexandra on the occasion of her marriage to the Prince of Wales in 1863. © The Trustees of the National Museums of Scotland

a single patron, as for example had the Gareloch hose industry, started during the potato famine years of 1846-48 by Sir Kenneth Mackenzie to alleviate distress, or the Harris Tweed Industry, whose success was largely due to the patronage of Lady Dunmore in the 1840s and later to that of the Duchess of Sutherland under the auspices of the Scottish Home Industries.

The gossamer filminess and exquisite workmanship, along with the inherent romanticism of hand wrought articles from the 'lonely isles', made Shetland lace items particularly suitable for entering competitions and displays at exhibitions. At the Great Exhibition, there were five exhibitors of Shetland lace (see fig. 4.13), Standen & Co., of London, Mackenzie of Edinburgh, and Linklater's of Lerwick and Edinburgh were the three merchant houses exhibiting, whilst the Lerwick Local Committee and the Marchioness of Westminster also exhibited Shetland hosiery. Twelve years later, the Lerwick Ladies Committee presided over by Miss Ogilvy - probably the relative of the Ogilvy family mentioned in Dr. Cowie's account of the origin of Shetland lace - presented to Princess Alexandra on the occasion of her marriage to the Prince of Wales, 'the handsomest collection of Shetland knitted goods ever brought together'.[31]

Fig. 4.15 shows a copy of the shawl included in this gift. Shetland lace knitting won medals at numerous exhibitions at home and abroad. The bridal veil shown in fig. 4.14, won a gold medal at the Great Exhibition. Catherine Brown formerly from Lerwick, one of the expert knitters who gave evidence before the 1872 Truck Inquiry, won a prize at the London Exhibition of 1870; she knitted a silk opera cloak for the Princess Alexandra, Princess of Wales. It was also at exhibitions that royal patronage could be forthcoming. For example, at the Edinburgh International Exhibition of 1886, Queen Victoria and the Princess of Wales were presented with Shetland lace shawls from Unst. They also made purchases from the Shetland stand (see chapter three, fig. 3.4). This stand won a gold medal diploma. Shetland lace was even shown at exhibitions abroad. For example, in 1893 a beautiful lace shawl knitted by Marion Nisbet of Unst, was displayed at the Chicago Exhibition. The shawl measured 2 1/2yds. square and was spun from 2 1/4oz. of wool. A correspondent, trying to describe the shawl, stated:

> It is impossible to give an adequate idea of the fineness of the thread and the delicacy and perfection of the work, but the thread - fine, it seems, as human hair - has all been spun twice, and if you untwist a strand of it you will find that it consists of two threads twisted together. Twelve miles of wool (single yarn) are knitted into this wonderful shawl; and the centre as well as the border is richly patterned...and took the best part of two years to knit.[32]

Shetland lace knitting has always had links with the British Royal Family. Several instances, starting with Arthur Anderson's gift to Queen Victoria, have been listed above. In the mid 1890s, Ellen Smith from near Lerwick, was commissioned by Queen Victoria to knit an exact replica of her favourite but worn-out black shawl. These small amounts of royal patronage, have always had the beneficial effect in either boosting sales, creating fashion trends or simply reminding the public of the existence of Shetland lace. Even after the First World War, *The Scotsman*, reporting on 'Shetland in 1925', finds space in this short article to report excitedly that:

> A rumour was current some little time ago that the Queen had her benevolent eye on the Shetland shawl industry, and intended to do her best to make these shawls fashionable, and so bring prosperity to the women of the islands.[33]

The popularity of Shetland lace was at its peak from around the time of the Great Exhibition of 1851 to that of the 1872 Truck Inquiry. From then until the turn of the century, there was still a steady, but reduced, demand for Shetland lace. For example, *The Shetland Times* in December 1885, stated that the Edinburgh International Exhibition of 1886, would "bring to light ...

Shetland shawls - not so much knitted lately because of change in fashion".[34] The change in fashion referred to is the decline in the vogue for crinolines - a fashion which was at its height from 1856 to 1868 - shawls being particularly suitable for wear with these bulky dresses.

Shetland lace has never totally gone out of fashion, being regarded as a classic form of knitwear, but twentieth century demand has never come near that of the nineteenth century. The First World War brought not only changes in women's fashions, but also a considerable upheaval to the social and economic circumstances of the more well-to-do, that is, the traditional purchasers of Shetland lace. During the War, Shetland hosiery sales enjoyed a boom, but practicality rather than elegance, was of paramount importance, with warm spencers, small haps and gloves, ousting lace knitting in popularity. Probably the most marked decline in the popularity of Shetland lace was noted during the inter-War years, when Fair Isle knitting became popular. The trend for delicate, feminine creations, seemed to die with the War and the women of the new society, less hidebound by class and inherited wealth, who emerged after the War, were free to enjoy a more physically active lifestyle. Fair Isle knitwear was ideal for sports and children's wear; also for the new jumpers and cardigans adopted by the more liberated female of the 1920s.

Attempts by Mrs Jessie Saxby and her cohort, Mrs L.D. Henry, to revive the dying Shetland lace industry were made in 1928. Both ladies wrote to the press appealing for support and patronage for Shetland knitters. Mrs Saxby's appeal highlighted the hard times the islands were experiencing, emphasising the effect such periods of unemployment had on the population with people drifting away to other parts of the country, and appealed for:

> ...some philanthropic person with a long purse and a wise head, will establish in our Isles a 'hadd' of native sheep, and the beautiful industry which has (for nigh a century) given employment to our women will be restored.[35]

In a subsequent article, Mrs Saxby proposed, that in the face of diminishing supplies of native wool, knitters should turn to using linen yarn for lace knitting; she stated that she had been in touch with a Glasgow firm specialising in linen goods. Nothing came of this scheme. Mrs L.D. Henry's article in *The Scotsman* appealed to ladies to lend their drawing rooms for Shetland lace sales to try and prevent the demise of this industry. Her attempts to revive Shetland lace knitting through an appeal in the *Sheffield Daily Telegraph* in October 1928 are of particular interest, as this article highlighted Shetland lace knitting as the victim of the 1920s craze for Fair Isle knitting:

> ... the furore of the Fair Isle jumper, which spread over the world like wildfire, and created an unprecedented demand for work, which offered them more money, and a quicker return than their lace shawls could bring them. In this way there has only been a small loyal remnant of lace knitter working in Shetland, during these post-war years, and at the present moment, there is a very real danger that the industry will disappear altogether, unless some help and guidance are given to it from outside the islands.[36]

The decline in fortune of the Shetland lace industry thereafter, was inextricably bound up with the Shetland hosiery industry and will be looked at as an integral part of the Shetland hand knitting industry.

References - Chapter 4

1. Norbury, J., *Traditional Knitting Patterns*, (Batsford, London 1962), p. 173. Also by James Norbury *The Penguin Knitting Book*, (Penguin, Harmondsworth 1957) - on page 18 of this book he repeats the 'Jessie Scanlon story' but also adds for good measure: "The Shetlanders, who were already ardent knitters, mainly following the Scandinavian tradition which had been taken to the islands by the Norse settlers in the ninth century..." There is of course no surviving evidence to suggest that knitting may have reached the Shetland Islands via these early Norse settlers.
2. Rutt, R., *A History of Hand Knitting*, (Batsford, London 1987), p. 3.
3. Walker, Barbara, *A Treasury of Knitting Patterns*, (Batsford 1968), p. 150.
4. Cowie, R., *Shetland*, (Edinburgh 1874), p. 185.
5. NMS, Henry, L.D. MSS. Letter from Mrs Saxby to Mrs L.D. Henry 21st April, 1928.
6. Edmondston, E., *Sketches and Tales of Shetland*, (Edinburgh 1856), p. 177.
7. SPRI, Ms. 248/240, unpublished *Journal of Sophia Cracroft in Shetland 1849*, p. 147.
8. Saxby, J., *Shetland Knitting*, (Lerwick - undated), p. 4.
9. 'A Lady Resident', *The Poor Knitters of Shetland*, (Paisley 1861), p. 9.
10. Op.Cit., p. 5 & 6.
11. SA, SA2/52. Unknown author. *An excursion to the Shetland Islands*. The extract quoted in the text, refers to Lerwick, 28th May, 1832.
12. NLS Gaugain, J., *The Lady's Assistant for executing useful and fancy designs in knitting, netting and crochet work*, (second edition, London 1840). The information in the text is taken from the inside front cover.
13. 'A Lady Resident', *The Poor Knitters of Shetland*, (Paisley, 1861), p. 2
14. *Official Descriptive and Illustrated Catalogue of the Great Exhibition 1851*, Vol. II, p. 585.
15. PP, Cd. 555-1, 1872 Truck Inquiry, p. 41, q. 2138.
16. Standen, E., *The Shetland Islands*, (Oxford 1845), p. 32.
17. Cowie, R., *Shetland*, (Second edition, Edinburgh 1874), p. 185.
18. Standen, E., *The Shetland Islands*, (Oxford 1845), p. 6.
19. Edmondston, E., *Sketches and Tales of Shetland*, (Edinburgh 1856), p. 177 & 178.
20. NMS, Henry, L.D. MSS., Letter from Jessie Saxby to Mrs L.D. Hentry dated 21st April, 1928. The Royal Museum of Scotland could find no trace of this shawl in March 1992.
21. Cowie, R., *Shetland*, (Second edition, Edinburgh 1874), p. 186.
22. SPRI, Ms. 248/240, unpublished *Journal of Sophia Cracroft in 1849*, p. 194.
23. Op. cit., p. 6.
24. NMS, Henry, L.D. MSS. Lecture given by Mrs. L.D. Henry on Shetland lace 30th March, 1932.
25. SPRI, Mss. 248/240, *Journal of Sophia Cracroft in Shetland 1849*, p. 144.
26. Edmondston, E., *Sketches and Tales of Shetland*, (Edinburgh 1856), p. 39.
27. Edmondston, A., *A View of the ancient and present state of the Zetland Islands*, (Edinburgh 1809), Vol. II, p. 2.
28. Munro, L., *Scottish Home Industries*, (Dingwall 1895), p. 117.
29. *The Scotsman*, 24th January, 1871. Report from 1871 Truck Inquiry held in Edinburgh - evidence of George Smith, Clerk of Supply.
30. 'A Lady Resident', *The Poor Knitters of Shetland*, (Paisley 1861), p. 7.
31. Cowie, R., *Shetland*, (Second edition, Edinburgh 1874), p. 187.

32 *People's Journal*, 27th August, 1889.
33 *The Scotsman*, January, 1926.
34 *The Shetland Times*, December, 1885.
35 *The Shetland Times*, 7th April, 1928.
36 *Sheffield Daily Telegraph*, October, 1928.

Chapter 5
Dawn of Modernisation 1872-1918

The period 1872-1918 was of vital significance to the development of the Shetland hand knitting industry, as increased communications with the south led to its great expansion. For Shetlanders in general, this was a period of oscillating and intermittent progress towards a modern Shetland, with truck declining, the old 'Shetland Method' disappearing, and in its place, a modestly prosperous economy emerging, largely based on the principles of free trade.

In 1872 Shetland's first regular weekly newspaper, *The Shetland Times*, appeared. Apart from local news, this paper carried much national and international news, culled from the pages of national 'dailies', like *The Scotsman*. From this date, not only could the inquiring Shetlander become more aware of what was happening in the next parish, but he could also keep abreast of events within Britain and throughout the Empire, thus helping to erode his sense of isolation, identifying more with Britain than with Scandinavia, and severing the last remnants of traditional Scandinavian ties.

Scanning the pages of the 1872 editions of *The Shetland Times*, it is apparent that the scene is set for a modern Shetland to emerge, but, not without a struggle. On the one hand, the papers carry numerous advertisements for imported consumer goods, such as patent medicines, provisions and imported worsted, as well as services like the direct bi-weekly steamer service with Aberdeen and the weekly service with the Northern Isles, and for the new Thule Hotel and the arrival of tourist cruisers in Lerwick, and interestingly, the arrival of large numbers of Dutch herring busses; whilst on the other, the columns are full of economic gloom and despondency, with for example, potato disease and sheep scab spreading, and the Unst chromate quarry closing down, with kelp alone showing a good return. The fact that kelp burning (fig. 5.1) was important enough to have been reported by *The Shetland Times*, was an indication of the hard times in which people were living. Kelp, one of the few industrial commodities which many of the crofting counties could produce, was economically viable only in times of hardship or destitution, when the meagre wages paid to kelp burners for this dirty, labour intensive work, meant that any form of remunerative employment was better than none, and like the sifting, sorting and recycling of rubbish commonly undertaken by women in urban districts during this period, was only feasible because of the very cheapness of human labour and the desperate need for employment.

Thus, this period opens with the islands' economy in a depressed state and destitution widespread. *The Scotsman*, reporting on the 1872 Truck Inquiry, referred to the living conditions and circumstances of the people of Shetland

KNITTING BY THE FIRESIDE

Fig 5.1 — Kelp burning was an indication of the hard times in which people were living.

as "deplorable".[1] Yet again destitution appeals were circulated by philanthropists from as far away as Glasgow and London. One such pamphlet entitled *Statement regarding the Poor in Shetland*, admirably summed up the situation:

> There are, we believe, few, if any, of the districts of Scotland where the poor are so numerous as in the Shetland Islands. This is attributable to various causes:- narrow circumstances in general, casualties in sea faring life, and to the small number in Shetland of that wealthier class by whose Christian charity the sufferings of the poor in other parts of the land are so much alleviated.[2]

The severity of fishing accidents, like the Gloup disaster of 1881 when 58 men and boys from North Yell, mostly from the one village, were drowned, diminished during this period as steam drifters replaced open boats for deep sea fishing, although war casualties during the 1914-18 War unfortunately redressed this balance. Little local charitable help for the poor continued to be the norm, with major landowners being absent for much of the year, or like Lord Zetland, strongly opposed to any increase in the overstretched poor rates, and regarding charity as an encouragement to the idle.

It was just prior to the beginning of this period, that Shetland's first wave of emigration started in the 1860s. Unlike many districts in the Highlands and Islands, Shetland had been spared full scale clearances (although some clearances did take place), which had caused social unrest and the break down of local administration in the Western Isles during the 1880s. Whether for this reason, or because of the symbiotic relationship between the land and sea which made it easier to survive periods of destitution, or the summer migration of some men to the Greenland whaling, or pluralism of employment - but not migration - for women, or simply because people were too poor to emigrate, Shetlanders as a whole, had in the past, failed to turn to emigration in times of hardship. The 1871 decennial census (appendix 1) showed, for the first time, a drop in population which was to continue throughout this period. This drop was in line with the other crofting counties but contrary to the national figures for Scotland, which rose by almost 10%. Rural depopulation was on the increase with the number of inhabited islands falling from 30 in 1871 to 24 by 1921. The steady fall in population can be attributed largely to advances in technology and increased communications with the outside world. For example, Shetlanders were able to take advantage of the availability of jobs outwith Shetland and were encouraged to do so by the lure of free or assisted passages to Canada, New Zealand and Australia. The demise of trucking in the fishing industry, followed by its rapid expansion and modernisation, generated considerable wealth, and with money replacing barter, allowed for greater mobility of labour. Whether through word of mouth, correspondence from migrant friends and relatives, or through the Press, Shetlanders were more aware of the world around them and the opportunities it offered. The rise in the Merchant Navy in the late 1800s, meant that many men were away from home for longer periods than during the fishing season, whilst many decided to settle in other ports as the strong Shetland community in Leith showed.

It was during this period that the advances in steam, postal and telegraphic communication which helped bring Shetland 'closer' to the Scottish mainland, were consolidated. The introduction of the parcel post in 1883, enabled knitters to break away from their local merchant, allowing them to sell direct to the public, to send their wool to the Scottish Mainland for spinning, and to order worsted by post. Fishermen in particular, benefited from the new telegraphic system, opened in 1870. This enabled them to ascertain in advance the most lucrative markets, which along with the introduction of steam drifters, contributed to Shetland being regarded in 1898 as "...the most important herring fishery in the kingdom".[3] Improved communications meant not only speedier and more regular services for travellers and traders, freight and news, but also a subtle shift in outlook from that of an insular and isolated island community, to the broader concept of Shetland as an integral part of Britain, governed from Westminster. Advances in education, parliamentary and land reform, enabled Shetlanders to better themselves, whilst the social benefits of increased spending in both local amenities and health, led to an improved quality of life. Often beset by the difficulties caused by distance and isolation, these changes slowly percolated to the crofting counties.

The 1832 Reform Act, which had given the vote to proprietors and tenants with land of an annual value of £10 or over, and truly represented Shetland for the first time, was followed by the 1884 Reform Bill, giving 3000 men in Shetland the vote. Arguably, the most significant of these legislative changes for Shetland, was the 1886 Crofters' Holdings (Scotland) Act, and not, as would be natural to expect, the Truck Amendment Act. Hopes had run high after the 1872 Truck Inquiry of impending reform and economic expansion, but in reality, life changed very little, as the vexed question of land tenure, the root cause of the 'Shetland Method', had not been dealt with by Sheriff Guthrie. The Napier Commission, sitting in 1883, recognised the importance of land tenure, and, following the passing of the Crofters' Holdings (Scotland) Act in 1886, the Crofters' Commission was established to travel throughout the Highlands and Islands to listen to appeals from crofters against their landlord, and in Shetland, began its hearings at Dunrossness in August 1889. Oppression and apathy were replaced by freedom of speech and enterprise. An educated and informed society was emerging, and one, which freed from the shackles of debt-bondage, was vociferous in demanding its rights and expressing its views.

In 1889 local government was reorganised, with the Commissioners of Supply largely being replaced under the terms of the Local Government (Scotland) Act. This act separated Orkney and Shetland into two counties and established a Zetland County Council made up of representatives elected by the people. Meantime, Lerwick was expanding and emerging as a modern port and bustling town. In a move to increase their respectability, many established merchants separated their dwelling and work places, by having substantial sandstone houses built on the outskirts of the town. For instance, Robert Sinclair's handsome "St. Clair Villa", Clairmont Place, was one of the first villas to be built in the late 1860s in Lerwick's 'New Town'. To accompany such refinements, foul smelling open sewers were replaced by a piped sewage system, a fresh water supply was piped down from Sandy Loch, streets and sidewalks, once little more than midden-heaps, were cleaned up and paved, and some even lit by the new gas installation. The Zetland County Council and Lerwick Harbour Trust were formed and an imposing Town Hall and new harbour built, along with leading lights, fog horns and lighthouses. Fig. 5.2 shows a modern, thriving port, comparable to many Scottish coastal towns of this era.

However, progress did not automatically bring affluence. Hard times continued into the twentieth century, with all 12 Shetland parishes declared congested by 1901. Towards the end of the century, the quartering of the poor gradually disappeared. In 1888 a Poor House was opened, although never fully utilised, and in 1908, the non-contributory old age pension, instigated for those with an annual income of less than £30 per annum, amounted to 5/- a week and greatly eased the problems of old age, the chief cause of poverty in the Highlands and Islands. Social conditions, highlighted in the Truck Inquiries, showed that life had changed little in rural areas. For example, houses with straw roofs were still being built in 1883, although, the houses of the poor in Shetland were considerably better than those in the Western Isles. The security occasioned by the Crofters' Commission meant that many tenants were carrying out minor improvements themselves, whilst emigration helped ease the problem of overcrowding in Shetland.

DAWN OF MODERNISATION 1872-1918

Fig 5.2 – Steamer day in Lerwick, late 1880s. *Photo: J. D. Rattar*

The Congested Districts (Scotland) Act of 1897 set up the Congested Districts Board to help develop rural areas of high unemployment and low living standards, but did little to help unemployment in Shetland. Whether through lack of enterprise or lack of capital, no new industries were created during this period, although Hay & Co., Shetland's largest company, and both the fishing and knitwear industries, continued to expand until the outbreak of the First World War. The three Truck Inquiries of 1872, 1888 and 1908, and the Poor Law Inquiry of 1887 and 1910, revealed that for many, life was still at a subsistence level, but against this, Shetlanders were spared the turmoil and social upheaval of an industrial society. By 1900 Britain was the most urbanised country in the world, with less than a quarter of its people living in rural districts, and there only 7% were engaged in agriculture. The crofting family with its land and boat, enjoyed a better and healthier quality of life than one, say in Paisley, where the whole family would possibly be engaged in working long hours in the damp, noisy and dangerous cotton mills, and living in squalid, overcrowded conditions, often isolated from their extended family.

The outbreak of the First World War finally removed any feeling of isolation. The islands were used as naval bases and Lerwick as an examination port, and rendezvous for the Bergen Mothil convoys, which travelled via Lerwick. Large numbers of service men were billeted locally. This influx of personnel brought with it increased job opportunities, particularly for women, who found employment in ancillary services. For fishermen, the War was the final blow to the, by then, ailing fishing industry. Restrictions in fleet movement, the difficulties of getting fish to market and the ever-present threat of enemy submarines, all hampered their activities. And it was really from this point that hosiery gained in economic importance as fishing revenues declined.

Role of Women

Details of the comprehensive role of women, so inadequately recorded by census returns, have been greatly added to by recent oral history studies, such as *Living Memory* and *Ahint Da Daeks*, but obviously deal only with living memory, and are thus confined to the late nineteenth and twentieth century. From Victorian times, and particularly from around 1880 onwards, photographs add a fascinating insight into the role of women. From these, it is possible to learn details of dress, appearance, living conditions, domestic habits, modes of employment and working conditions, along with a plethora of other details which are generally thought too insignificant to record, but added together, give a realistic picture of the life style of a bygone age. Three photographs from the Shetland Museum's collections are shown in Fig. 5.3 - 5.4 and are representative of the main occupations of women throughout this period; that is knitting, fish and croft work.

The many chores and burdens which fell to women in a fishing-crofting community remained largely unchanged until the First World War. The establishment of naval bases on the islands gave women additional employment outside the home. Prior to this, temporary absences at the fishing and whaling, taking men rather than women away from their homes, meant that during these prolonged absences, the cares of the home and labour of the croft, still fell to women. It was only during seed-time and harvest, that Shetland men - never noted for their energies on land - gave anything like steady assistance with the croft. That many women had to look to themselves for help is illustrated by an extract from *Ahint Da Daeks*:

> At one time she [mother] was on her own, and half a dozen o kids, so dey maybe helped some; but dere wisna much dey could do. So sho aye did a lok o croft work - I don't know how she managed, but she managed. My oldest sisters was maybe left da school, or coming dat stage, so dey'd a been a big help. But there were a lok o work for da women folk on dis crofts.[4]

The list of onerous tasks which women were expected to undertake seems daunting by today's standards:

> Whin I left da school, oh, I god oot here apo da rigs ta wark, hoe taaties an neeps, dell taaties and dell eart, an go ta da hill ta raise peats, an turn peats, an stack peats, and carry peats home; I milked cows too. We kirned and made butter.[5]

DAWN OF MODERNISATION 1872-1918

Fig 5.3 – Fishwives at the farlins, Lerwick, 1920.　　　　*Photo: R. Williamson*

Fig 5.4 – Delling at Springfield, Fair Isle, c.1910.

Fig. 5.4 taken c.1910, illustrates the back breaking work of delling*
undertaken by teams of women. The burdens which fell to women were
further aggravated by the continuing imbalance of the sexes with for instance,
111.9 women :100 men in 1901 (appendix 1), as many women would remain
unmarried and have to look to themselves for their own support. However,
'May you geng manless to the grave' wasn't such a dire curse during the war
years, as the large concentration of servicemen helped, at least temporarily, to
improve marriage prospects for local women.

Occupations undertaken by Shetland women during this period, varied
little from earlier periods. Census returns are a poor source of information in
giving a true picture of the work of women, and even children, as they fail to
take into account monotonous and constant, unpaid domestic and crofting
work, seasonal and secondary occupations; nor do they include the labour of
children, who often helped out with domestic and crofting chores. That
knitting was the single largest occupation is clear from census returns. For
example, in the 1901 census, out of the 7445 females of 10 years and upwards
who were returned in the census as engaged in occupations, no less than
5045 were working at hosiery; that is, 67.8% of the work force. Women seem
to have been reluctant to leave the islands and seek employment elsewhere -
even temporarily as was stated by Mr Henry Pearson Taylor, Medical Officer
for the North Isles district of the Zetland County Council. Giving evidence
before the Royal Commission on the Poor Laws and Relief of Distress in 1907
he stated that Shetland fishwives would not go beyond Baltasound and
Lerwick, nor would they leave the islands to be trained as nurses, being able
to make a reasonable living from gutting in the summer and knitting in the
winter. Women gutters could easily earn £1 a week during the season, but
less than 10/- a week from knitting during the winter. In Whalsay, a team of
two women and three children, could make £25 during the kelp season.

Pluralism of employment - for Shetland women this meant invariably,
knitting in the winter and fish, land or kelp work in the summer - continued
as an important theme in female employment and undoubtedly made a
significant contribution to staving off rural depopulation. However, despite
the fact that the role of women had apparently remained unchanged until the
outbreak of the first World War, times were changing. By 1909, Lerwick had
both a Suffragette Movement and a Women's Working Association. The War
brought an unexpected, if only temporary, fillip to the hand knitting industry.
Shortages and rationing acted as a catalyst to price rises. Knitters had never
had it so good!

The Shetland Hand Knitting Industry 1872-1918

This was a period of great expansion and radical change for the Shetland
hand knitting industry, but also one of fierce competition from machine-made
imitations. At the time of the 1872 Truck Inquiry Shetland lace and
undergarments were in great demand. Shetland hand knitted hosiery had

gained such national acclaim for its warmth, softness and high quality workmanship, that the word 'Shetland' had become a prestigious symbol of quality knitwear. Unfortunately this led to manufacturers all over the world flooding the market with spurious 'Shetland' hosiery causing great damage to the Shetland hand knitting industry.

Information from the 1872 Truck Inquiry, suggests that veils were the most popular item being made at that time, with large quantities being knitted for both Robert Sinclair & Co. and Robert Linklater & Co. But as the demand for the 'health' properties, popularly regarded as inherent in Shetland wool, increased from c.1890, so too did the merchants' production and range of underwear and outer garments rise to meet the demand of this lucrative market, kindled by Dr. Jaegar's 'woolleners' in the late 1880s[6], and commented on by Cathcart Wason, MP for the county:

> Your Shetland goods, your Shetland hosiery, have great peculiarities of their own...but there is a softness and elasticity about Shetland goods, and also medicinal properties about them, which make them extraordinarily useful to many people, who are perfectly willing to pay considerably more money...than they would pay for machine-made goods.[7]

During this period the export value of the trade rose from an estimated £10,000 in 1871 to £100,000 by 1920. Appendix 2 gives a full list of estimated valuations of the hosiery industry from 1790 to 1950. This great expansion in the trade can largely be attributed to the rise in communications, particularly the mail service which not only opened up the market to the trade, but also allowed wool to be sent to Scotland for spinning from c.1890 and knitters to sell direct to the public with greater ease. For instance, between 1890 and 1905 the number of parcels posted from Shetland rose from 23,036 to 75,920, whilst those received also rose considerably. Improved communications highlighted the relative economic advantages of different locations. The inter-island steamer service started in 1868 helped open up the Scottish market to small hosiery traders, as for example, records from the Old Haa', Burravoe, Yell, show, with local dealers trading with Arnott & Co., 19 Jamaica Street, Glasgow, and John W. Black of 25 North Bridge, Edinburgh. Ease of communications increased the volume of wool being sent to the Scottish mainland for spinning, and from 1872 onwards, advertisements regularly appear in the local newspapers and trade journals for machine spinning at 'moderate charges'. By 1884 Alexander Laing, Wool Merchant, Aberdeen advertised that orders would be executed with promptness at moderate charges due to "the most improved machinery".[8] As the practice of sending wool off the islands to be spun became more common, the number of commission agents working for Lerwick merchants and for Scottish woollen mills, grew, so that, for instance, by 1909, Hunters Woollen Mills, Brora, Sutherland were employing 14 agents in Shetland and advertising for agents in unrepresented districts.

The rise in tourism, with the regular steamer services, considerably expanded the retail side of the hosiery merchant's business as hosiery shops were a great tourist attraction. For example, writing in 1871, Dr. R.Cowie stated:

> To the tourist the most attractive place of business is that of the hosier, whose shop presents a tempting display of the far-famed Shetland goods, of every size, shape, pattern, and shade.[9]

These increases in communications were however, not without their teething troubles as the following extract from an appeal to the Congested Districts Board in 1898 for assistance to improve postal services, showed:

> The hosiery trade has greatly developed in recent years...The introduction of the parcel post has been of great assistance in developing this industry, and an increase in the certainty and frequency of mails, would...lead to further development by enabling the merchants and knitters to execute orders with promptness and regularity which are now impossible.[10]

The document goes on to instance a case where the same post bringing a letter ordering knitted goods also brought a second one, demanding why this order had not been executed. However, despite these teething troubles, and little extraneous help - this proposal was turned down by the Congested Districts Board - the Shetland hand knitting industry continued to adapt and expand.

The Shetland hand knitting industry remained a cottage industry dependent of female labour, and one on which the female population, given its excess number of females to males, relied on heavily for employment. Knitting remained a valuable supplementary source of revenue for many crofters and cottars in providing the additional comforts of life, like tea and new clothing, as well as the basic necessities. Knitting undertaken during slack periods, fitted in between times or combined with other tasks such as carrying kishies of peat, was time gainfully employed which would otherwise have been unprofitably spent. It was only in Lerwick, with its prevalence of 'Shetland housewives', that knitting continued to be prosecuted full time and as the sole means of support. These knitters worked long hours for very poor returns. For instance, in 1909 it was rare for a good knitter to be able to make an average of $7\frac{1}{2}$d. a day, which compared unfavourably with £1 a week which gutters could easily earn. It was this group of town knitters, totally dependent on their labours and without capital behind them, which was caught in the truck poverty trap, as they could not afford to give up dealings with their local merchant.

Between 1872 and 1918, several major changes took place in the structure of the industry. Firstly, there was a marked increase in the number of knitters by-passing Shetland merchants, selling direct to the public or to home industry associations, like the Scottish Home Industries Association, made possible by philanthropic interest and improved mail services. Secondly, by the end of this period, as trucking diminished so too did merchant domination of the hosiery trade, and many merchants made good this loss by expanding their businesses to include wool broking, particularly during and after the war, when wartime conditions sent the price of raw wool soaring. Thirdly, machine spinning was gradually replacing hand spinning, so that by c.1914, most wool was being sent away to be spun. However, the most significant development during this period was the growing competition from the ever increasing number of Shetland imitations which undercut the price of genuine Shetland articles and threatened to annihilate the Shetland hand knitting industry.

Merchants were slow to respond to this threat and failed to take action until the early 1920s, although proposals for a protective organisation had been mooted in 1909. This problem of failing to adapt from a position of monopoly to one of competition, was a common one faced by many British merchants around the turn of the century. The growing number of foreign imports was also causing concern in many spheres, and was a problem from which the Shetland hosiery trade was not exempt. Adverts for Shetland wool made in Germany and South America were not uncommon (fig. 5.5). Unscrupulous competitors were capitalising on the term 'Shetland' being synonymous with quality knitwear. Machine-made imitation Shetland shawls

WARRANTED BEST QUALITY
AA SHETLAND
4oz. FULL WEIGHT
Manufactured in Germany.

Fig 5.5 — Adverts for Shetland wool made in Germany and South Africa were not uncommon

were produced in such quantities that consumers came to accept them as the genuine article, and knitters of good quality, genuine Shetland lace, were in the same position as the Devonshire Honiton lace makers, whose trade had been so severely hit by machine-made imitations, that purchasers would not accept a good piece of Honiton lace as genuine. The inevitable temptation to cut prices by lowering quality proved too great for many Shetland merchants and knitters. Substantial numbers of poorly executed and mis-shapen knitted garments, often made from non-Shetland yarn, appeared on the market so that not infrequently London dealers were returning unsatisfactory work to source. This short-sighted lowering of standards and lack of enterprise, acted against the industry by destroying the precise qualities on which it had established its high reputation, a state of affairs recorded in the 1914 Home Industries report:

> It would be difficult to find an industry of a similar comparatively small magnitude upon which so many and sustained attacks have been made - some of them insidious, some clumsy, but all tending to diminish the reputation of, and the demand for, the original hosiery.[11]

The difficulties of competition from machines and the subsequent lowering of standards facing the Shetland hand knitting industry, were problems being felt by other rural industries and the importance of rural industries to help sustain life in the Highlands and Islands was one of the concerns of the Congested Districts Board. In an attempt to halt rural depopulation and regenerate the Highland economy by encouraging and assisting rural industries, Professor W.R. Scott of St. Andrew's University, was appointed by the Congested Districts Board in 1911, to investigate and report upon the Home Industries in the congested districts and, in particular, on the relation of these industries to the life of the people of the Highlands and Islands. The following definitive statement is taken from this report and aptly summed up the importance of hand knitting in Shetland at that time when all its 12 parishes were designated congested.

> Rural industries occupy a distinct and important position in the economic life of country districts...In particular, where the crofts are small or poor, and where there is a large cottar population, home industries are necessary for the support of the people, while any considerable extension of such occupations will have a material effect in raising the standard of comfort. Indeed, the nature of the work in the vicinity of the home constitutes an adaptation of the people to an environment which, from the point of view of agricultural production, is an unkindly one.[12]

This was particularly true in Shetland with its large landless cottar class and excess female population, many of whom had settled in Lerwick.

It is apparent from this report that it was textiles which formed the backbone of the cottage industry in the Highlands and Islands. These textile industries ranged from the very small production of lace at Tarbert, Loch Fyne, and knitted hose at Gareloch, Portree and Lewis, to the Shetland hand knitting industry and the large and well established Harris Tweed Industry; it is interesting to make a brief comparison of the latter two.

Both the Shetland lace and Harris tweed industries had their origins in the hard times of the 1830s and 40s, when the failure of the potato crop, together with bad fishing seasons and evictions, led to severe distress in these districts, districts where the standard of living was already very low. As can be seen from chapter four, lace knitting emerged because of the interest of local MPs, local ladies and Edward Standen, all of whom were anxious to help alleviate distress amongst destitute knitters, caused by the stagnation in the hose market. Similarly, the Long Island, in particular, Harris, had a well established reputation for the excellence of its weaving, which, up until the middle of the nineteenth century, had been mainly produced for home use or the local market. In 1844 the Earl of Dunmore directed some of the Harris weavers to copy the Murray tartan. This they did so successfully that it was adopted by him for his own family and staff's use. Thereafter, Lady Dunmore spent much of her time improving the production of the tweed and in introducing the tweed to her aristocratic friends. Like Shetland hosiery, the reputation of Harris tweed was based on production being entirely by hand, that is, hand carded, hand spun, home dyed and hand woven. Harris tweed differed in one major respect with regards to the native wool; this wool did not have the high reputation of the native wool, unlike the Shetland hosiery industry whose native wool was regarded as one of the finest in Britain. Harris tweed enjoyed the direct support of the Scottish Home Industries Association (SHIA) and the aristocratic patronage which went with it. Shetland hosiery was very much on the periphery of this inner circle and never wholeheartedly experienced this good fortune.

By the turn of the century, both industries were beginning to fall prey to machine imitations and the subsequent temptation to lower standards to survive. In Lewis, tweed makers resorted to including machine carded wool in their work, but as this did not have the same soft feel as hand carded wool, it changed the character of the tweed. This illicit practice led to weavers having to sign a declaration stating that their tweed was "entirely hand-spun, hand-woven, and home dyed Harris tweed". This system did not prove satisfactory and a registered trade mark was applied for from the Board of Trade, which led to Harris tweed being legally defined as "tweed hand-spun, hand-woven, and dyed and finished by hand in the islands of Lewis, Harris, Uist, Barra and several purtenances, and all known as the Outer Hebrides",[13] A trade mark was registered in 1911 and a Harris Tweed Association formed to undertake the stamping of webs. Thus by 1911, Harris tweed had not only established a high reputation but also, a Board of Trade registered trade mark, its own association to safeguard its interest, plus the patronage and market outlet of the SHIA, who established two local depots, one at Tarbert in Harris and the other in Stornoway, Lewis, to accommodate this industry. This was a much stronger and more favourable position than the Shetland hand knitting industry enjoyed, although interestingly a *Report on Social and Economic conditions in the Highlands and Islands (Congested districts) of Scotland*, pin-pointed both Harris and Shetland as the main centres of successful domestic industries by 1924.

The Shetland hand knitting industry lagged behind the Harris tweed industry, not forming a woollen industries association until 1922, nor gaining its own trade mark until 1925, nor even consolidating its position with the Scottish Home Industries Association — a local depot was never opened, and Shetland knitters had to market their hosiery through the SHIA's Inverness depot. Attempts to set up a protective organisation had come to nothing. In 1909, Cathcart Wason, MP for the county, proposed setting up a Shetland Hosiery Association in conjunction with the SHIA. The proposed association, whose objectives were to promote Shetland hand spinning, hand weaving and hand knitting, got as far as obtaining as its president, the illustrious surgeon, Sir Watson Cheyne, Bart, who had been Lord Lister's chief assistant before succeeding him as Professor of Clinical Surgery at King's College, London. In addition, they had enlisted several other distinguished patrons, including the Marquis of Zetland and Captain Laing, Lieutenant of the County. What is surprising, is that nothing came of this apparently well planned organisation. The influx of machine-made goods and yarn marketed as real Shetland, which had initially sparked off the need to establish a protective organisation, had, in no way diminished. Professor Scott who had visited Shetland during 1912, whilst researching material for his *Report to the Board of Agriculture for Scotland on Home Industries in the Highlands and Islands*, and urging Shetlanders to form such a protective organisation, made no reference to this proposed association, which seems to have inexplicably, vanished as quickly as it had appeared. In this report Professor Scott had recommended the setting up of a body to supervise the industry and to look into the advisability of establishing a trade mark. He outlined suggestions for nine possible trade marks which would clearly indicate the exact nature of the manufacture of the garment. Professor Scott's recommendations for a protective organisation, were taken up by the Board of Agriculture, who called a meeting of all concerned in the hosiery industry, for 18th August 1914, but had to be cancelled because of the war. As a result, Professor Scott's proposals were shelved.

Cheap imitations continued to flood the market, and rather than uniting to combat this fierce competition, merchants turned to using more and more machine spun Shetland worsted and imported yarns. A steam operated carding mill, owned by T.M. Adie of Voe, Delting, was in operation c.1912. Purists resisted such yarn believing that, as it took away the natural softness of the wool, people would question whether the finished article was of Shetland manufacture or not, and this in turn would lead to falling sales. The dilemma here was that machine spinning allowed a greater quantity of Shetland yarn to be used, but in debasing its qualities, made it easier for machine made copies, which could be produced at half the cost, to be put on the market as 'real Shetland'. Out of this confusion, some Shetland wholesalers felt a need to attach labels to their hosiery bearing such statements as "Real Shetland Wool", "Hand Knit" etc., to try and regain public confidence in the genuine article. No common policy was adopted. Meantime, concern was being expressed at the diminishing purity of the native breed of sheep and ultimately the quality and reputation of the hosiery. The formation of a 'flock book' was suggested which would perform the same function as a 'herd book' for cattle. However, like many suggestions for the survival of this important industry, failure to agree amongst themselves, apathy and the difficulties facing post-war farmers, ensured that it came to nothing for some years.

During the 46 years spanned by this period, inevitable changes in fashion took place. Lace knitting, so fashionable amongst the privileged classes in the era of Queen Victoria and crinoline dresses, was badly hit by the War. Warmth, comfort and practicality, were the features required in wartime and Shetland lace was too delicate and impractical for anything but drawing room wear. Changes in fashion became more available to a wider set of people, a more mobile and physically active woman, whose lifestyle was reflected in her clothes. Skirt hems rose to ankle length to allow greater freedom of movement, and it was only for evening wear, that the more elaborate and restricting garments were worn. The market for Shetland lace never died away completely, but never regained its prestigious position in the fashion world.

Organisation of Labour 1872-1918

The domination of the Shetland merchant on the hand knitting industry gradually faded as circumstances more favourable to the knitter emerged. The advent of the parcel post in 1883, the anti-truck lobby following the 1872 and 1888 Truck Inquiries in Shetland, the slight shift of public focus and attention from the Highland Clearances in the Western Isles and Sutherland, to the Land Reform Movement throughout the crofting counties, and the rise in the number of organisations through which hosiery could be sold, all helped to emancipate the Shetland knitter and slowly free her from truck. Those knitters fortunate enough to obtain cash sales for their hosiery were able to organise their expenditure, be more discerning in their sales, and seek more profitable markets. Thus much of the better quality hosiery was being syphoned off, leaving the poor and mediocre to the Shetland merchant. Meantime, Shetland was going through a consumer revolution. The rise in monetary payments in almost every sphere of the economy increased demand for imported goods and allowed far greater mobility of labour, and as the new century opened, hosiery was gradually ceasing to be used as a substitute currency for money.

The Delting Truck Inquiry of 1888, showed great similarities with the 1872 Truck Inquiry as regards the industry's organisation of labour. From the evidence given at the three Truck Inquiries held in Shetland between 1872 and 1908, it would appear that the number of knitters employed by merchants fell during this period, and when knitters were employed, it was usually for a special article required for a specific order. There are no statistics to back up this assumption, merchants being particularly wary of divulging the actual number of knitters they employed, as in so doing they could be fined under section 10 of the 1887 Truck Amendment Act. This fall in numbers was partly due to repeated slumps in the hosiery trade, the extra work involved in employing knitters upping the cost, and the prosecutions under the Truck Amendment Act; which, taken with the quantity of quality knitting by-passing local merchants and the undercutting of prices by machine-made knitwear, led to the demise of the three largest hosiery merchants who ran their businesses in the 'old style'. Robert Linklater died in 1876, Robert Sinclair emigrated to New Zealand in 1885, and Arthur Laurenson died in 1890, although his firm continued in business until 1917.

Spinning

As the amount of locally grown wool and the hand knitting industry expanded, hand spinning could not meet the demand for home spun worsted. And from around 1890 the amount of raw wool being sent to the new power mills springing up along the north east coast of Scotland, steadily increased.

Pringles of Inverness and Hunters of Brora were the two mills most popular with Shetland hand knitters. The reasonable rates charged by the steamer *Earl of Zetland* and the introduction of the parcel post, meant that it was not only merchants but also knitters who could take advantage of this facility.

Woollen Mills
Alexander Rennie, Mill of Aden, Mintlaw, Aberdeenshire.

Alexander Rennie, woollen manufacturer, having now appointed James Aitken, merchant, Lerwick as his agent for Shetland, for the receiving of parcels of wool to be manufactured, and settling the accounts thereof, would respectfully, solicit an increase of orders from that county. Parties forwarding their wool to Mr. Aitken, will have it forwarded every few weeks in one package, per steamer, thus affecting a saving on carriage as well as ensuring its safe conveyance. All freights and carriages from Lerwick to Mill of Aden paid by A.R.

Consigners will favour to send their wool clean, washed and orders, name and address inside parcel.

Wools dyed any colour, and made into blankets, plaidings, serges, tweeds, jerseys, crumbcloths, winceys, twill, sheetings, worsted etc.etc.
Good workmanship, quick despatch and moderate charges guaranteed.

Mill of Aden, Mintlaw, Aberdeenshire.
Fig. 5.6 Mill of Aden advert 1872.

Fig. 5.6 shows an advertisement for the Mill of Aden to which both merchants and knitters could send their raw wool. Knitters could send their wool direct to the mills, use their local agent or send it through merchants who freighted it in bulk at reduced rates. The trend for private knitters to send their wool to Scotland grew as knitters found that machine spun worsted went further and was easier to knit. This practice of sending wool to be machine spun led to the demise of hand spun Shetland wool except for the fine lace yarns, which no machine could surpass. Spinners of the very fine cobweb yarn became scarce and by 1922, spinning wheels were little more than curiosities.

Dressers

Hosiery had to be dressed before it could be valued, and as goods were priced and ticketed before leaving Shetland, it meant that this was always done in Shetland. *Mansons' Shetland Almanac and Directory*, under the heading of 'Trades in Lerwick', listed 'cleaners and dressers of Shetland hosiery', and for example, gave four dressers in 1892, and six in 1902. This list would have represented the independent dressers in Lerwick. There are no records to indicate the number of employee dressers, but as the trade was expanding, presumably so too did the number of its ancillary workers rise. Fig. 5.7, taken in 1910 by the well known Shetland photographer, J.D. Rattar, shows the Petrie family at work. P.E. Petrie is listed in *Mansons' Almanac* as 'a cleaner and dresser of Shetland hosiery', at Albany Street, Lerwick in 1892, but by 1905 was specialising in shawl dressing. This is significant, as the move to specialisation would indicate considerable developments in the trade. The parcel post had also given a boost to this side of the hosiery industry, as there are several references to customers being advised to send their hosiery back to Shetland for cleaning and dressing. Shetland dressers had such a high reputation that, even outwith Shetland there was a demand for their skills. For example, in the 1895 report of the Central Branch of the SHIA based in Edinburgh where there was a considerable Shetland colony, reference was made to "The art of washing Shetland goods is only known to the Shetlanders, and thus much employment is also given by the Association".[14]

Knitters

Throughout this period, knitting remained a home-based activity, but one which was gradually changing from a subsistence activity to a secondary occupation. The family unit was still the backbone of this cottage industry, although even this unit was being eroded by the advances in modern technology, with wool being sent off the islands for spinning. By 1918 there were still no knitwear factories/units or knitting machines, nor was there any division of labour in the factory sense, in Shetland. Knitters were mainly

Fig 5.7 – The Petrie family dressing shawls, c.1910.   *Photo: J. D. Rattar*

knitting and marketing as individuals, with no united body of representation behind them. This is corroborated by a statement taken during the 1908 Truck Inquiry. When asked if the workers had any co-operative movement, trade or workers' union or organisation, Mr A. Newlands, factory inspector, replied "There is no organisation among the workers".[15] Nor had workers banded together to protect themselves from exploitation. This lack of representation is surprising when it is remembered that Shetland had both a Working Women's Association and a Suffragette Association by 1909. Shetland women seem to have been slow to band together and voice their grievances, as in both the fish and hosiery industries, it was the women who held the upper hand - without their labour there would have been no product to market. At the heart of this apparent apathy lay poverty, isolation and the difficulties of rural travelling, coupled with the volume and multiplicity of tasks in which women were constantly involved. Time was of the essence - animals still had to be tended, peats flitted, leaving little time in reserve. The attempt made in 1909 by Cathcart Wason, to promote a Shetland Hosiery Association "...to encourage and foster this great industry, which is of such enormous importance to Shetland"[16] - had come to nothing; and it was not until 1943, that knitters were to form their own co-operative, protective association, the Shetland Hand Knitters Association (SHKA).

Marketing and Knitters

One of the most marked features of this period, was the increase in direct sales between knitters and the public. These sales, which had been rising since around the mid 1880s reached unprecedented heights during the War. And it was these wartime conditions, allowing knitters to by-pass their local merchants and sell direct to servicemen for cash, which were the final blow to the merchants' supremacy and dominance of the Shetland hand knitting industry, splintering the industry into two separate marketing factions: that is, knitters selling direct to the public, and merchants selling wholesale to retailers and to a lesser extent, retail to tourists and visitors to the islands.

At the time of the 1872 Truck Inquiry, the differentiation of knitters into two groups, had been made up of self-employed knitters and those who knitted with the merchants' wool. However, after this date, these two groups were gradually restructured into those who sold to, or knitted for local merchants, and those who sold their work independent of them. Looking at the former, there is ample evidence in the 1888 and 1908 Truck Inquiries, and the Press, to confirm that, apart from their drop in numbers, their organisation had otherwise changed very little. This group invariably represented the poor or inferior knitter, for whom life was a continual hard struggle against the system and survival. Moreover, it was this group, and its inferior workmanship, which was playing into the hands of industrialists by lowering the high reputation of Shetland knitters. It was also this group who, relying on their merchant for credit in times of need, could not have survived without the aid of truck. Many merchants were kindly in their transactions, but basically they were both trying to survive in a changing world in which there was no place for either them or for the products of their labours. Machines had usurped this type of knitter and her inferior products - poor shaping and workmanship, lack of uniformity and in general carelessness, were the disadvantages which gave machines, with their uniformity of production, superiority over hand knitters. There was no intrinsic value in this type of hand knitting.

Marketing and the Independent Knitter

By-and-large, this group was made up of superior knitters who increasingly enjoyed many opportunities to market hosiery independent of local merchants, as is shown in the chart on the following page:

Unlike the Harris tweed industry, whose success can largely be attributed to the help and guidance of patrons, Shetland knitters had never benefited to any large extent from such attentions, with the Shetland Knitters' Repository in Edinburgh, being the nearest Shetland knitters had come to enjoying direct patronage (see chapter three). Other local patronage came from Sheriff Thoms and local ladies like Mrs Jessie Saxby, Lady Lyall, Mrs Traill, Mrs Grierson and others.

Shetland was fortunate in developing ties with the SHIA, albeit modest ties compared to the Harris Tweed Industry. Founded in 1889, this Association, whose chief patron was HRH Princess Louise, with the Countess of Rosebery as President, had three main objects: To find markets for the produce of home industries, to improve quality by providing instruction and circulating information, and to pay workers a fair price for their labours. The Association was run on philanthropic lines, whilst recognising that it was only as a self-supporting business that the success and permanent existence of the Association could be secured. It was hoped that good and artistic work would sell for satisfactory prices, and that only a sum sufficient to cover the cost of bringing goods to the market on an economical scale would be deducted and that the rest would go to the worker - Shetland hosiery with its wide range of popular garments and beautiful lace work, was well suited to fulfil their criteria.

The SHIA was divided into four geographical branches - northern, eastern, western and central counties - with a shop at 132 George Street, Edinburgh and depot at 14 Lower Grosvenor Place, London. The northern counties branch, which had the benefit of the pioneer work which had been done for the previous 30 years in aiding workers in the Harris Tweed Industry, proposed bringing the hosiery of Shetland to a wider and better market than it had hitherto reached. In the SHIA's 1895 publication, *Scottish Home Industries*, Lady Lyall, wife of Sir Leonard Lyall, MP for the county from 1885-1900, is credited with having done this:

Lady Lyall has done much for our industries - not only bringing us into touch with the

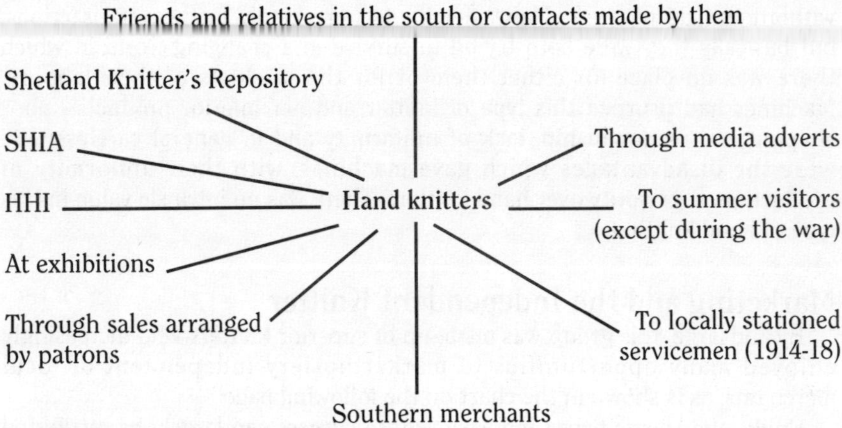

KNITTING BY THE FIRESIDE

```
            Friends and relatives in the south or contacts made by them
Shetland Knitter's Repository                    |
                                                 |
SHIA ─────────────────\                      /─── Through media adverts
                       \                    /
HHI ──────────────────── Hand knitters ──────── To summer visitors
                       /                    \   (except during the war)
At exhibitions ───────/                      \
                                              \
Through sales arranged /                       \ To locally stationed
by patrons                                       servicemen (1914-18)
                                 |
                         Southern merchants
```
Fig. 5.8 Marketing and the independent knitter.

SHIA, but also selling quantities of our work - she has further helped to improve its quality by obtaining better prices.[17]

Alice Grierson, wife of Andrew Grierson, landed proprietor of Quendale and Deputy Lieutenant of Zetland, was Shetland's local SHIA's representative - Shetland came under the jurisdiction of the SHIA's northern counties branch, based at Inverness. In her 1895 report to the SHIA, Mrs Grierson, stressed the time consuming nature of hand carding, spinning, and knitting, and brought to the public's attention the desperate plight of many knitters left with no other means of support but their knitting, and emphasised that the truest charity was to pay well for work. What her report failed to give, was an annual valuation of sales made through the SHIA. Sales with the SHIA must have been quite considerable if the endless list of articles knitted is anything to go by. These included shawls - lace and haps - sleeping jackets, bed stockings, head squares, chest protectors, cholera belts, cardigan jackets, spencers, sleeves, leggings, respirator veils, helmets, gloves, mitts, wristlets, for ladies; there are also extensive lists of articles made for babies, children and gentlemen.

Two other references to the SHIA would suggest that Shetland knitters continued to market hosiery through the SHIA until its termination in 1914. Firstly, a note from a Miss J. Cochrane, dated January 1909 and enclosed with the Delting Inquiry file, referred to her sales of Shetland hosiery, through Miss Rae, Manageress of the SHIA's shop in Edinburgh - Miss Cochrane undertook these sales as a private philanthropist and not as an emissary of the SHIA and had been selling to them since 1900, sending on average £100 back to knitters between 1900 and 1907, but £160 in 1908. Secondly, Cathcart Wason's abortive proposals for a Shetland Hosiery Association to be formed in conjunction with the SHIA.

Further help for Shetland knitters with organisation and marketing, came during the War, from the Co-operative Highland Home Industries (HHI), set up in 1909. In a bid to alleviate unemployment and hardship occasioned by the War and from the restrictions on the use of wool, the Board of Agriculture for Scotland, recognising that Shetland women were expert knitters, proposed that they be employed to knit socks etc. for the Army, and approached the HHI to organise this scheme, with the offer of a grant of £100. This scheme was successfully undertaken by the HHI, and by May 1915, over £2,300 had been paid in small sums to individual workers. This amount represented the actual proceeds of the sale of the different articles made, as the cost of postage, packing material, carriage, storage, advertising etc. as well as the salaries of the organisers of the scheme, were met from the funds of the Co-operative Council. The Board, being satisfied that the scheme was helping in a practical way and ensuring the continuance of Home Industries in the islands, gave another grant of £100.

Hosiery Merchants 1872-1922

Working on a combination of the store and consignment principles, merchants bought goods - paying for them in either cash or Shetland hosiery - from Scottish Mainland wholesalers, both to stock their retail drapery shops and to pay their local knitters through the store system. Hosiery was sold on the consignment principle, to wholesale and to retail hosiery dealers throughout Britain. It was particularly this latter practice which hampered mercantile expansion. Shetland hosiery merchants, by 'buying' hosiery, even when out of season from knitters, had large amounts of capital tied up in their hosiery stock and by selling to wholesalers by consignment, shouldered the risk and delay in payment, often having to wait up to 18 months to secure payment. For example, at the time of their deaths, Robert Linklater and Arthur Laurenson, were owed £1,173-18/1d. and £1,668 respectively; these sums were in addition to their shop stock. Lack of capital and delayed payments, continued to be the scourge of Shetland trade, and protracted trucking in the Shetland hosiery industry, with the smaller merchants lacking the capital to break away from a barter economy, being themselves trucked by their suppliers. Lack of statistics and paucity of business records, make it impossible to judge the extent to which merchants expanded their businesses during this period. Valuations of the hand knitting industry, albeit a doubtful source of information, indicate a steady expansion (appendix 2). Information from Commissary Records, contemporary writers and Scottish Office files, make it possible to piece together a comprehensive picture of the complicated nature of marketing used by Shetland merchants.

The hosiery trade in Shetland continued as a symbiotic affair with most merchants, regardless of size and status, involved to some extent in hosiery, with merchants helping each other out for rushed orders, employing travellers to buy up or fulfil orders in country districts. Hosiery was still used as a form of currency in country districts, whilst, to a lesser extent, lines filled this function in Lerwick - at least at the beginning of the period. The small country merchants, with which the islands abounded, continued their dual roles, buying hosiery and other home produce, whilst retailing by barter, shop goods.

Hosiery Merchants - Their Organisation and Marketing

As a result of the complex nature of their business dealings and the symbiotic nature of the hosiery trade in Shetland, it is enlightening to take several case studies of different merchants, representative of the main types of business activities undertaken during this period. To this end the following have been chosen: Robert Linklater of R. Linklater & Co., Shetland hosier of Lerwick and Edinburgh, and Robert Sinclair, the principal partner of Robert Sinclair & Co., Shetland hosiers and drapers, Lerwick, both of whom were examined at the 1872 Truck Inquiry, and Anderson & Co., one of the few firms which has survived to the present day. In the country districts, Wm. Pole of Pole Hoseason, fish curers and general merchants dealing in hosiery - and an ardent protagonist of truck - and Mrs. M. Smith, a small-time dealer who sold hosiery to agents in London, for cash. Outwith Shetland, the case study chosen is John White & Co., Frederick Street, Edinburgh.

Robert Linklater (1811-1874)

Robert Linklater set up in business as Shetland hosier at 173 Commercial Street, in 1836. These old and dilapidated premises were demolished and rebuilt between 1837 and 1844. The lower portion of the building was used by Robert Linklater as a dwelling house and shop. In 1868 he moved his business to 112 Commercial Street. In all, Robert Linklater had three shops - a retail store in Princes Street, Edinburgh, and two in Lerwick, one acting as a buying depot and warehouse for Shetland hosiery and the other as a drapery store, both trucking with knitters and selling to the public. In Lerwick, he employed at least one shopman, Robert Anderson, a dresser, an agent in Unst to undertake orders for lace knitting, and an agent to dispose of job lots of inferior goods. Robert Linklater bought much of his Shetland worsted from Laurence Williamson of Mid Yell. He also employed over 300 knitters, mainly from the country districts. Robert Linklater dealt mainly in veils (fig. 5.9) and to a lesser extent in shawls and underclothing (fig. 5.10), but only employed knitters to knit fine Shetland lace, not coarser hosiery. Knitters were paid in goods, although a little cash was given occasionally. Robert Linklater kept a work book where a debit and credit account of each knitters' transactions was recorded. Knitters were given pass books if required, but not lines. Judging from the large number of small debts outstanding at the time of his death in 1874, knitters were allowed to run up accounts to a limited extent - for example, Margaret Anderson from Lunnasting owed him 7/5d., whilst Agnes Williamson and her sister Christina, of Whiteness, between them, owed Robert Linklater £18-18/-. Robert Linklater's testimony at the 1872 Truck Inquiry, gave detailed information on the knitting, finishing and marketing of

DAWN OF MODERNISATION 1872-1918

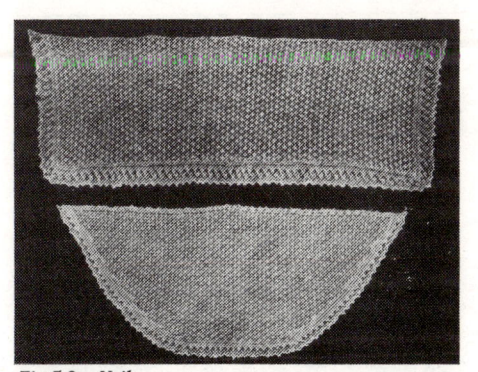

Fig 5.9 – Veil.

Ladies Underclothing Department

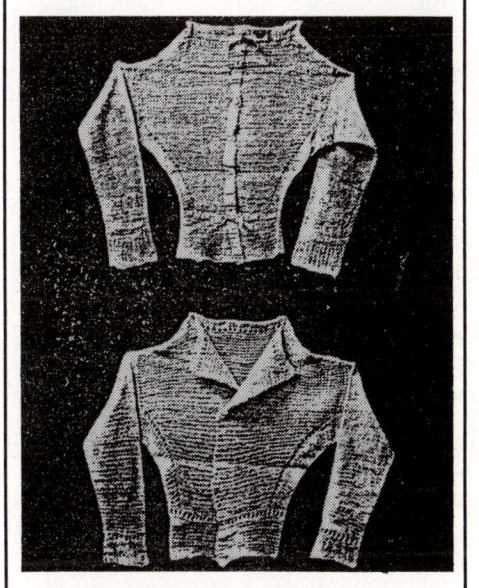

1. Trimmed Spencer 2. Untrimmed Spencer
Ladies' Spencers in White, Grey and Brown,
   Small Size, 2/- each, trimmed 2/- each
   Medium Size 2/3 " , "   3 "
   Large Size, 2/6 " , "   3 "
Ladies' Spencers in Black,
   Small Size, 2/3 each, trimmed 3/- each
   Medium Size, 2/6 " , "   3 "
   Large Size, 3/- " , "   3 "
Ladies' Short-sleeved Spencers, in Grey and White, 1/8,
   Trimmed, 2/6 each.
Ladies' Short-sleeved Spencers, in Black, 2/-,
   Trimmed, 2/9 each.

Fig 5.10 – Linklater dealt in shawls and underclothing to a lesser extent

veils. Veils were graded from one to seven with a no. one, being the finest type and were knitted in Shetland worsted or mohair and then dressed, before marketing.

Robert Linklater employed at least one agent on Unst to whom he sent orders, as he felt that Unst was the home of the finest knitting. He also bought hosiery from self-employed knitters. Once received, hosiery was dressed before it could be valued and ticketed, ready to send to his retail shop in Edinburgh. R. Linklater & Co. did not confine its marketing to the Edinburgh store. They sold wholesale to Peace and Low, Kirkwall; Knox Samuel and Dickson, Edinburgh; Marshall and Snelgrove, London; and to numerous retailers as far apart as Wick, Liverpool, Rothesay, Harrogate, Manchester, Leith, Inverness etc. and interestingly, to Pole Hoseason & Co., Delting. This latter rather unusual sale, may be accounted for by merchants helping each other out when a rushed order for which they had insufficient stock, was received. Not all work was of a marketable standard and an agent, paid in shop goods at wholesale prices, was employed to get damaged and shoddy hosiery sold in job lots.

Robert Linklater, a senior member of the Town Council and Parochial Board as well as Shetland hosier, died in 1874, leaving £3,945-16/6d. Commissary Records list the value of "the cash in house and shop" at £12-10/- and "the stock in trade and other effects in his shops" in Lerwick at £1,423-8/8d. and in Edinburgh at £465-4/9d., these sums representing his total personal estate, excluding £1,173-18/11d. worth of debts due to him. Of these the 'good debts' amounted to £1,056-10/- and represented the amount outstanding from retailers, to whom his company sold wholesale, small Shetland firms, and Shetland knitters. This was a considerable sum to have tied up in the 1870s and must have had a crippling effect on his business. An advertisement by Knox, Samuel and Dickson, dated c.1875, referred to their having bought up a second and third consignment from the late Mr. Robert Linklater. As his Shetland

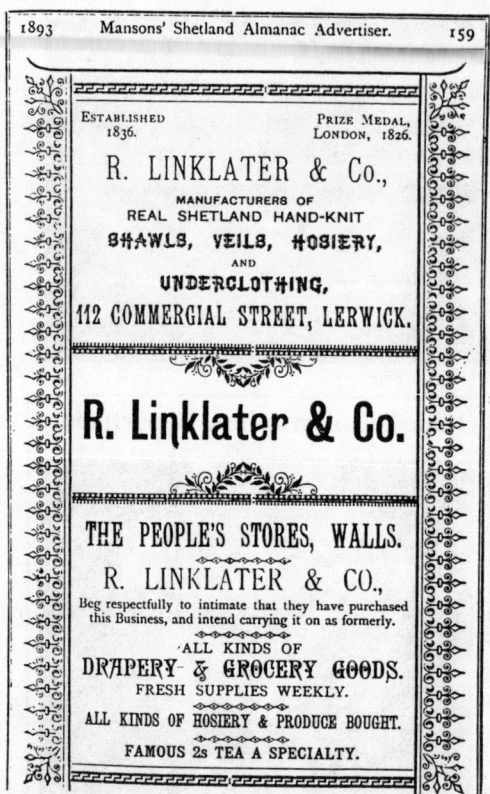

Fig 5.11– Advert from Manson's Shetland Almanac Advertiser, 1893.

business continued until at least 1893, it would seem likely that this stock was from his Edinburgh shop which may have closed down. Fig. 5.11, dated 1893, shows his business as "Manufacturers of Real Shetland Hand-Knit shawls, veils, hosiery and underclothing", as continuing and expanding as drapers and grocers out to Walls, in north west Mainland.

Robert Sinclair (c.1815-?1900)

Robert Sinclair, a farmer's son, was born in Twatt, in the Parish of Aithsting. He later moved to Lerwick to learn his trade, working for James Linklater, draper, of Queen's Street. In 1852, he set up as Robert Sinclair & Co., at 60 Commercial Street, Lerwick, and at the time of the 1872 Truck Inquiry, had two shops in Lerwick - a cash and a truck shop. He was obviously a very successful business man as, in the late 1860s, he had an impressive villa built on the outskirts of Lerwick. T. Manson, editor of *The Shetland News*, described his shop as:

This shop seemed always to be packed with people selling their wares, with Mr Sinclair, a fountain bubbling over with fun and good humour behind the counter, cracking

DAWN OF MODERNISATION 1872-1918

jokes, and telling stories.[18]

This statement seems to be verified by the information in Fig. 5.12.

Robert Sinclair ran his business in much the same combined store/consignment system as Robert Linklater. The principle difference between the two, was in the issuing of lines and pass books. Mr Sinclair issued lines and only occasionally issued pass books. According to his evidence Robert Sinclair would have preferred not to give out lines but was obviously unsuccessful in dissuading knitters from taking lines as his line book for the first four days of December 1871 records 74 lines issued. Robert Sinclair had perfected an extensive system for marking lines with the knitter's initials, the amount due and the date. These particulars were also entered in his 'line book'. When knitters exchanged their line for goods, the line was destroyed and the

OLD LERWICK WORTHIES

The above is a portrait of the late Mr Robert Sinclair, who carried on an extensive business in Lerwick as a draper and hosier for many years, first in the premises now occupied by Messrs J. B. Anderson & Goodlad, Solicitors, and latterly in the Union Bank Buildings (the buildings that were burned down). Mr Sinclair was the soul of geniality and good humour, and was widely known for his pawky, but never ill-natured, wit and old-fashioned sayings, his jokes, and stories. He was leisurely and dignified in his movements, but was nevertheless a keen and successful man of business. He it was who built St Clair Cottage on the South Hillhead.

Mr Sinclair had strong literary tastes and was an omnivorous reader. He wrote a very interesting story called "Da Tief o' da Neen", which attracted considerable attention at the time. Exceedingly fond of music and having a very pleasant tenor voice, he regularly attended the choir of the Congregational Church, of which he was a devoted member. Mr Sinclair had a large family, most of whom emigrated to New Zealand in 1885. A fine type of man was Mr Sinclair – shrewd, kindly and "jokesome", with a kindly word for everyone.

Fig 5.12 – Mr Robert Sinclair (Shetland News, 1937).

amount due in the 'line book' marked off as paid and dated. Robert Sinclair issued more lines than any other merchant, issuing 6-8,000 lines between 1870 and 1872. Like Robert Linklater, he was extensively involved in veil making, employing country people to knit these for him. Mr Sinclair sold mainly to the trade and to visitors in the season. In 1885 Robert Sinclair and his family emigrated to New Zealand.

Anderson & Co.

Anderson & Co., 'Manufacturers of real Shetland wool hand knit shawls, veils, hosiery and underclothing' was established by Thomas Anderson at 60 Commercial Street, Lerwick in 1873. The firm's rather cumbersome title was later shortened to Anderson & Co., Shetland Warehouse. The business later moved to its present site at Market Cross and is one of the oldest firms still in existence today. Fig. 5.13 shows the cover of the firm's 1894-6 mail order catalogue. This catalogue contains an almost endless list of articles from their firm's many departments viz. children's underclothing, glove, hosiery, gentlemen's, veils and scarfs, underclothing, heavy wrap shawl, lace shawls and handkerchiefs, Fair Isle (fig. 5.14) and finally silk knitted goods department. Even at this early date the firm advertises "All kinds of Shetland goods sent on approbation".[19] Several of the photographs shown in chapter four are taken from the above mail order catalogue. Mail order continues to be an important part of most Shetland hosier's business dealings.

William Pole (1839-1921)

William Pole was the eldest son of William Pole, merchant at Greenbank and Ann Sandison, daughter of Alexander Sandison, merchant, Delting. William Pole junior, started work at the Union Bank Lerwick, and then joined Mr James Hoseason to form Pole Hoseason & Co., Merchants and Fishcurers at Mossbank, Delting. In addition, they had a shop at Greenbank, North Yell and owned and ran two fishing stations at Feideland and Gloup. The 1872 Truck Inquiry showed that William Pole had been in charge of the Greenbank shop sometime before 1872, whilst his father ran the Mossbank shop; but by 1872, he was the managing partner in the Mossbank store.

The firm's largest business concern lay with fishing and fish curing. The local men fished for him, and bought or hired their gear and provisions through Pole Hoseason's stores, running up accounts which were settled annually. The firm hired women from the end of May until the end of September to work at the fishing stations - about twenty women at Mossbank and ten at Greenbank to gut and pack fish. These women were paid by the day. They also ran up accounts with Pole Hoseason who kept a separate women's ledger. The women's wages could be settled weekly, every five or six weeks, or at the end of the season. Much of their pay was taken out in provisions, that being convenient to the women and the accustomed understanding - the nearest other shop was one mile away. Both Mr Hoseason

DAWN OF MODERNISATION 1872-1918

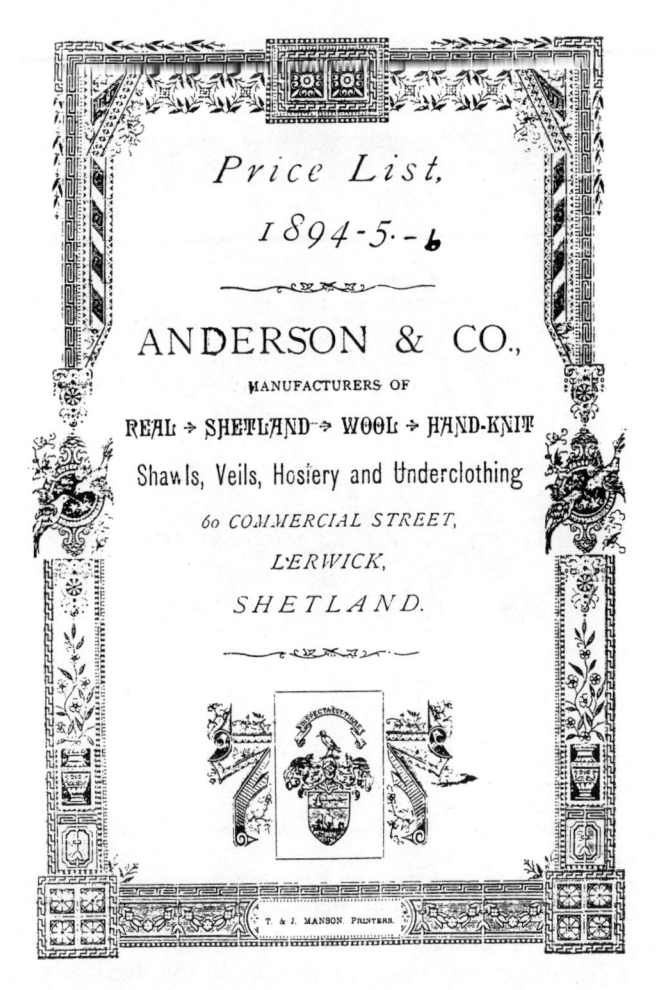

> **Price List,**
> **1894-5.-6**
>
> **ANDERSON & CO.,**
> MANUFACTURERS OF
> REAL ✣ SHETLAND ✣ WOOL ✣ HAND-KNIT
> Shawls, Veils, Hosiery and Underclothing
> 60 COMMERCIAL STREET,
> LERWICK,
> SHETLAND.
>
> T. & J. MANSON, PRINTERS.

Fig 5.13 — Cover of Anderson & Co.'s 1894-96 mail order catalogue.

and Mr Pole, were landed proprietors, and acted as factors for George Hoseason of Basta, North Yell, and one or two small properties. Mr Pole was also a tacksman for Aywick, East Yell and Sellafirth and Sandwick in North Yell, whose tenants were obliged to fish for him, this being part of the contract for their land. If not required, these tenant fishermen were allowed to go to the whaling or Faroe fishing.

In 1872 Pole Hoseason dealt with hosiery only to a very small extent; not turning over more than £100 worth a year - what proportion of the firm's total turnover this represented, is impossible to ascertain, as no figures were given for his fishing returns. William Pole did, however, deal in Shetland worsted and was the only merchant mentioned in the 1872 Truck Inquiry who sent it south, and so doing, met with his fellow merchants' displeasure, due to

KNITTING BY THE FIRESIDE

Fig 5.14 – Fair Isle goods on offer from Anderson & Co.'s 1894-96 mail order catalogue.

the scarcity of Shetland wool. But, by the time of the Delting Truck Inquiry in 1888, William Pole was dealing extensively in hosiery. This shift of emphasis from fishing to hosiery was undoubtedly due to the decline in the haaf* fishing around the mid 1880s, the failure of the fishing in 1886 and 1887, and to the terrible fishing disaster at Gloup in 1881. This was not just a loss of man power to Pole Hoseason but a considerable loss of capital, tied up in boats and fishing gear, to say nothing of the accumulated debts of these men and the greater dependence of their women folk, left destitute. Reluctant as William Pole may have been to deal in hosiery, in hard times of trade depressions and fishing disasters, to keep in business he probably had little option but to accept hosiery as the only form of currency in circulation locally. In the Delting Truck Inquiry, he referred to a knitted garment as "...a value put on it, and it was just franked the same as a pound-note or a shilling, and we had nothing more to do than to pass the goods over the counter".[20] William Pole's father-in-law, T.M. Adie of Voe, merchant and fish curer, who in 1872 stated that he had given up the hosiery trade two years earlier as there was no profit in it, had gone back to dealing in hosiery by 1888.

William Pole, who it will be remembered was the chief instigator of the Delting petition, was very much in favour of truck and felt quite justified in exchanging shop goods for hosiery - to ensure some profit - for his troubles. As he stated to Sheriff Mackenzie:

> The first class knitted goods are comparatively easily sold, and at good prices, but the medium and inferior goods are most difficult to sell. I have known us travel to London and back again to sell that class of goods, and not able to sell £20 worth. And, on the other hand, when we had got it sold, it was generally to parties requiring a long credit. It is very often 12 months from the time we put it into their hands until we get our money.[21]

He also stated that the bulk of the knitters were sending their best stuff away and that he was left with the rubbish, which had to be sold in the south by auction, and pointed out that if all the hosiery was of the best quality, the hosiery trade would be a very different one. As William Pole also ran the post office, he would have a fair idea of the amount of work knitters were sending south. For all that William Pole was obviously a tough and astute business man, he was highly spoken of by his knitters, many of whom were dependent on him for their hosiery sales, and realised that despite the poor prices being paid for hosiery, they would have faired no better anywhere else. For example, Ann Blance from Mossbank, said "If it was not for the hosiery we would be very badly off", whilst Mrs Ridlon from Toft, who had knitted to Mr Pole for twenty years, and had been employed as his dresser for the last twelve, was well aware that it was only through trucking that the poor people could survive. "The merchants take things from the poor that they have very little chance of getting sold, so we cannot be down altogether on the merchants".[22] 'Things' refers to poor quality hosiery.

Nineteen years after the fishing disaster in Gloup, Delting also suffered a major fishing tragedy. At Christmas time 1900, 22 men were drowned and four boats were lost, leaving 15 widows and 61 other dependents. It was through the telegraph service installed at Pole Hoseason's Mossbank store, that the news of the survival of one of the boats came. Shetland country life still centred round the country merchant. Such disasters and their appalling social consequences, ensured that trucking would linger on despite any legislation from 600 miles away. William Pole's truck activities continued unchallenged until 1902, when he was fined the paltry sum of £1 for infringements of the Truck Amendment Act. Still undaunted, he continued to believe that the Truck Act was harmful to Shetland interests and that Westminster should not poke its nose in to matters that he felt did not concern them. At the 1908 Truck Inquiry, the Commissioners were told that Pole Hoseason & Co. at Mossbank were the worst offenders, constantly contravening the law by extensive trucking.

A letter to James Clerk, Camb, Mid Yell, illustrates that Pole Hoseason & Co., had expanded their hosiery dealings, selling wholesale to retail dealers in the south and employing local agents on a commission basis to help fulfil orders. The letter asked for one dozen 'nice white hap shawls' ranging from 3/- to 6/- each, with the promise of prompt payment in cash. This would infer that Pole Hoseasons were being paid in cash and not goods from their wholesale source. These varied types of marketing arrangements, seem to have been common, with Shetland merchants helping each other out to complete orders. This type of order was much valued as a sale was assured.

For all that William Pole felt that trucking was the only way in which this risky business could survive, he did extremely handsomely out of it. When he died in 1921 he left the vast sum of £20,474-2/4d., much of it invested in stocks and shares - it is not possible to estimate what proportion of this can be attributed to the hosiery side of his multifarious business dealings. After his death, Pole Hoseason & Co., continued in business and was the first Shetland firm to use knitting machines. The firm was bought over in 1946 by Standen & Co. London, whose founder had opened up the London market to Shetland hosiery just over one hundred years ago.

Mrs Mary D. Smith. (1839-?1910)

Mary Smith's hosiery and household accounts book, lodged in the Shetland Archives, is the only extant Shetland hosiery merchant's ledger. The term 'hosiery merchant' is in fact rather too grand a title for Mary Smith, who was no more than a small-time dealer selling Shetland hosiery to agents in the south by post. She is recorded in the 1881 census, as a 42 year old widow (and head of the household), residing at 'Waterside', Gluss Ayre, Northmavine. Her occupation is listed as 'grocer', although her account book, running from 1876-1883, gives little indication of such activity. She conducted her business by employing women to knit for her, then sending parcels on approval to agents in the south. She used the *Earl* for freighting - that is, the steamship, *Earl of Zetland* - and sent hosiery to agents in London, Edinburgh, Suffolk, Cheshire and as far afield as Quebec. It seems likely that these agents were in reality patrons of Shetland knitters, selling Shetland goods amongst their friends. This assumption is based on several factors. Firstly, all the addresses of her clients are private addresses, as for instance, Mrs Henderson, 19 York Place, Portman Square, London. Secondly, this Mrs Henderson seems to have extended her patronage at the London end, as their are several entries of shawls and other hosiery being sold to Mrs Irons of 5 York Place, Portman Square, and notes to the effect that other people were to be invoiced along with Mrs Henderson. Lastly, enclosed in the ledger was a short letter, evidently not sent, which can hardly be described as written in an impersonal business manner:

Jan/82   "Waterside", 3

My Dear Mrs Henderson,
    I send this parcel to you to look at at your convenience - you will just send what you think most suitable and charge whatever price you please. I

got the P.O. for which accept of my grateful thanks.
With kindest love to you both,
from M.D. Smith, (Excuse haste)

Fig. 5.15

Mary Smith dealt mainly in clouds and shawls of all sizes and styles. Her parcels also included stockings, ties, petticoats, a muffler and wool. She was paid promptly, that is within two or three months, receiving postal orders, bank cheques drawn on the North Bank, Zetland, cash and postage stamps; employed women to knit for her and had her wool spun on the Scottish mainland. Her records show that the proceeds from her hosiery business and rents were her main sources of income. For example, her 1880 Household Accounts show her outgoings as £54-15/9d. and her income as £55-9/-. Fig. 5.16 shows the break down of these figures.

Mary Smith's Household Expenses 1880

	Debit	Credit
Work people's wages	£13-10/-	
Robert Mouat for work	£1	
Lerwick accounts	£3-14/8d.	
For spinning	£2	
Paper and books	£1	
Meal, tea and barley etc.	£25	
Account from Fulham (? rather illegible)	£6-14/-	
Taxes, roads etc. (smudged entry)	£1-17/1d.	
Money received for shawls		£10-15/-
For wool 6, for lambs 1		£7
Money for shawls		£9-14/-
" " 4 "		£4
Rents		£24
Totals	£54-15/9d.	£55-9/-

Balance = 13/3d.

Fig. 5.16

By present day standards, an annual balance of 13/3d. appears meagre, but when it is considered that in 1910 the poor role allowance was between 1/- and 1/6d. and a dresser earned 5/- a week for her labours, Mrs Smith was fortunate to have a surplus, and may well have had savings in the North Bank, Lerwick.

John White & Co. (1830-1988)

Much is known about this prestigious company thanks to two sources of information, one extant and the other lost in the 1980s - the former being an article published in *Scotland of To-day and Edinburgh its capital*, and the latter, John White & Co.'s 1908 mail order catalogue. Fig. 5.17 shows an old advertisement for John White and Co. based at 10 Frederick Street, Edinburgh.

This hosiery business was founded as far back as 1830 by Mr W. B. Mackenzie at 126 Princes Street, Edinburgh. Fig. 4.14 (see chapter four) lists the range of Shetland articles which he exhibited at the Great Exhibition in 1851. William Mackenzie was credited with having pioneered the sale of Shetland hosiery in the south and has been described as the 'Father of the Shetland wool trade'.[23] He is mentioned in the 1872 Truck Inquiry by Mrs Andrina Anderson of Lerwick, as purchasing direct from Shetland knitters both in Edinburgh and when visiting the Shetland Islands. These purchasing visits can be dated to at least 1847. William Mackenzie was succeeded in 1860 by John White, who running the business under his own name, substantially enlarged it, establishing extensive trade links with the Continent and America. John White continued Mackenzie's custom of visiting the Shetland Islands to purchase hosiery direct from knitters. There is, however, no mention of any partnership with Shetland merchants.

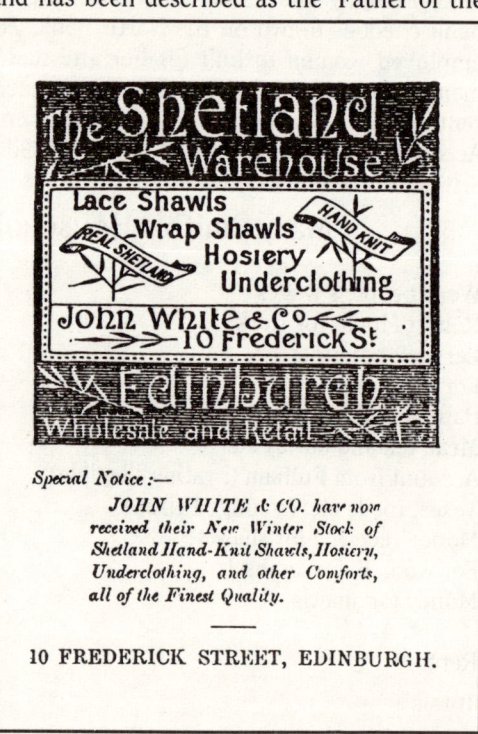

Fig 5.17 – John White & Co. advertisement

In 1882, John White was succeeded by his nephew, a Mr Ramsay, who whilst retaining the old title of John White & Co., continued to extend the scope and influence of his business, increasing the volume of its trade operations year by year. Mr Ramsay had "large numbers" of knitters knitting for him all over the islands, some of whom had been knitting for John White & Co. for generations; this would imply that not only did Ramsay's predecessors visit Shetland to buy hosiery 'on spec', but had also engaged local women to knit for them. The list of articles stocked by John White & Co. in 1890 included under and outer garments, Shetland lace and Fair Isle garments described as "...peculiar by reason of their curious colours and patterns".[24] The following extract illustrates the high esteem in which this prestigious company was held throughout the world:

DAWN OF MODERNISATION 1872-1918

...Messrs. John White & Co. stand in the front rank of those engaged in distributing the products of this vigorous island industry... (and) do a very large trade in the beautiful and serviceable goods that constitute their speciality, and maintain valuable commercial connections throughout the United Kingdom, Germany, France, Austria, America, and all British colonies of any importance. Their goods are known to be exclusively of the most excellent quality, and their reputation has for many years been their best and only advertisement.[25]

Around 1904 John White & Co. moved from 10 Frederick Street to more spacious premises at 30-32 Frederick Street (Fig. 5.18). The company dealt in both wholesale and retail trade, carrying on its retail trade on the ground floor and wholesale business on the upper floor of these new premises, and in addition established a considerable mail order business. Their mail order catalogue contains a wealth of detailed information on the type and extent of the company's hosiery business and provides an interesting social review on the types of clothes worn by Edwardians at that time.

John White & Co.'s 1908 mail order catalogue comprised 50 pages with not only photographs and descriptions of the goods for sale, but also details of Shetland life and traditions. The catalogue described Shetland wool as soft, light and warm and greatly sought after for its 'health' qualities and related how famous sanatoria used Shetland shawls as bedcovers because of their lightness and warmth. Numerous shawls are listed. For example, a one yard square shawl cost between 3/6d. and 7/6d., and a two and a half square shawl, 28/- to 38/- with black shawls an extra 2/-. Many, many other types of Shetland hosiery are listed: motoring scarfs and neckties, clouds (fig. 5.19) and long scarfs, circular and square veils, all in lace knitting were just a few of the more elegant items available by

Fig 5.18 – John White & Co.'s premises in Edinburgh.

125

mail order. Shetland wool was felt to be particularly suited to underwear, as in addition to its warmth and lightness, its porous and elastic qualities allowed it to adapt to the shape of the wearer, so that such garments could be worn 'invisibly', with no trace of additional bulk. Precise measurements were requested for underwear - and if this was not possible, customers were requested to state whether stout, short and so on! Vests, socks, drawers, knee caps, abdominal and cholera belts, gloves, belts and spencers in summer and winter weight were available for babies, children, men and women, with a large choice in each category, as for instance, spencers (vests) came with high or low necks, with or without sleeves, waisted or not. Fair Isle garments were also available. Savings could be made by ordering from the 'cheap goods department'. In addition to hand knitted Shetland hosiery, John White & Co. dealt in machine knitted waistcoats, Shetland 'claith', blankets and rugs.

Patrons were requested to order by letter or telegram, and orders over 10/- were sent post free in Britain and Ireland. When returning goods which had been sent on approval, customers were asked to send a separate letter in advance. Customer files were kept, detailing previous orders and noting temporary summer addresses. New customers had to send cash with their order. Precise washing instructions were given at the end of the catalogue, along with a request that fine Shetland lace should be sent back for dressing. The cleaning and dressing department guaranteed no shrinkage and quick service - washing day was Wednesday, so no garment took longer than eight days to be returned. White garments were treated with sulphur fumes to whiten and disinfect them.

Fig 5.19 A knitted 'cloud'.

DAWN OF MODERNISATION 1872-1918

In the days before central heating, it is easy to understand the appeal of Shetland garments and how this business thrived. The parcel post and cheap labour - both Edinburgh employees and hand knitters - had been the essential ingredients which had enabled John White & Co., to develop this side of the business. This thriving business, which drew on the wealth of the middle and upper classes and their interest in health, Shetland garments being "...much recommended by medical men as beneficial to health on account of their lightness and warmth"[26], had been made possible by the advances in modern communications.

John White & Co. was taken over by John Smith & Co. (Wools) Ltd. of 6 Frederick Street, Edinburgh, who continued in business trading as John Smith & Co. (Wools) Ltd. until c.1988. (Latterly John Smith & Co. dealt mainly in knitting yarns and needlecraft materials).

From 1906 to the end of the period, there is a dearth of reliable information on the marketing of Shetland hosiery by Shetland hosiers. Professor Scott's 1914 report on the Home Industries in the Highlands and Islands gives a very comprehensive summary of the Shetland hosiery trade, but is limited in its information on merchants and how they marketed their hosiery. To a very small extent this gap can be filled in from articles in *The Scotsman* and *The Shetland Times*. From around 1910, there seems to have been a slight shift of emphasis from hosiery to wool dealing, as there are several references to merchants outbidding each other and forcing up the price of native wool. This was possibly because of the competition from machines undercutting hand knitted hosiery to such an extent that there was little profit in it. There are still references which indicated that quantities of poor quality hosiery had to be sold through auction sales which were damaging the reputation of Shetland hosiery.

Shetland, so literally a backwater of Britain for centuries, had been opened up by the tremendous advances in modern communications, both within the archipelago and with Britain and her colonies. The herring boom of the 1880s, peaking around 1905, lasted until the outbreak of the War, and had done much to aid these developments. With 174 curing stations scattered around 26 Shetland ports, 46 of them in Baltasound, Unst and 36 in Lerwick - the two most important centres for the hosiery industry - ease of communication was essential to transport fish rapidly to the most lucrative port. Pedestrian travel had been improved by paths funded by the Congested Districts Board, whilst extensions to the 'meal' roads made cart and stage car travel possible by land (fig. 5.20); and by sea, the inter-island steamer service greatly facilitated local mobility and brought enormous developments to the import and export trades. The herring boom transformed Lerwick; the new harbour and docks, coupled with the ample supply of water and imported coal, needed for steam drifters, established Lerwick as the 'Herringopolis' of the north. Inevitably this migrant population, with money to spend, boosted sales of every description in Lerwick. Shortage of cash gradually became less

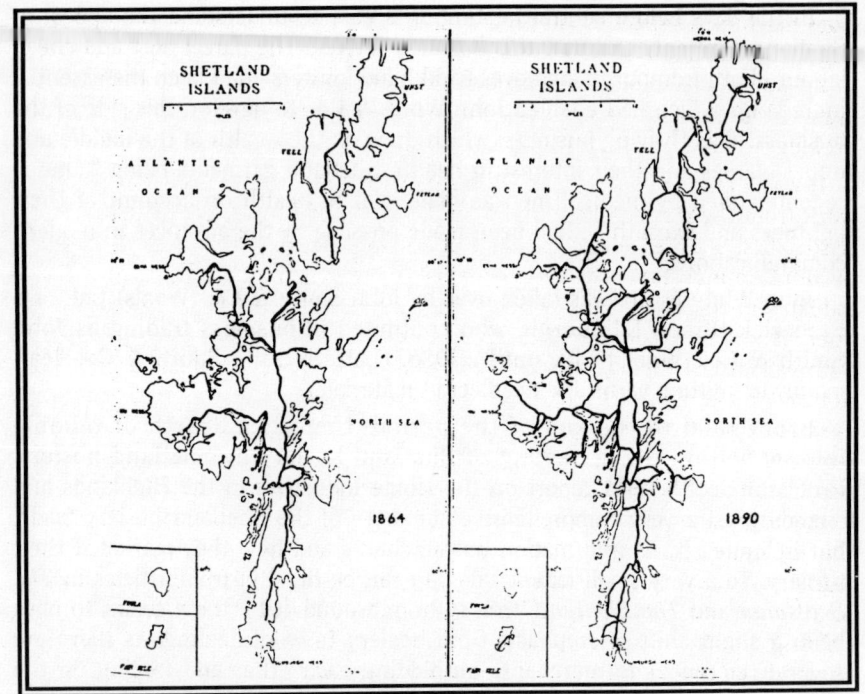

Fig 5.20 – Shetland road plexus, 1864 and 1890 (after O'Dell).

of a halting factor to trade expansion, and as the amount of cash in circulation increased to all spheres, Shetland slowly moved from a community tied to the land and dependent on crofting for subsistence, to one independent of the land, relying on cash for their 'daily bread'. Increased cash brought increased mobility reflected in the falling population in rural areas and the rise in Lerwick's population. Hosiery merchants had not been slow to take advantage of this money supply. They benefited from the wealth generated by the growth of the fishing industry, and in fact, owed much of their success to the opening up of Shetland spurred by the fishing industry. To the hosiery industry in general, advances in communications were its life blood, whilst the advances in modern technology, were a mixed blessing. For example, whilst machine carded wool saved Shetland spinners time and allowed more worsted to be spun on the islands, it detracted from the soft, fine texture of the native wool, and made it easier to imitate; this was also true of machine spun worsted. However, it was the knitting machine, with its growing number of cheap imitation, which posed the greatest threat to the industry - a situation fuelled by the large quantities of inferior Shetland goods still finding their way on to the market, and aggravated by trucking. As has been shown in the case study of William Pole, it was the destitute, the bereaved, the old and infirm, who unable to help themselves, were acting as a cancer on the islands' hosiery industry. The industry's ability to develop and survive competition

DAWN OF MODERNISATION 1872-1918

from machines, depended on producing quality products aimed at the luxury slot in the market. There was no place for mis-shapen, inferior workmanship in an age of machines and modern technology. The time had come when survival depended on jettisoning these inferior knitters, a very difficult problem when it was their livelihood at stake.

It was a problem facing many home industry associations, as it was so often work from them which kept many out of the Poor House. The Midland Lace Association is an excellent example of a dying industry which had managed, by unrelenting standards of excellence, to revive the cottage lace making industry in the Midlands. Run on purely business, rather than philanthropic lines, it was able to compete with machine made lace, and even up to the outbreak of the First World War, make a profit. However, such success was not accomplished without its victims - the old and infirm, whose failing eyesight and strength, prevented them from meeting the high standards required by the Association. Extant business records and accounts of this Association, include sad, inarticulate little notes from workers no longer able to meet the standards of the Association. Were the Shetland merchants doing the knitters a kindness by accepting inferior work and threatening the industry's survival, or was the Midland Lace Association's policy of excellence at all costs, the soundest policy? In the event, it was the Shetland hand knitting industry which survived, whilst the Midland Lace Association limped along after the First World War, finally terminating in the mid 1920s.

It would be untrue to deduce from this comparison, that the Shetland approach was the correct one. Several factors must be taken into consideration. First and foremost, knitting was a part-time/spare-time occupation for the majority of knitters, which fitted in with the crofting way of life; secondly, as islanders, Shetlanders, unlike Midland lace workers, were unable to pick up employment in nearby towns and cities; thirdly, the Shetland knitter had her own supply of raw material and did not depend on an agent to supply her - she could use or sell the wool, in each case a net gain - and lastly; knitting skills were so greatly developed and so many island women involved, that even if several hundred women had given up knitting or migrated to other parts of the country, the effect would have been little felt. A more valid comparison would be with the Harris Tweed Industry's strategy in dealing with spurious 'Harris tweed'. The Harris Tweed Industry, as inextricably enmeshed in trucking as the Shetland hand knitting industry for much of this period, managed to overcome machine competition by maintaining the high standards laid down and enforced by its Association. As the Government Inquires had invariably shown, living and working conditions in the Hebrides, were marginally worse than Shetland. The social and economic conditions which had been the initial cause of truck, did not disappear in the Long Isles during this period, but equally, they had not been allowed to interfere with and ruin one of the few valuable assets the islands possessed. By attention to detail and vigilant quality control, the Association was able to survive and expand by capitalising on its reputation by selling to the luxury market in Britain, diversifying into the American market during British trade recessions. It was of critical importance that all concerned with the Shetland hand knitting industry should unite to fight their common enemy - the knitting machine - by forming a protective organisation, and thereby gaining their own trade mark.

References - Chapter 5
1. *The Shetland Times*, 28th September, 1872.
2. SA, D6/292/24, p. 66.
3. SRO (WRH), AF42/263. (1898).
4. Mitchell, I., (editor), *Ahint Da Daeks*, (Shetland 1987), p. 6.
5. Ibid.
6. Newton, S.M., *Health, Art and Reason*, (London 1974), p. 98 -100. Dr. Jaegar, a German from Stuttgart, revised and had his *Essays on Health Culture* translated into English in 1887. Although he had some very curious ideas about the health properties of animal and vegetable fibres for clothing, he had a great following in Britain - called 'woolleners' - who were anxious to adopt his theories of the beneficial effect of wool next to the skin, not only for warmth and comfort, but also to aid slimming and avoid the noxious vapours he claimed were given off by vegetable fibres!
7. *The Shetland Times*, 4th September, 1909.
8. *Peace's Orkney and Shetland Almanac* 1884, p. 192.
9. Cowie, R., *Shetland*, (Edinburgh 1874), p.126.
10. SRO, (WRH), AF42/263.
11. PP, Cd., 7564, (1914), Report of the Board of Agriculture for Scotland on Home Inudstries in the Highlands and Islands, p. 91.
12. Op. cit., p. 141.
13. Op. cit., p. 49 and 50..
14. Munro, Lewis, *Scottish Home Industries*, (Dingwall 1895), p. 173..
15. PP, Cd., 4443, (1908), Minutes of Evidence taken before the Truck Committee (days 1-37), q. 3448, p. 137 & 138, evidence of Mr A. Newlands.
16. *The Shetland Times*, 4th September, 1909.
17. Munro, Lewis, *Scottish Home Industries*, (Dingwall 1895), p. 123.
18. Manson, T., *Lerwick During the Last Half Century*, (1991 edition, Lerwick), p. 13.
19. SA Reid Tait Collection. D6/263/1. Anderson & Co.'s 1894-6 mail order catalogue.
20. SRO (WRH), HH1/848, Delting Truck Inquiry, evidence of Wm. Pole.
21. Ibid.
22. Op. cit., evidence of Ann Blance and Mrs Ridlon.
23. *Scotland of To-day and Edinburgh its capital*, (London and Edinburgh 1890), p. 81.
24. Ibid.
25. Ibid.
26. Ibid.

Chapter 6
Modernisation
1918-1950

During this period Shetland experienced the high unemployment and economic depression common to the rest of Britain, as well as further extensions in the field of communications, a restructuring of traditional Shetland life, an overall rise in the standard of living brought about by the Crofters' Commission and a rise in public spending. At the outbreak of the Second World War, Shetland, a virtually forgotten backwater in the United Kingdom, was rediscovered by London and became the northern base of the war effort, playing a vital role in the North Sea blockade. The influx of servicemen, with troops possibly outnumbering civilians, led to a welcome increase in well paid full- and part-time local employment, and thereby to an increased standard of living; even in rural areas, basic amenities like water, electricity and roads - taken for granted almost everywhere else in Great Britain - were gradually installed. In short Shetland continued to develop into a modern society in line with other Highland and Island regions.

Socio-economic Conditions in Shetland During the Inter-war Years

Until the outbreak of the First World War, the majority of the islands' active man-power had been involved in fishing. Shetland's position of supremacy in the herring industry was finally toppled by the increased use of steam drifters which few Shetlanders could afford, and by the trade disruptions caused during the First World War. The fishing industry never recovered fully after the War. And as fishing, traditionally regarded as the cornerstone of the Shetland economy, declined in economic importance after the First World War, and the unpredictable returns, together with the long hours and hard labour of crofting, compared unfavourably with waged employment, Shetland economic life went through a considerable upheaval. With the move from a barter to cash economy, great advances in communications, and a general rise in the standard of living, other forms of employment, particularly the service industries, presented themselves. Fig. 6.1 shows the fishing industry becoming subordinate to the textile and the service industries, although agriculture still remained Shetland's largest primary employer.

Nor did agriculture remain unscathed by twentieth century developments. The croft, still the home base for many, had changed from essential

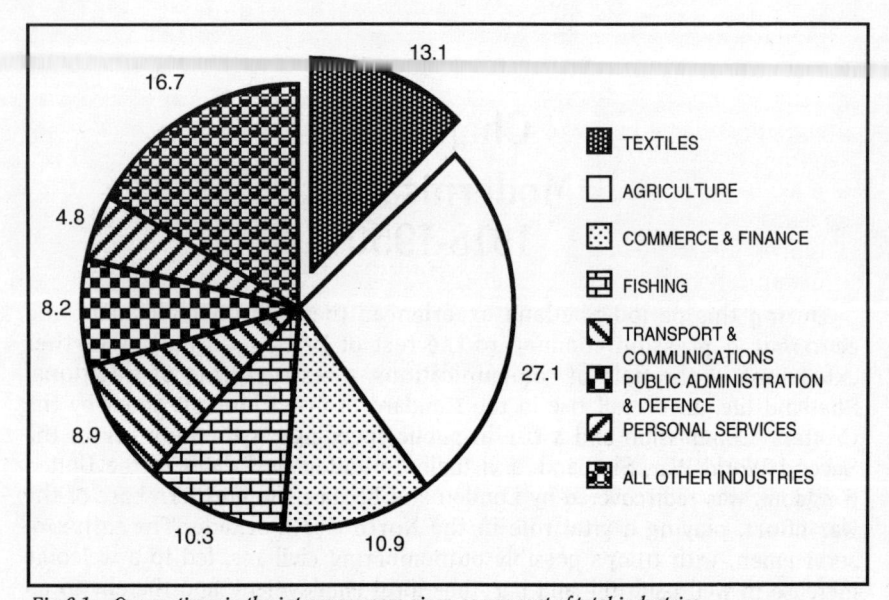

Fig 6.1 – Occupations in the inter-war years given as per cent of total industries.

subsistence food production to the spare-time occupation of those who chose to continue this way of life, which in the words of the first report by the Highlands and Islands Board "appears to be a form of living and working which gives deep satisfaction to those who follow it".[1] The crofter-fisherman's dual way of life tended to become separated into two distinct occupations; this separation was generally felt to be marked by the passing of the heyday of the Shetland sail drifter, with the number of sail drifters falling from 2,263 in 1911 to 938 by 1931. Those with large enough crofts concentrated on the land whilst many fishermen-crofters joined the merchant navy or emigrated. The Shetland croft was too small to provide more than a mere subsistence living - a legacy from the splitting of outsets in the days of the fishing-tenures, and a system perpetuated by the security provided by the 1886 Crofters Holding (Scotland) Act, and encouraged by the Smallholders (Scotland) Act of 1911, and the Land Settlement (Scotland) Act passed eight years later. The crofter who was able to make a living from the land, did so generally by acquiring several crofts and, in addition, by reclaiming hill land.

The herring boom of the 1880s, the general expansion of trade with Britain and her Colonies, and full wartime employment, were responsible for a much needed cash injection into the Shetland economy, and as the imports of staple foods rose, the land was used less for subsistence agriculture and more for the rearing of livestock. As crofting declined the number of acres given over to arable farming fell, whilst those devoted to sheep farming rose. This increase in wool production aided further expansion in the textile sector, and gave fresh impetus to the expansion of wool marketing, the continuing expansion of internal and external communications greatly helping both sectors.

MODERNISATION 1918-1950

And it was this continuing progress in communications which arguably had the greatest overall impact on island life. Road travel within the islands was greatly improved under the Crofters Counties Scheme, which gave 100% grants for the building and upgrading of existing roads. This scheme, which ran from 1935-1942, was responsible for no less than 63 miles of class 1 roads and led to an increase in the number of motor vehicles in the islands. From a dozen or so cars in pre-First World War Shetland, the number had risen to 1,146 by 1938. Shetland, so dependent on the sea for its main lines of communication, continued to enjoy a three runs a week steamer service in the summer time, with two a week in winter. This route which was subsidised, was operated by the North of Scotland, Orkney and Shetland Steam Navigation Company which, from 1931, gradually replaced all its steam ships with motor vessels. Travel to the smaller islands was made easier by the inter-island overland ferry service to Unst and the North Isles, which started in 1932. Even remote Fair Isle at last enjoyed a regular ferry service provided by the *Good Shepherd* - twice weekly in summer and once a week in the winter. Despite these improvements in modern communications not all islands could rely on rapid contact with the outside world - for instance, the people of Fetlar celebrated Edward VIII's coronation in 1936!

American aviation pioneers, Cramer and Pacquette, landed in Shetland in 1931 in their quest to find a North Atlantic air route. (They disappeared after leaving Lerwick en route for Denmark). A regular air service was not far behind. In 1936, a regular air service between Aberdeen and Shetland, via Orkney, was established and flew an incredible three return flights a day until the outbreak of the Second World War (an erratic air service had in fact started in 1934). Gradually air services were extended to many of the more remote islands. Alternative means of transport provided a safety net in times of emergencies, but also helped accelerate emigration.

Postal, telegraphic and telephone communications developed markedly. By 1937, Shetland had a daily airmail service in the summer, reduced to three flights per week in the winter, although during the war postal deliveries were upped to two a day. The regularity of the postal service boosted trade and led to the expansion of mail order firms - an ideal way to market goods, particularly hosiery, in a remote community. The basic telephone and telegraph network provided by the GPO during the early part of the century, steadily expanded. Radio-telephone links were established with Out Skerries, Papa Stour, and Foula in the mid 1930s. However, it was not until after the War, that Shetland was fully incorporated into the national telephone circuit.

Great improvements were made in housing conditions after the First World War. In 1919 the Town Planning (Scotland) Act concerned with housing, became law and the formidable task of improving living conditions started. Except in Lerwick and Scalloway, there were no drainage facilities or public water supplies. Wells - often little more than shallow holes collecting surface water - were covered and their walls lined with concrete. Despite local opposition, water closets were gradually erected throughout the islands. House walls were heightened and lined, windows enlarged and designed to open, earthen floors covered over, porches built and other improvements made. Health facilities steadily improved. The Gilbert Bain Hospital, built in 1902, was extended in 1921. In 1924 R. H. Rose-Innes Shetland's first consultant surgeon was appointed, and greatly reduced the number of severely ill people having to undertake the hazardous sea voyage to Edinburgh for treatment. Further improvements were carried out after the War and plans drawn up for a new hospital.

These improvements were not without their repercussions. Many people left the islands, as for instance, between 1921 and 1931, no less than 2,500 people emigrated, that is 9.8% of the population; census figures for 1931 and 1951, show this trend continuing but at a reduced rate by 1951 (appendix 1). Many emigrated to seaports like Leith within Scotland or the north east of England, as well as to the Dominions. Heavy losses during World War I left some of the smaller islands so short of young manpower that essential services like ferries could not be operated and caused the removal of whole communities. Within this period, the smaller islands of Havra, Hildasay, Papa, Linga, Oxna and Langa were all abandoned.

The loss of young people by emigration and war led to a low marriage and birth rate in Shetland and in turn to an ever increasing proportion of elderly people and a high death rate. War casualties did little to help Shetland's troublesome sex imbalance. During the years 1921 to 1951, females averaged a 9% surplus over men. This disparity, with its underlying consequences of lowering the status of females in the community, also gave rise to a lower marriage and birth rate than Scotland as a whole, and to a subsequently higher death rate. This social imbalance tended to contribute to rural depopulation, particularly of some of the smaller islands, and to the withdrawal of services like schools, mobile shops, and buses, and to a downward spiral which inevitably caused an acceleration in the number of people leaving rural areas. Population changes in Shetland have in the post-war period continued the trends started two generations earlier when many migrated from isolated rural areas to Lerwick or emigrated to Scotland and the Dominions.

Role of Women

All too often, the contribution of women has gone unrecorded. The oral history project started during the 1980s and funded by the Manpower Services and Shetland Islands Council, has done much to remedy this omission by the publication of *Living Memory* and *Ahint Da Daeks*, both of which were compiled from many hours of recording the memories of the older generation. Such oral history studies show how little the role of women had changed since the last century.

Women's role in society was usually a double one - being frequently mothers and workers. Motherhood and work left little time for much else; as one old woman put it when asked during the 1986 Oral History Project in Shetland what she did with her free moments replied: "Spare time?...I hed none".[2] The demands of motherhood were invariably accompanied by the constant financial and physical struggle to keep the house going whilst working on the croft or paid employment. Girls helped out at an earlier age than boys with domestic affairs, and in fact many boys escaped entirely from such mundane chores. Even in rural areas where there was more equality in the division of labour between the sexes, job-sharing rarely encroached on the boundaries of the kitchen:

...we'd be working in the fields maybe...on a fine day I'd be sent in to make something to eat while they [the boys] went off and had a quick dip".[3]

Traditionally young women, particularly the youngest girl in the family, stayed at home to help the old folks, only leaving to get married. The prospect of meeting a suitable partner in these circumstances was limited because of Shetland's continuing unbalanced sex ratio, and for this reason, despite the hard work entailed, many young women looked forward to the fishing season, as it was at the curing stations that many found a marital partner.

Arguably it was the two wars which did most to improve the quality of life for many Shetland women. The increased job opportunities offered by wartime conditions in the First World War, were greatly extended during the Second World War. Not only were they outnumbered by men but the unique opportunity of well paid full- or part-time employment in ancillary services was available without leaving the islands or, sometimes in rural areas, even their local township. Emancipation from truck, from immobility, from domestic drudgery suddenly presented itself when knitters found this ready market on their doorstep anxious to buy virtually all the hosiery they could produce, and pay cash for it.

The Shetland Hand Knitting Industry During the Inter-war Years

For several years after the War, hosiery prices remained artificially high as shortages continued in Britain and the Empire. Keen to ensure their survival, Shetland merchants competed against each other buying up all the available Shetland wool. Competition between merchants forced up the price of wool, so that wool, which in pre-war days would have cost 1/5d. per lb., was now costing 3/- per lb, making it very difficult for the Shetland knitter who did not have her own source of wool, to purchase wool and then sell her hosiery profitably. It was felt that even allowing for the increase in the price paid for knitted articles, knitters did not receive sufficient for their work. The poor returns to knitters were of greater consequence than formerly as the collapse of the fishing industry led many families to rely on knitting as their main means of support.

The creation of new and the development and resurgence of existing rural industries, was recognised by the Government as a vital ingredient to the success of its post-war reconstruction schemes in the Highlands and Islands. Conscious of the difficulties arising from these times of change, the Scottish Office, although greatly hampered by under funding, endeavoured to aid cottage and rural industries with a view to creating employment and economic stability to prevent rural depopulation. To this end, many small inquiries were commissioned, much advice given, but little action taken.

Each of these reports recognised the importance of the hand knitting industry and the vital role it played in both providing and supplementing the domestic economy as fishing and agriculture declined, and where the War, or death from other causes, and rising unemployment, had left rural areas with many families dependent on the earnings of its women, and not on its traditional male breadwinner. And it was during this period of change that the hand knitting industry in Shetland, so often under valued by historians and economists, was at last recognised as one of the strengths and mainstays of the Shetland economy. This situation was aptly summed up in the *New Shetlander:*

> Take the hosiery industry from the islands and her life blood will ebb, her crofts will be deserted, her islands depopulated, for crofting and fishing are industries of a season providing a background for a home, but in themselves inadequate for a reasonable amount of comfort and leisure.[4]

Scanning the Scottish Office files dealing with rural textile industries, four weaknesses in the Shetland hosiery industry become apparent. Firstly, the deterioration in the native breed of Shetland sheep; secondly, the difficulties crofters experienced in marketing their products; thirdly, the harm done to these industries by careless, shoddy workmanship; and fourthly, the serious nature of the increased competition from machines. In addition, it was felt that Shetland would be better able to safeguard the future of its woollen industry by establishing its own spinning mill - this was at the time when the Lewis branch of the Hebridean tweed industry was experiencing marketing problems through their use of machine, and not, hand spun yarn. In an attempt to overcome these difficulties the Shetland Woollen Industries Association was to be formed in 1922, the Shetland Flock Book Society in 1926, and in the 1940s, a knitter's co-operative, the Shetland Hand Knitter's Association, was to be started, followed by a local spinning mill in 1947.

After a brief period of post-war prosperity due to continuing shortages, Shetland hand knitters were to find their world irrevocably changed as competition from mass produced machine-made articles undermined their way of life. There was virtually no demand for Shetland lace on a commercial scale, whilst hand knitted underwear had been replaced by the cheaper machine knitted goods, and if it hadn't been for the 'discovery' of Fair Isle knitting by the outside world - which knitting machines could not copy - the Shetland hand knitting industry would not have survived. This distinctive method of colour-stranded knitting which used native wool dyed from local natural dye stuffs, and had originated in Fair Isle possibly sometime during the seventeenth century (Gunnister Man's purse was worked in colour stranded knitting - fig. 1.7), was suddenly in great demand as a fashion garment. The covers of fashion magazines such as *Vogue*, showed Fair Isle golfing outfits, pullovers, cardigans etc, in an infinite variety of designs and colours (fig. 6.2)

The following extract from the *Shetland News* attributes much credit for the development of Fair Isle knitwear to Provost James Smith, one of the founder members of the SWIA.

Fig 6.2 — The golfers' craze for Fair Isle, mid 1920s.   *Photo: Bob Inkster*

WHEN THE PRINCE OF WALES WORE A FAIR ISLE JUMPER

It is of interest to recall that when in 1922, Shetland women decided to send a parcel of fine Shetland hosiery to Princess Mary on the occasion of her marriage, Mr Smith, who supplied some of the goods, put a Fair Isle jumper in the parcel. Apparently, it came into the hands of the then Prince of Wales (now the Duke of Windsor), who wore it playing golf which immediately popularised it as a new sportswear, with the result that the demand for these brilliantly-coloured jumpers increased enormously, much to the benefit of Shetland knitters, who for a time were scarcely able to cope with the demand from retailers in the south.[5]

In the years that followed, the regional specialisation of the hosiery was largely discontinued in favour of an almost exclusive production of Fair Isle knitting. Many Shetland knitters adapted quickly to this form of knitting by copying patterns from Fair Isle pullovers, and for the first time in the history of Shetland knitting, some knitters resorted to the use of pattern designs charted on graph paper, although many used the traditional Shetland method of copying from other knitters. An interesting measure of this rapid change over to Fair Isle knitting was mentioned by Dr. Bennett in a paper on the Shetland hand knitting industry. A Mrs Henry who had come to Shetland to learn the art of Shetland lace knitting from the women of Unst, was unable to do so, as in response to unprecedented orders from American and British buyers for thousands, rather than the usual dozens, every available knitter had been urged to abandon her usual style of knitting in favour of Fair Isle work. Quick to see the marketing potential of this exclusive form of hand knitting, an enterprising Lerwick man produced a pattern book to help knitters learn the basic Fair Isle designs.

At the same time the industry was changing from what had been a wholly home-based cottage industry into a more organised and structured one. This long overdue change had been precipitated by the need for protection against spurious, cheaply produced machine-made 'Shetlands'; as whilst the demand for Shetland hand knits was high, so too were prices. Cost wise, hand knitting compared unfavourably with machine-made articles which could be mass produced at a fraction of the cost. The time consuming nature of the hand knitted goods meant that the prices for them were high, yet represented a poor return to the worker for the many hours spent knitting and finishing. It was this vulnerable position that prompted all concerned in securing the future of the Shetland woollen industry, to come together in 1922 to form the Shetland Woollen Industries Association.

Shetland Woollen Industries Association

The SWIA was the first voluntary co-operative scheme to attempt to organise and protect the future of the woollen industry in Shetland. The initial idea for such an association was instigated by a group of merchants and other interested parties, led by Provost James Smith. The objectives of the Association, which specifically excluded the buying or selling of Shetland hosiery, were as follows: Firstly, to encourage the growth of pure Shetland

MODERNISATION 1918-1950

wool in the Shetland Islands; secondly, to revive and encourage the hand-loom weaving of Shetland tweed cloth and Shetland rugs, and thirdly, to protect, improve, and promote the interests of the hand knitting and woollen industries in the Shetland Islands. The latter the Association hoped to achieve by the acquisition of a trade mark which would be applied to all goods of approved quality after inspection.

The story of the SWIA is largely one of the islands' fight against 'Shetland' imitations and its unsuccessful struggle to have the word 'Shetland' exclusively kept for articles manufactured in the Shetland Islands. Professor Scott, in his 1914 Home Industries Report, had advocated the use of a distinctive mark for various classes of hosiery and suggested a trade mark be applied for and the marking of goods carried out by local inspectors appointed by the Board of Agriculture for Scotland. However, the War intervened and the scheme was shelved. The SWIA applied for and was granted, its own trade mark - registration number 437482 - in August 1925. This mark depicted a Norse galley, and as well as the Association's name, bore the words "Shetland hand knit", and for Fair Isle knitting "Fair Isle - Made in Shetland". (fig. 6.3)

In 1926-27 the SWIA was given a grant of £400 by the Board of Agriculture for Scotland towards the cost of advertising its trade mark and a Shetland Flockbook Society formed; it looked as if the future of the islands' knitwear industry was at last on a sound and secure footing. However, despite efforts by the Association to help and to protect the Shetland woollen industry, it was clear by the early 1930s that a new threat lay at their doorstep - competition from machine-made articles produced in Shetland itself. Moreover, these articles were apparently being passed as hand knitted ones.

Fig 6.3 – The SWIA trademarks which were granted in August, 1925.

This disturbing situation led to the SWIA, backed by the Zetland County Council (ZCC), endeavouring to enlist the Government's help to force Shetland machine-made hosiery to bear a label to that effect and to exclude it from using a plain 'Made in Shetland' label. A very full account of the SWIA's unsuccessful struggle to this end is recorded in the Scottish Office's Highland Development Files.

The story started with the secretary of the SWIA, J.R. White, writing on 29th March, 1932, following the Association's AGM, to the Secretary of the Board of Trade, London, requesting an inquiry into:

> ...the present condition of the Shetland hand-knit industry and its vital relation to the life of the people of the islands... petition is being made because the hand-knit industry is now seriously threatened by the introduction into the islands of machines operated by hand and that these machines are increasing in number year by year.[6]

White further stated that the Association's trade mark had done much to combat successfully spurious imitations of Shetland hosiery in the south, but that the introduction of machines to the islands constituted a much graver danger. The Association set out their reasons as follows:

1. Every article made by machines here can be labelled ... "hand-knit" or "hand-finished" and also "made in Shetland from Shetland wool", and this so nearly approximates to the Association's trade marks in its descriptive matter that it makes the latter ineffectual as distinguishing marks.

2. When hand-knit and machine-knit garments from Shetland are put on the market the advantage lies in favour of the latter owing chiefly to lower costs of production, regularity of texture and uniformity in designs etc.

3. The industry in a normal year has an export value of approximately £80,000. Under the hand-knit regime every home in the islands gets a share of this sum which considerably supplements the earnings of crofters and cottars alike. In fact it is doubtful if crofting agriculture can exist in Shetland apart from the support of the hand-knitting of the crofter's wife and daughter, and herein lies the threatened danger to the islands from the mass production of knitting machines.[7]

The request led to a Government inquiry, conducted by Mr John C. Russell of the Scottish Department of Agriculture. Russell travelled all over the mainland and islands, interviewing numerous representatives, merchants and knitters, in order to obtain first-hand information regarding the present state of the industry and its prospects, as well as inspecting the new hand-driven knitting machines. Reporting on Russell's visit the *Daily Express* wrote:

> The object of Mr Russell's visit is to ascertain whether any steps can be taken to restore the prosperity to this important cottage industry, in which more than ten thousand women and girls are engaged.[8]

This report was concluded early in 1933. It was brief but concise. Russell recognised that with the decreased earnings from agriculture and the fisheries, the majority of the households in the country districts had become more and more dependent on the earnings of the women and girls from knitting. Russell estimated that there were more than 9,000 knitters in Shetland, which accounted for 75% of the total female population. He did however, point out that only 3,049 of these knitters were members of the SWIA and stressed that:

> ...all concerned in the Industry should recognise the value of the Association's work and the urgent necessity for supporting their efforts to organise the industry on a sound basis.[9]

He also pointed out that only ten years ago, all hosiery exported was done by hand, but now in 1932-3 there were 13 knitting machines on the islands turning out good uniform work at relatively low prices, and were selling well in America, where a strong demand existed for correct shaping, standard sizes and an even, regular texture. Poor quality goods, lacking the uniformity to make up set orders were telling against hand knits, and led to a diminished demand. Russell felt that co-operation with the Women's Rural Institute in teaching knitters to remedy faults would help, and that knitters should be prepared to change their styles to meet fashion demands.

Moving to the question of the trademark, Russell rightly pointed out that two-thirds of the knitters did not use the existing trademark, and that less than one-third of the total production of Shetland hosiery was trademarked with the Association's sewn-on label, many bearing no label at all, whilst others bore a manufacturer's label. In other words, a total lack of uniformity, which he felt prejudiced the marketing of Shetland hosiery. Russell emphasised that the hand knitting industry must protect itself from machine imitations by fostering a distinctive differentiation between its own characteristic product and the machine-made article, "...whether the latter is produced in Shetland or outside Shetland". He strongly advocated the use of the existing trade mark to this end, as the Galley mark had the virtue of being already registered. The effective utilisation of the trade mark depended on good workmanship, adequate inspection and on the power of the Association to defend its trade mark by taking up cases of infringement. These requirements necessitated a large increase in the Association's membership to strengthen its resources and organisation, to enable it to carry out inspection of work and if need be, defend its trademark in the Courts. Finally Russell touched on the industry's Achilles' heel:

> ...real co-operation and a united effort by all concerned in the industry to remedy existing defects of workmanship, organisation and marketing and to prevent a decline from which all would suffer.[10]

Accurate as it was, this report was not well received by the Shetland people, who had set much store on the Government's ability to solve their problems. In essence all concerned were furious with the Government for not, in effect, sending out an edict enforcing all machine knitted articles to carry a 'machine made in Shetland' label or even forbid the use of machines in the islands! An extraordinary meeting of the SWIA was called to consider the report. Great disappointment was expressed at the Department's "throwing all the work of differentiating hand-knit from machine-made goods on to the Association, while requiring nothing from the owners of the machines", who could legally but ambiguously, label their articles to the detriment of hand knitted ones. The SWIA was insulted at the suggestion of there being a decrease in demand for hand knits due to carelessness and pointed out that as far as help from the Shetland Women's Rural Institutes was concerned, the Rural was composed almost entirely of knitters. The meeting ended with the SWIA curtly thanking the Department of Agriculture for the inquiry and report, but stating that:

> ...they were greatly disappointed at the Department's failure to deal effectively with or supply any solution for the problem of knitting machines in Shetland, and they pressed for further consideration of this matter.[11]

It is fascinating to read the 'behind the scenes' version of this story from the Highland Development files. The Government's basic stand point was that it was not illegal for hand-frame machine knits to use a 'hand knitted in Shetland' label unless so determined by the Courts under section 2 of the Merchandise Marks Act which dealt with 'false trade descriptions'. And secondly, that self-help, that is, improvement of standards, and the expansion of the SWIA membership should be sufficient to nullify the detrimental competition from machines. They were also aware that the Shetland hand knitting industry was the only hand knitting industry left in Britain in 1933, and that as a means of providing subsidiary employment, it played an important part in the domestic economy, fitting in with the rhythm of the crofting seasons, as well as helping to stave off rural depopulation, and that knitting machines, which employed far fewer people, were indeed a real threat to life in country districts, but were adamant that they couldn't, and wouldn't, intervene to stop the march of progress. In a letter from the Board of Trade to the Scottish Office, dated 28th March, 1932, regarding the introduction of knitting machines to the Shetland Isles:

> ...the Board would point out that the industry in Shetland is undergoing a normal process of industrial evolution under which machinery is being introduced to assist hand labour, and while the result, as in other instances, may be a temporary diminution in the volume of employment, it is difficult to see how this process can be retarded ...or should be".[12]

Although unwilling to intervene over the question of the labelling of knitwear, the Government was not unsympathetic to the Shetlander's plight but wary of creating a precedent by making Shetland a special case, when most other crofting counties were also experiencing economic difficulties. The Scottish Office, whilst spending more per head of population on the crofting counties, represented Scotland as a whole, and could not ignore the repercussions of State interference which might well adversely affect the Scottish hosiery industry in general.

The outcome of this bid for survival, amounted to offers of ineffectual help from the Department, who suggested trying to obtain help for the islanders through the Rural Industries Bureau to enable an assistant from the Highland Home Industries Ltd. to make a short tour in Shetland and advise the knitters about the defects in their way of making garments - of little help when the

MODERNISATION 1918-1950

Scottish sub-committee of the Rural Industries Bureau had been abolished early in 1932! In true Civil Service style, the next move was to suggest taking a little money from an already allocated roads grant to help the hand knitting industry. In the letter containing this proposal, Rose, the Scottish Office official dealing with Shetland affairs, referred to the disappointment the Shetlanders felt in having "...to work out their own salvation in this matter. Apparently some of them would have liked a dictator to prohibit machines".[13]

The Government felt strongly and rightly that it was only by producing a quality article that hand knitting could compete with knitting machines. And it was at this unsatisfactory, stale-mate situation that the whole matter was left. *The Shetland Times* devoted much space to this issue, but apart from a lot of heated talk by a lot of people, the SWIA moaned and groaned about the Government's unhelpful response and rather than turn their anger to action, failed to follow up the sound suggestions put forward by Russell's report. The SWIA was obsessed to the point of blindness by the iniquity of hand-flat knitting machine users labelling their products as 'hand knits', whilst the knitters were still smarting at the Government having had the temerity to criticise the standard of Shetland hand knitting. Poorly knitted, and particularly poorly finished hand knitted hosiery, looked extremely unprofessional beside even the most inexpensive mass-produced knitwear. At the heart of the whole issue lay a violent antagonism, based on fear, to the introduction of hand-flat knitting machines and it was felt that under the corrupting influence of these machines the Shetland hand knitting industry would collapse. Knitters, and many merchants, failed to realise that hand knitting and knitting machines could, and should, complement rather than compete with each other to transform this valuable but outdated industry into the new cornerstone of the Shetland economy.

The SWIA, did not increase its membership, and thereby, the use of its trade mark, nor did knitters change their old ways - a perfect recipe for self-destruction in a changing world. And from the mid 1930s, the Association appeared moribund and its trade mark suspended in 1937. From a strong position of unity in the 1920s, the Shetland woollen industry, represented by the SWIA, backed by Government support, and further strengthened by a Board of Trade registered trade mark, let this advantage slip through its fingers by failing to sustain unity. Many dealers were not in this voluntary organisation, others allowed their allegiance to dwindle, feeling they were not reaping any marked benefits from belonging to the SWIA, whilst many knitters were disinclined to pay a membership subscription and 1d. label fee for their hosiery if they could obtain sales elsewhere. A lot of hand knitted hosiery was leaving Shetland labelless and unpromoted, exposing it to the vulnerability of market change. Both parties were short sighted in their neglect of the Association; neither bothering to look to the future so that in the bad times they would be able to batten down the hatches and pull together. This weakness of grabbing what the present had to offer - a legacy of hard times and isolation - rather than planning for an assured future, was nearly the downfall of the Shetland woollen industry.

Interestingly, during this period of struggle against progress, the Scottish National Development Council (SNDC) published a report in 1934 on rural industries in Scotland. Rural industries were defined as small rural factories employing no more than 100 people, and domestic or cottage industries. This enlightened and perceptive Report, reiterated much of what had been said by Professor Scott in his 1914 Home Industries Report, but where it differed from this and other predecessors, was that it compared Scottish rural industries with those of England and Wales. In the Report's preface, the working committee stated their optimism in hoping that the report would be widely read, and urged that recommendations be translated into practice as soon as possible. It took the committee no more than two sentences to sum up the difficulties experienced by rural workers. Firstly, workers were scattered and found it difficult to combine; secondly, their resources were too slender to allow for advertising and/or high pressure salesmanship; thirdly, craftsmen were out of touch with prices etc. being long distances from markets; and lastly, and of paramount importance "In conditions of hard competition rural industry encounters the almost irresistible temptation to lower its quality and thus wreck itself".[14]

The committee suggested that a Scottish Rural Industries Bureau be created with representatives from Government Departments, from the Highland Home Industries Ltd., the Scottish Women's Rural Institutes, with the addition of three or four men and women interested in the subject.

No action was taken by the Scottish Office. This succinct and excellent report was presumably filed away and its recommendations forgotten. If all the money which had been spent on producing these reports had been channelled into grants to cottage industries, or to funding the discontinued Rural Industries Bureau, the tax payer would have had better value for money through the consolidation of rural industries. In the crofting counties, rural industries were imperative to supplement agricultural or fishing returns. This was particularly important in the changing times of the twentieth century when many crofts had become too small to be economically self-supporting, and depended on ancillary employment to make ends meet. As people moved from the land to towns and cities gaining an enhanced standard of living, it was important that those left behind did not feel themselves too disadvantaged when compared with their migrant friends and relations, as this in itself, would have further encouraged rural depopulation. Logistically, crofting life lent itself to the utilisation of spare time being turned to profit through home industries. Rural industries were of paramount importance to sustain rural life.

The Shetland Flock Book Society

Of greater and more lasting success than the SWIA was the Shetland Flock Book Society formed in 1926 by Dr. Bowie, a medical practitioner, and some progressively minded stockmasters, notably Mr Andrew Tait. This group of men set about the long overdue task of saving the Shetland breed of sheep from extinction. The purity of native Shetland wool which had given cause for concern as far back as the days of Sir John Sinclair, continued to do so, as constant cross-breeding and the breeding of cross-bred sheep with Shetland 'types' diminished the purity of the native Shetland breed, threatening to make it extinct. As the average fleece from a Shetland sheep was considerably lighter than that of the black face or Cheviot sheep, it was not surprising that many wool growers were turning their backs on the native breed in favour of the more lucrative non-native breeds. The price of Shetland wool was higher than for other breeds, but pound for pound per sheep, the heavier fleeces of the non-native breeds gave a better overall financial return, which understandably was more attractive to the wool grower, especially those with small flocks. The Flock Book Society endeavoured to protect the Shetland breed from extinction by breeding flocks of rare purity of conformation, colour and quality of fleece. Premiums given by the Department of Agriculture for Scotland for the breeding of high quality tups, which along with help from the Flock Book Society, led to an increase in the number of pedigree tups being used for breeding. Prophet Smith, Convener of Zetland in 1958, felt that in addition to the work of the Flock Book Society, the holding of agricultural shows, as for example, in the Walls and Sandness district, had helped raise standards as they were an ideal opportunity for displaying high quality breeds and provided a forum for discussion amongst wool growers. This Society, so necessary with the ever-increasing numbers of sheep being bred on the islands, did much valuable work, and is still in existence to date.

Proposed Spinning Mill

Attempts to establish a local spinning mill, first advocated by the SWIA and encouraged by the Board of Agriculture in 1924, failed to come to fruition. In 1939, Dr. T. Manson, Chairman of the SWIA, proposed that hand spinning sets which teased, carded and spun wool, be established at small co-operative units dispersed throughout the islands - co-operation was essential as the basic cost of each set was £700. This attempt to establish local machine spinning came to nothing as the War intervened. During the inter-war years it was customary for crofter-knitters to send their wool for spinning through a local agent. For example, R.& I. Henderson, hotelier, shopkeeper and post master at Spiggie, Scousburgh, Dunrossness, acted as agents for Hunters in Sutherland, collecting raw wool and sending it to Brora by post. The worsted was returned cash on delivery; 37 c.o.d. parcels were returned to the Hendersons between 25th May and 9th October 1928 from Hunters of Brora.

The Shetland Hand Knitting Industry During "The Knitting Years" (1939-45)

Wartime knitting wis good because da prices went up again. Hit wis only in wartime dat we started to get whit looked like money for our hosiery. Because quite honestly, before that it wis such a mere pittance dat you got, all you wir havin ta live on.[15]

The 1940s were regarded as the 'knitting years', as during the Second World War, hosiery was sold at realistic prices, rather than exchanged for goods at local shops. The Second World War marked a watershed in the organisation of the Shetland hand knitting industry, and it was during these War years that the Shetland hosiery trade was catapulted into the twentieth century. Many hand knitters finally broke away from marketing hosiery through their local merchant by forming their own protective organisation, the Shetland Hand Knitters Association - subsequently changed to a marketing organisation - whilst merchants, in the absence of sufficient hand knitted hosiery to fill their orders, were forced to rely more heavily on hand-flat knitting machines. As has been shown, the Shetland hand knitting industry had failed to capitalise on its strong position created by the First World War, and it was only by consolidating the unique marketing conditions created artificially during this period, that the hand knitter and the hosiery industry in general, could modernise sufficiently to compete with the mass-production market. Thousands of servicemen were based on the islands, and despite shortages and austerity, this captive market needed services and supplies and was prepared to pay for them, so that hand knitters enjoyed an unprecedented boom created by wartime shortages doubling, and even trebling, the prices paid to knitters. This situation was summed up by *The Scotsman* in its annual review:

> The outstanding feature of the Shetland hosiery trade in 1941 was a very marked switch-over of sales from the regular dealers to men in the Services in the county and also a further increase in the direct trade between knitter and wearer. The demand was more than maintained, but on account of this transition, which of course is a war-time development, the dealers in town and country were able to get only a comparatively small percentage of their requirements. The keen demand coupled with the enhanced prices, greatly benefited knitters, even although they had less time for knitting owing to having to do more work on the crofts because of their men folk being away on service. This applied in varying degrees and according to the labour and time available from crofting duties.[16]

Knitting had become so lucrative that some knitters found it paid better to stay at home and knit rather than to go into the ancillary services.

Shetland hand knitters got off to an apparently good start at the beginning of the War when it was announced on 26th October that Shetland wool, along with native wool from Orkney and the Hebrides, was to be exempt from the Wool Order issued on 12th October, 1939,[17] - decontrolled wool did however, lead to a steady rise in wool prices throughout the war years. All went well for knitters and merchants until June, 1940 when it was made known that the Government was about to control Shetland hosiery. Representation by the ZCC to the Board of Trade for exemption from the system of wool control was made on the grounds that hand knitting was the main means of livelihood for a large proportion of the population. The outcome was satisfactory. In a letter

MODERNISATION 1918-1950

to the ZCC, dated 5th August, 1940, the Board of Trade stated that the independent knitter would not fall under the Limitation of Supplies (Miscellaneous) Order 1940, as she was exempted under the provisions which excluded small manufacturers.

For Shetland hosiery merchants, the outbreak of war brought increased steamer freights - as high as 20% in some cases - and the new 'war risk insurance' placing a 10% tax on goods owned by retailers, which in addition to the normal insurance required for goods being exported to the south, added considerably to their overheads. This resulted in higher prices being charged for hosiery with, understandably, no increase being passed on to the hand knitter. Wool prices rose but wartime conditions meant that many brokers found themselves with large quantities of valuable wool which they were unable to turn into yarn. Spinning mills had been forced to curtail their output of Shetland worsted as priority was given to fulfilling army orders. Government work commandeered up to 75% of the machinery in the mills, leaving only one quarter of the spinning mill able to execute orders for yarn for both merchant and knitter. This shortage of yarn led to merchants being unable to match their supply of knitwear with demand - a situation marginally alleviated by the wartime trade disruption in overseas trade cutting off the supply of continental machine-made goods, thereby increasing the demand for hand knitted hosiery. For example, in 1940 *The Shetland News* stated that "due to war conditions, the supplies of practically all kinds of goods were increasingly insufficient for the demand"[18] with pre-war stocks exhausted. Although there was still great difficulty in obtaining yarn, interestingly, the main reason for merchants having difficulty supplying their orders was attributed to the women lacking time to knit, as in the absence of their menfolk, they had much more crofting and other work to attend to. One hosiery dealer bemoaned the fact that:

> The majority of the knitters are knitting for the Forces in the islands, and the tax on the goods and the question of coupons are not affecting sales at all. I have never had such a sustained demand for hosiery in all my experience, and just now not more than 50% is going through the usual channels - the merchants. I am afraid that there will not be any change until the war is over. I am not getting more than 25% of the goods I got before.[19]

Not all locally knitted hosiery was offered for sale. Both the ZCC Minutes and *The Shetland Times* record many generous gifts of knitting to the services.

The next hurdle for the industry to overcome - that of Board of Trade coupons issued by the Crofter Wool Committee of the Department of Agriculture for Scotland's Wool Control Board - led to untold complications with knitters making illicit, but welcome, sales to servicemen, profiteers selling coupons on the 'black market', and hosiery merchants withholding coupons due to knitters for their hosiery. The collection and distribution of coupons had got so out of hand by the autumn of 1941, that the Board of Trade intervened with the loan of coupons to allow the coupon scheme to get off the ground and all concerned to extricate themselves from this muddle. However, after representation to the Board of Trade by the Shetland Chamber of Commerce, it was proposed that a central distribution point for coupons be established in Lerwick and managed by a full-time official paid for by the whole trade, or alternatively, coupons could accompany wool sent to the spinning mills, the mill acting as a collecting agency. This ultra-complicated situation was never wholly resolved in a manner acceptable to the Government but did not affect, in fact positively helped, knitters in their sales. Illicit sales to the public were difficult to trace when knitters had their own supply of worsted.

However, hand knitters were flourishing. Freed at last from trucking, thanks to their direct sales with servicemen, they found themselves in an enforced semi-organised position brought about by the distribution of coupons. Backed by the National Farmer's Union, many knitters started to organise their own sales independent of local merchants, realising that a great opportunity had been missed after the First World War when the SWIA had failed through lack of proper support. The high hopes accompanying the formation of the SWIA in 1922 had long since evaporated. Lack of support meant, that in real terms, the SWIA had had a minimal impact on the woollen industry, plus marketing, the most crucial aspect of the industry, had not been included in the Association's remit. The Shetland Hand Knitter's Association would surely heed the many warnings for the need for a trade mark, the need for unity and for a structured marketing policy.

Shetland Hand Knitters Association

The Hon. Robert Bruce, in his report entitled "Some impressions of the Shetland Woollen Industry" and published during the war, made the following suggestions:

> It is possible that a scheme might be formulated whereby the population taking part in the industry, an organised system of collecting, grading and pricing, together with facilities for offering immediate cash payments on a scale which adequately approximates to market values, appears to be absolutely necessary; although participation in the scheme should be on a voluntary basis.[20]

It was on similar principles to these, that the SHKA was established in 1943. It was initially set up as a protective organisation to campaign for the removal of the coupons from Shetland hand knits, to maintain high standards and to lobby for set realistic prices for hosiery. The membership fee was 2/6d.; members were issued with a copy of the SHKA's constitution. In December 1943 the SHKA's members voted unanimously to change the Association to that of a marketing organisation, selling direct to the retailer through agents appointed by the Association. It was hoped that this development would "put the whole Shetland hosiery trade into the hands of knitters".[21] This move necessitated changing the Association's constitution and registering it under the Industrial and Provident Act.

The SHKA was registered on 7th February, 1944, and had its headquarters at 58 Commercial Street, Lerwick. It operated as a non-profit making workers' co-operative with members purchasing shares costing £1 each (fig. 6.4). In its first year the Association had 36 branches scattered throughout the islands - each branch sending a representative to the Association's meetings at the Lerwick headquarters. The Association's turnover for the year 1944-45 was £43,634, rising to £55,678 the following year. When it is remembered that the entire Shetland woollen industry had been valued at £80,000 in 1932, this was a very encouraging start. A Sales Committee was appointed and it was decided to sell hosiery on a 10% commission basis to cover running costs, any surplus being paid out in dividends.

The SHKA had four main objectives. Firstly, to protect the interests of the knitters and others engaged in the woollen and hosiery industry in Shetland;

Fig 6.4 — An old SHKA share certificate from 1944.

KNITTING BY THE FIRESIDE

A MESSAGE TO SHETLAND KNITTERS.

KAYS OF SHETLAND, LTD., welcome the SHETLAND HAND KNITTERS' ASSOCIATION. In it we see an instrument which, if handled wisely and with vision, could in the course of time ensure the prosperity of these Islands.

With the exaggerated demand for Shetland hosiery during war time, the immediate problem is probably justice in prices and coupons for the individual knitter. Here we would suggest that the Association take definite steps to ascertain from the Board of Trade the highest permissible prices that can be paid, and to advertise these. This would give a square deal to every knitter.

But what about after the war ? During the war, of course, it is so easy for the knitter to sell her hosiery, but surely every knitter in Shetland can remember those tremendous slumps in Shetland hosiery when little or no hosiery was sold. What caused these slumps, and can the Shetland Hand Knitters' Association do anything to avoid these in the future?

The main point about these lean years in the sale of Shetland goods was the dependence of the Shetland knitter on a certain and particular type of knitting. When this was unfashionable the knitter, or rather the majority of the knitters, could not get away from the type of hosiery they had been educated to knit. They found it impossible to break out and to knit in accordance with the fashion of the time.

> IT IS ALL A MATTER OF EDUCATION. IF WE HAD IN SHETLAND TRAINED FASHION DESIGNERS TO DESIGN SPECIAL GARMENTS FOR EACH SEASON, AND IF WE HAD KNITTERS WHO COULD FAITHFULLY AND QUICKLY COPY THESE DESIGNS, THEN EVERY YEAR THE NEW SHETLAND MODELS WOULD STORM THE FASHION WORLD AND THE SHETLAND KNITTER COULD DEMAND SUCH A PRICE AS NEVER BEFORE HAS BEEN ANTICIPATED.

These things, unfortunately, cannot be done at present, but the Shetland knitter should look into the future for the sake of her daughter or even her grand-daughter. For instance, is it possible for such a revolution to happen, say even in twenty years' time ? We definitely say "Yes."

> EVERY GIRL SHOULD BE TAUGHT KNITTING AT SCHOOL. FROM THE VERY EARLIEST TO THE VERY LATEST AGE. COMPETENT TEACHERS, DESIGNERS AND SPECIALISTS SHOULD SO CONDUCT THESE CLASSES THAT WHEN A SHETLAND GIRL LEAVES SCHOOL SHE IS MISTRESS OF A TRADE THAT WILL ENSURE HER LIVELIHOOD THE REST OF HER LIFE. A TECHNICAL COLLEGE OR CLASSES SHOULD BE OPENED IN THE ISLANDS TO ENSURE THIS. GIRLS SHOWING A SPECIAL FLAIR FOR DESIGN, COLOUR, ETC., SHOULD BE SENT ON A SPECIAL COURSE OF STUDY. THESE GIRLS, WHEN THEIR EDUCATION HAS BEEN COMPLETED, WILL, IN TIME, BE THE FASHION DESIGNERS, IN FACT, THE FASHION DICTATORS, OF SHETLAND HOSIERY.

Fig 6.5 Kays message to the SHKA.

secondly, to negotiate fair prices for all classes of knitwear, and to improve the methods of marketing such goods; thirdly to encourage, secure and maintain the adoption of distinctive marks for all classes of woollen goods reaching the standards of quality, design, manufacture and finish approved by the committee of management of the Association; and lastly, for the aforementioned purposes, to carry on business as agents for, and buyers and sellers of yarn, woollen and hosiery goods used or manufactured by members and others in Shetland and such other products and/or requirements as the Committee may direct. In conjunction with the Association's third objective, the Association encouraged innovation and design, a point felt strongly by Kays of Shetland Ltd. to be lacking in the industry; a point which had been voiced by many in the past. Fig. 6.5 shows Kays message to the SHKA. Interestingly, the points made by Kays, formed the basis of the ZCC's Post-war reconstruction committees' report to the Crofters' Woollen Industry the following year and is dealt with later in this chapter.

The Association was particularly concerned about the threat posed by locally based knitting machines. It realised that although the pre-war demand for Shetland machine knits had been mainly from America, in peace time Shetland machine made hosiery might very well be in demand in Britain and that highly priced hand knits would compare unfavourably with Shetland machine knitted hosiery. In a bid to protect the hand knitting industry, knitters voted to establish their own spinning mill, advocated by Prophet Smith, Secretary of the SHKA and a trade union leader, and supported by the NFU and Shetland Flockbook Society, which would be run by the Association for the exclusive use of knitters and weavers the worsted being available exclusively to members. The Association was equally determined to obtain their own protective trade mark, exclusively for hand knits which would be a guarantee of workmanship and quality. To this end they intended to petition the Board of Trade for the exclusive use of the word 'Shetland' as a mark on hand knitted goods to be used only on hosiery produced in Shetland. Neither of these ambitious schemes were successful, although by 1947 the SHKA did have an 'approved house mark' but not a Board of Trade registered trade mark. Shetland did obtain its own spinning mill in 1947 but despite the combined efforts of the ZCC, NFU, SWIA, SHKA and Jo Grimond MP, the Board of Trade was not prepared to grant the industry the exclusive use of the word Shetland, as under present statute it was inadmissible to register a geographical name as a trade mark. To overcome this state of impasse the SHKA adopted the SWIA's Galley mark.

By 1948 the SHKA had 4,000 members and judging from a 1947 SHKA advertisement (fig. 6.6), the Association's members seem to have realised at last that it was only by uniting and acting as a corporate body, that they would be able to strengthen their position, stabilise prices, and finally rid themselves of the remnants of truck and merchant domination. The Association laid down set, realistic piece work rates for knitwear, although it

Four and a Half Years!

OBJECTS.

(a) To protect the interests of handknitters and others engaged in the woollen and hosiery industry in Shetland.

(b) To negotiate fair prices for all classes of knitwear and to improve the methods of marketing of such goods.

(c) To encourage, secure, and maintain the adoption of distinctive marks for all classes of woollen goods manufactured in Shetland and their application to all goods reaching the standard of quality, design, manufacture and finish approved by the Committee of Management of the Association, and

(d) for these purposes to carry on business as agents for and buyers and sellers of yarn, woollen and hosiery goods used or manufactured by members and others in Shetland and such other products and/or requirements as the Committee may direct. The Association shall also, subject to the approval of members in General Meeting, carry on any kindred forms of trading or other activity likely to protect, improve or promote the interests of all engaged in the woollen and hosiery industry in the Shetland Islands.

(a) Since it was founded the S.H.K.A. has represented knitters on all Committees formed to aid the Industry, and has been recognised by Government departments as the competent body to speak collectively for the knitters.

(b) We have continuously campaigned for stabilised prices and took the leading part in negotiations that resulted in fixing minimum prices to knitters.

(c) The S.H.K.A. has been in the forefront of the fight for a Trade Mark, which should be in operation soon.

(d) The S.H.K.A. formed the first trading business owned and controlled by the knitters themselves.

> **We have done our bit.**
> **It is up to YOU to Support us.**

WHEN YOU SEND YOUR HOSIERY, REMEMBER WE HAVE A REPUTATION TO UPHOLD

THE SHETLAND HAND KNITTERS' ASSOCIATION LTD
58 COMMERCIAL STREET · LERWICK · SHETLAND

'PHONE 46.   'PHONE 46.

Fig 6.6 – A 1947 advertisement for the SHKA.

would be misleading to paint a rosy picture of fair prices being paid to knitters, that is, fair in terms of workers being paid on an hourly rate economically commensurate with the work involved in producing a garment. This stability in turn gave the knitter some leeway to try out new designs, styles, shapes, all of which were encouraged by the Association. In the past there had been little point in spending precious time on innovation and raising standards, when this effort was not financially rewarded. Trucking, low rates of pay, and price fluctuation all acted against the hosiery industry to stifle enterprise and the raising of standards.

Oral history sources suggest that some knitters felt that they gained little benefit from the Association. Problems had arisen with members who had regular customers in the south. The Association felt that all hosiery had to be channelled through their depot in order to stabilise prices. Prophet Smith believed that if the Association did not control the industry after the war it would cease to exist. However, like the SWIA, the continuing story of the SHKA becomes one of its struggle to compete with 'Shetland imitations' and their subsequent action to try to have the word 'Shetland' kept for exclusive use of the indigenous woollen industry.

ZCC Post-war Reconstruction Committee and Calder Report

As early as the summer of 1942 the ZCC, in a forward-looking move, appointed a post-war reconstruction committee to draw up plans to ensure employment and prosperity in peace time. A woollen industries sub-committee was appointed with representatives from knitters, the Flockbook Society, smallholders, and dealers, to look into the state of the Shetland hosiery industry and plan a strategy to ensure its post-war survival. The central committee regarded the hosiery industry as the most important of Shetland's three traditional industries "...as there is hardly a household in the Islands which does not depend, to a greater or lesser extent, upon the sale of hand knit and hand woven goods".[22] The woollen industries sub-committee felt that the crux of the industry's survival lay in establishing a national mark to be allocated for use on all woollen or tweed goods manufactured in the islands - hand knitted or otherwise. From this the committee felt that the establishment of a local spinning mill and the development of cottage industries would follow as a natural consequence. The committee, advertising in the local press, invited all those interested in these schemes to submit their ideas in writing.

The sub-committee looked into the feasibility of establishing a dispersed system of spinning using the hand sets suggested by Dr. Manson in 1939, and into the cost of establishing a central spinning mill. Each small mill required for spinning sets was reckoned by the committee to require a capital outlay of £700 per unit, whilst a central mill would require an initial outlay of £63,000. Meantime, the Crofter Woollen Industry Committee - set up by the Scottish Council of Industry - was conducting an inquiry "into the present position of all branches of the woollen industry in the Highlands and Islands with reference to wool production and manufacture both of factory and home-made origin".[23]

This inquiry was published in 1945 and is generally referred to as the Calder Report, so named after the secretary of the Crofters' Woollen Committee. Anxious to protect the future of rural industries and rural employment after the war, the committee recognised that the woollen industry in the Highlands and Islands depended on a distinctive trade mark, local spinning mills, improvement in design and technique, and a structured system of marketing. In response to the request from the Crofters' Woollen Committee for suggestions which would foster progress in the Shetland woollen industry, the ZCC post-War reconstruction committee's woollen industries sub-committee compiled a lengthy memorandum outlining their suggestions. In essence, the committee suggested the use of a distinctive trade mark, the establishment of a local spinning mill, instruction in design and technique and the formation of a Protection and Development Board to look after the marketing of wool and hosiery.

The only positive outcome from the many utopian and over-ambitious suggestions put forward by the ZCC sub-committee representing the woollen industries, was the establishment of a local spinning mill. As is shown later in this chapter, even this outcome was of limited value as the mill quickly proved itself incapable of producing quality worsted. The proposals put forward by the sub-committee amounted to no more than a reiteration of those points proposed by Professor Scott thirty years earlier. Sadly, post-Second World War Shetlanders followed the same course as their First World War predecessors.

Initially after the War, the boom in the hosiery industry bred complacency. Few knitters or dealers were prepared to look to the future when the inevitable post-war depression would place expensive hand knits out of the reach of many of their traditional purchasers. Shetland hand knits had enjoyed a prolonged wartime boom largely because of the lack of competition from machine made goods. When the cheaper machine made goods reappeared on the market, Shetland knitters were unprepared.

The Shetland Hand Knitting Industry 1945-50

For two years after the War the demand for Shetland hand knits was high; in 1947 the Shetland hosiery trade, along with the wool clip, was estimated at having a gross annual value of nearly a million pounds. However, some large firms felt that the industry had reached and probably passed its peak, as reports from selling agents in the south suggested that many southern merchants felt that Shetland hand knitted hosiery was too highly priced. This situation was brought to a head by the exceptionally severe winter of 1947, which devastated sheep flocks and substantially depleted wool stocks, with the result that the price of wool rocketed from 3/- per lb. in 1940 to 9/- per lb in 1947. Despite this threatening situation, the Shetland woollen industry was still regarded as:

... the sheet anchor of the islands... bringing in very much more money to the country than any other industry, and brings it in in a manner which gives the maximum benefit to those engaged in it. It is a great cottage industry and entirely the opposite of a huge factory employing a similar number of workers, with its endless overhead expenses and management, deterioration of machinery and plant, 42 to 45 hour week and wages of 60/- to 70/- per week. The houses in Shetland where the knitters work have no additional "overheads", no plant to maintain, no restrictions of working hours, and almost no limit to what may be earned.[24]

This extract from the 1948 annual review in the *The Shetland News* went on to state how gratifying it was that all concerned with the industry, that is, the SHKA, resuscitated SWIA, the National Farmers Union, the Flock Book Society, merchants, dealers and knitters, were more unanimous in their drive to consolidate the industry on a sure and safe foundation. *The Shetland News* felt that such unity would lead to price stability, the formation of a wool marketing board and the constant use of a distinctive trade mark, all aided by the new spinning mill recently opened in Unst.

Spinning Mill

The use of decentralised spinning sets, suggested before the outbreak of the War, was again pursued, but after trials to process Shetland wool using spinning sets were made in Leeds, the resultant yarn was found to be inferior, and the project abandoned. However, a local spinning mill was established in 1946 and the company of "Shetland Spinners and Weavers" registered on 7th September, 1946, with Charles G.D. Sandison of Haamar, Baltasound, Unst as director (fig. 6.7). In December, 1946, the majority of the shares were held by five members of the Sandison family. Old War Department buildings left over from the Second World War were chosen for the site, which unfortunately being at Baltasound, Unst, Shetland's most northerly inhabited island, put it at an immediate disadvantage, as the cost of freight from Lerwick to Baltasound, was exactly the same as that from Lerwick to Aberdeen. It was also hoped that the mill would help relieve post-war unemployment on the islands. Whilst in operation, the mill employed a maximum of 60 people. Owing to the delay in the provision of machinery and the post-war difficulties of obtaining wood for building purposes, the mill did not start production until 1948, which coincided with a depression in the wool trade. One misfortune followed the next. Initially there had been insufficient Shetland wool coming in to keep the mill going, and the management had been compelled to mix it with other wools. This factor, coupled with some low standard work when workers were learning, led to a lack of confidence in the mill on the part of the Shetland wool trade who were, understandably, reluctant to lose their existing connections with outside firms unless the Shetland mill could pro-

**SHETLAND SPINNERS
AND WEAVERS, LTD.**

For Shetland Yarns

MADE FROM SHETLAND WOOL,
PROCESSED IN SHETLAND BY
SHETLANDERS

THULE MILLS, BALTASOUND

Fig 6.7 Shetland spinners.

duce equally good work. The fineness of Shetland wool made it difficult to spin by machine, and other types of wool were often added to it to overcome technical problems. In essence the workforce did not have the technical expertise nor its management the business acumen to compete with long established Scottish spinners. Despite attempts to have experts from the Wool College at Galashiels visit, and even offers of help from a small rural mill in Wales, the company went into voluntary liquidation in August, 1950.

Structural Changes in the Shetland Hand Knitting Industry 1918-1950

The traditional framework on which Shetland merchants had run their hosiery businesses during the last hundred years, changed during this period because of the effects of war-time marketing and increased communications both within and outwith the islands. The Lerwick merchant specialising in hosiery and the general merchant in country districts dealing in hosiery, suffered a nasty jolt when First World War knitters sold much of their hosiery independently, and later during the Second World War, when knitters formed their own co-operative, which taken with the increase in direct selling by knitters to Shetland based servicemen, finally brought the last remnants of merchant dominance of the hand knitting industry to an end. Merchants responded by purchasing more hand-flat knitting machines, setting up factory units and, unrestricted by the limitations of the hand knitter, branched out into manufacturing a wider range of fashion knitwear. For example, Pole Hoseasons and T.M. Adie diversified into machine knitting and set up factory units employing both knitters and non-knitters in these factories. In addition, many knitters were employed as outworkers with hosiery producers organising this workforce on the factory putting-out system. Worsted and orders were delivered by van on set days to outlying workers; hosiery was collected and payment made for the previous week's knitting. By 1938 six knitting units had been established on the islands - Urafirth, Voe, Aith, Lerwick, Scalloway and Hoswick - in which a total of 90-100 women had full-time employment. This expansion continued after the War so that by 1949 three more knitwear units had been set up in Lerwick.

With the arrival of hand-flat knitting machines, came division of labour. Knitters were employed to finish garments by hand knitting Fair Isle yokes and cuffs on to machine knitted jumpers and cardigans. Hosiery was finished or dressed in the merchants' factory units, some merchants even sending out cars to collect workers living in remote areas. Flat, piece-rates were paid by employers, and represented a more formal and progressive approach to the employment of workers. The knitting machine, regarded by pessimists as the downfall of the Shetland knitting industry, enabled this traditional industry to be transformed in to a modern industry, able to keep knitting alive by having the ability to compete on an equal basis with the cheaper mass-produced hosiery of the south. Successful operations in the post-war years were based on factories and marketing units where merchants had invested in buildings and equipment, and competed for sales with a realistically priced product backed by a professional management organisation. The hand knitting industry was still very much alive in 1950 and although threatened by machine knitting, was not displaced by them until well into the sixties.

Fig. 6.8 outlines the basic structure of the Shetland knitting industry by 1950 when hand knitting in Shetland was still an important form of supplementary employment, being complemented by full-time and part-time employment in, or as outworkers for, factory units run by merchants such as Tullochs of Urafirth and T.M. Adie of Voe.

The structure of the Shetland knitting industry by 1950

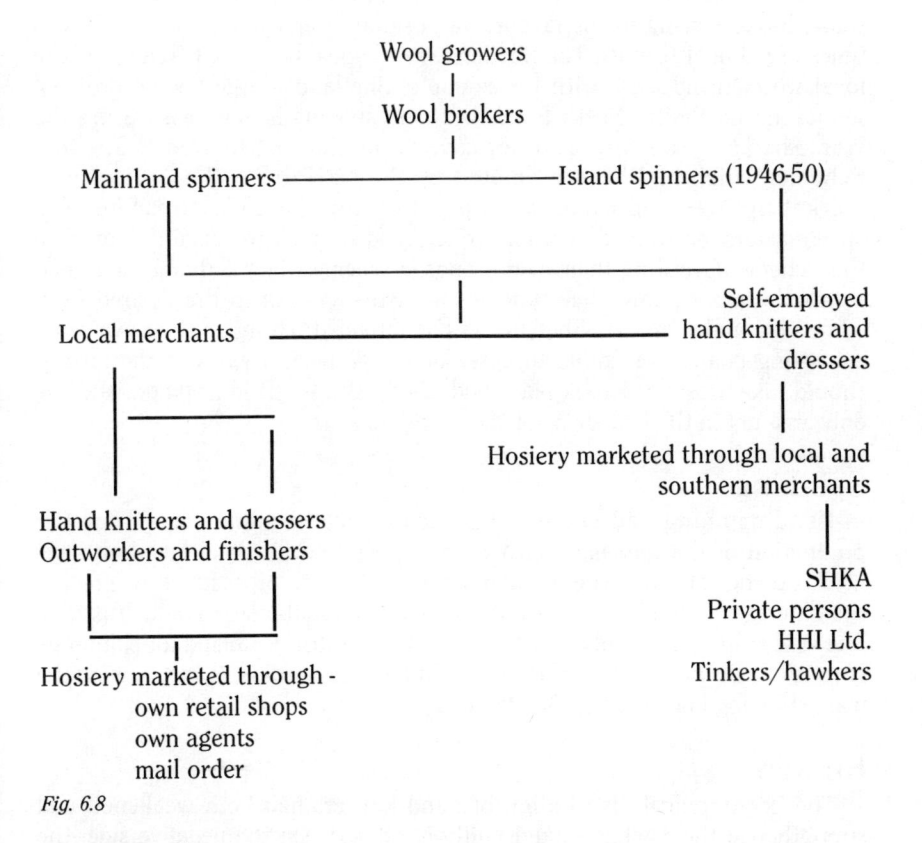

```
                        Wool growers
                             |
                        Wool brokers
                             |
Mainland spinners ──────────────────────── Island spinners (1946-50)
        |                                          |
        |─────────────────────────────             |
        |                            |             |
                                     |      Self-employed
Local merchants  ──────────────────────────  hand knitters and
        |                                          dressers
        |──────────────────                        |
        |                 |                        |
                                   Hosiery marketed through local and
                                         southern merchants
Hand knitters and dressers                         |
Outworkers and finishers                           |
        |         |                              SHKA
        |_____|                       Private persons
             |                                HHI Ltd.
Hosiery marketed through -                 Tinkers/hawkers
    own retail shops
    own agents
    mail order
```

Fig. 6.8

Wool Brokers

Not all the wool grown in Shetland passed through brokers' hands; much was still kept by the crofter-knitter for her own use. The small crofter-knitter could sell her wool to her local merchant or exchange it for ready-made goods such as blankets etc. By 1907, wool brokers had started selling pure Shetland wool in the south - a practice traditionally frowned on. An article in *The Shetland News*, stated that: "it is rumoured that certain firms in the south have started to manufacture Shetland hosiery in Shetland yarn, and this is regarded locally as a sinister development".[25] To have Shetland 'imitations' manufactured outwith the islands in Shetland wool meant that they were not imitations in their fibre content, nor impostors by name, as the term 'Shetland' was not protected by the Board of Trade for exclusive use by products made in the islands. Moreover, this new type of 'Shetland' hosiery, being machine-produced, could be sold more cheaply than hand knitted garments and would therefore pose a very serious threat to the Shetland hosiery industry.

The War acted as a stimulus and temporary salvation to the Shetland wool trade; brokers being in the favourable position of enjoying inflated prices in times of national scarcity. The Shetland wool clip was entirely taken up by the local woollen industry, with for example, Shetland's largest wool brokers, Jamieson and Smith, North Road, Lerwick, starting in business during the War. Shetland wool was also not covered by the British Wool Marketing Scheme, which had been promoted by the NFU under the Agricultural Marketing Acts and came into operation for the 1951 clip. Shetland stockmasters, crofters, and wool brokers had decided to remain aloof from this scheme, favouring their own proposed scheme which although designed primarily to safeguard their woollen industry was not in the desired form admissible under the Act. Shetlanders had intended setting up their own wool marketing board, but failing to agree amongst themselves as to the form it should take, this never took place and Shetland was left in isolation, and the only area not in the British Wool Marketing Scheme.

Spinning

Hand spinning had ceased to be economically viable, except for the production of the gossamer yarn used in very fine Shetland lace knitting - itself a dying art. This type of hand spinning was still prosecuted by a few of the older generation, the most notable being the Sutherland family (fig. 6.9). The vast bulk of the wool clip was sent to the Scottish mainland for spinning - Hunters of Brora, Pringles of Inverness and in the Borders, Munro's, were the main spinning mills used by Shetlanders.

Knitters

The geographical distribution of hand knitters had both weakened and strengthened the Shetland hand knitting industry. On the negative side, the isolation of many knitters contributed to their continued lack of organisation and acted against unity, whilst on the positive side, it is most likely that in a more densely populated area, hand knitting would have been totally usurped

MODERNISATION 1918-1950

Fig 6.9 – The Sutherland family at work. *Photo: J. D. Rattar*

by machine knitting, and would have become centralised on a factory basis, as had happened with the Aberdeenshire hosiery industry at the end of the eighteenth century. Knitters who were scattered in sparsely populated rural and island communities, found that distance and the difficulties, cost and time taken to travel to centres like Lerwick, made it unlikely that they could meet up to discuss common grievances, marketing policies and other issues. Where the knitter was a crofter-knitter, the demands of the croft and the tie of farm animals, coupled with the old and ubiquitous problem of lack of capital, all acted as deterrents to this possible squandering of precious time. It must also be recognised, that although many knitters grumbled about the poor prices they received for their hosiery, they were partly to blame as they were not prepared to change their ways and knit the new designs or styles which both the hosiery merchants and the public desired; particularly where knitting was a part-time occupation, being fitted in between times, knitters often could not be bothered or just were not prepared to spend the relatively small amount of extra time it would have taken, to become familiar with a different style. If it is remembered that Shetland knitters did not use knitting patterns but knitted the pattern 'out of their heads', it partly explains their reluctance to change, as it is easier to change from one style to another if written instructions are being followed. The Shetland knitter knitted so fast that it would have been a terrible frustration and waste of time to have to translate written instructions into stitches; the nearest she came to following a pattern was in the charting of Fair Isle designs. This reluctance to change to new styles was a serious shortcoming common to most hand knitters. For example, the SWIA held a knitting competition with prizes for new designs and fashions; very few knitters entered the competition, and fewer still were prepared to change to knitting the prize winning designs, or as one dealer found, rushed up the work, spoiling the design:

> Most knitters and districts stick to conventional patterns. I am always looking for new and better ones. The trouble is that when I find an acceptable one and want more, the next supply is too hurriedly done, or others copy and spoil it.[26]

The Shetland hand knitter obviously did not realise that in a modern world where machines were displacing workers, this cussed approach was a sure recipe for extinction. People, including non-knitters, could be trained to work machines to produce a desired design and then churn the same pattern out uniformly and indefinitely.

Marketing 1918-1950

Self-employed knitters continued to market their hosiery through the HHI Ltd., private persons at home and abroad, local merchants, tinkers/hawkers and latterly through the SHKA. The work of the HHI was praised by many, including the Scottish Office, for its work in alleviating distress in rural areas, by providing practical assistance on a sound business, rather than charitable basis, and by helping to stamp out truck by setting up purchasing depots through which knitters could market their hosiery at guaranteed prices, independent of their local merchant, totally free of truck. The HHI had its headquarters at 34 Charlotte Square, Edinburgh, with purchasing depots strategically placed in rural areas to serve different parts of the Highlands and Islands with Shetlanders dealing through the Strathpeffer depot (fig. 6.10). Unfortunately only snippets of information of the HHI's dealings with Shetland hosiery are to be found in the Scottish Office files. One interesting entry for 1933/34 refers to an order having been received from the 1/4th Gurkha Rifles in the Punjab, for Shetland jerseys specially designed for their officers.

An HHI report, compiled by Miss Sutherland of the HHI's Strathpeffer depot, concerning Shetland hosiery

Fig 6.10

in 1935 bears out, that as fishing was declining, knitting was taking its place as a major contributor to the family income, not just to supplement it:

> Last year (i.e. 1935), we had a considerable increase in the number of workers, especially in Shetland, and since my tour of these islands in the early summer, we had of necessity to increase our purchases, in order to meet to some extent, the economic situation, where the last few bad years fishing seasons had deprived the Shetlanders of their means of support. This fact impressed itself on me again and again during my visit, and the need of giving as much individual employment as we could...[27]

During that year Shetland knitters sold £4,310 -14/6d. worth of hosiery through the HHI. Only the very highest standard of hosiery was accepted by the HHI, so that although "Almost every woman in Shetland can knit, only a limited number can knit really well".[28] Personal visits were paid regularly to ensure that work was of a high standard. As well as this, conscious of the need to progress and compete in the world of fashion, the HHI were constantly working out new designs and sending them to their workers, which were scattered all over the islands. 120 knitters were dealt with directly and about the same number through collectors. This structured approach, with its high standards, ensured fair prices to skilled knitters, and was a great benefit in stabilising prices and taking the uncertainty out of marketing.

The greater mobility of the Shetlander, the steady influx of tourists (except during the war years when servicemen replaced tourists) and the greatly improved parcel post, enabled knitters to sell to private persons. Many emigrant Shetlanders and relations in the merchant navy, sent orders back home for Shetland hosiery. Christmas was a particularly busy time for such sales. With much of the dire economic pressures of life alleviated by pensions, allowances and subsidies from the public sector, knitters could establish their own markets and many had developed a clientele of 'regulars'. Advertisements in local newspapers asked endlessly for a large variety of hosiery, with for example, hosiery dealers from as far afield as Cornwall advertising in *The Shetland Times*. The knitter was still at the basic disadvantage that the merchant set the price for the work to be done. It was the knitter of poorer quality hosiery that mainly used her local merchant, as by this time there was an increase in more profitable outlets for hand knitters and an organisation like the HHI only dealt with high quality work.

Shetland Hosiery Merchants

Despite the increase in sales outlets for private knitters, a large proportion of hand knitted goods was still sold through local retail merchants or hosiery dealers such as Anderson & Co., Anderson & Smith, Kays of Shetland Ltd., A.I. Tulloch, H.C. Adam, Stewarts of Shetland and many others; from 17 hosiery dealers in 1938 the number of dealers rose to 31 by 1966. The hosiery industry became more dispersed as factory units and retail shops were set up throughout the islands, although Lerwick continued to remain the centre of the hosiery industry in Shetland.

Merchants sold their hosiery in three main ways - through their own retail shops or to wholesalers through their own agents, and by mail order direct to the public. This latter gained in importance after the First World War with many merchants sending knitwear 'on approval' to customers throughout the British Isles. During the inter-War years, many merchants were exporting their knitwear to America, Italy and France; the increase in orders from America was one of the main reasons for the decline in demand for hand knitted goods. Not only did the American market demand the very best quality of knitwear to a stated design and uniformity, but they ordered it in large quantities with specific delivery dates. If the completed order could not be fulfilled on time, buyers were not interested. Shetland hand knitters it will be remembered, were not good at being told what to knit and using knitting as a supplementary form of employment, did little knitting during the crofting season - the time of year when American dealers wanted to take delivery of their orders for the autumn/winter. Managers of hosiery factory units did have problems with their workforce, but on the whole it was possible for them to plan their orders when using machine produced hosiery rather than hand knitted hosiery.

A sample of Shetland hosiers has been chosen as being representative of the varied types of business dealings undertaken during the period dealt with in this chapter i.e. 1918-50.

Anderson & Smith

In 1909 James A. Smith and Mr Thomas Anderson started business at Aith as Shetland hosiery dealers and general merchants trading under the name of Anderson & Smith. In 1915 a second similar business was opened at Ravensgeo, Mid Yell. Then in 1919 James Smith moved to Lerwick to open "a country shop i' da toon" in Commercial Street.[29] Here Smith steadily developed his hosiery business and soon became one of the biggest hosiery dealers in the islands, buying and selling large quantities of Shetland hosiery and wool each year, in addition to doing a good grocery and general trade. James Smith was not only a committed business man but a great champion of the Shetland knitwear industry, helping to found the SWIA and acting as its chairman for many years, sitting on many committees, judging at local shows etc. as well as being elected to the posts of provost and ZCC convener. As has been mentioned earlier in the chapter, it was he who was largely instrumental in developing the trade in Fair Isle goods, particularly jumpers, which were in great demand and realising excellent prices, for several years after the War. He also endeavoured to introduce new designs and patterns for jumpers etc. to keep the demand up by creating new fashions.

Kays of Shetland Ltd

This firm, whose premises were situated on Commercial Street beside the Grand Hotel, ran a grocers shop and a drapery and hosiery store side by side. Fig. 6.11 shows the interior of the drapery and hosiery store. As fig. 6.5 has

MODERNISATION 1918-1950

Fig 6.11 – The interior of Kays shop, c.1920. *Photo: Theo Kay*

already shown, Kays was committed to educating knitters to enable the industry to survive in the post war period. Kays sold hosiery to Harrods, Fortnum and Mason, Marshall and Snellgrove etc.

A.I. Tulloch

A.I. Tulloch joined the firm of D. & G. Kays about 1918 as an office boy. In the early 1920s he was sent to Kays' Mid Yell shop as manager. Later he bought Kays' Burravoe store and then the Mid Yell one. In the 1920s and 30s he started selling knitwear, at first wholesale but later by direct mail order. The mail order organisation was run from Burravoe until only a few years ago. 'Kays of Shetland' was renamed 'Tulloch of Shetland' in 1946 and the mail order business was rapidly expanded, so that by 1953 over 1,000,000 circulars were mailed. In the late 1950s and early 1960s a wholesale manufacturing and export side was successfully developed until the arrival of oil resulted in the loss of many knitters. The wholesale side was then closed so that production could be concentrated on the direct mail order business. Even in the 1970s, quarter of a million circulars were still being mailed twice a year. But with the increased postal charges of the 1980s, this number was reduced to 50,000 by the late 1980s.

Stewarts of Shetland

An interesting and amusing episode in the saga of the marketing of Shetland hosiery is that of 'Stewarts of Shetland', hosiery dealers. Mr. E.C.

Stewart, a journalist by trade, came to Shetland in February 1943 to edit *The Shetland Times* following the sudden death in 1942 of its proprietor, R.M.Y. Johnson, but unwisely started a hosiery business in August 1944, at the same time as editing *The Shetland Times*, and was sacked two months later! He was, however, not sacked for attempting to do both jobs at the one time, but for cheating the Inland Revenue (and his employers) by employing soldiers, who had been printers, to work on a casual basis, the firm paying them, whilst Stewart pocketed the payment for the small jobs done on the side and ignored the Purchase Tax. He was found out by an observant Excise officer!

However, to return to the Stewart's hosiery business, they had no experience of the hosiery trade, but anxious to capitalise on Shetland's lucrative war-time hosiery trade, decided to start up with a capital of £100. During their first year's trading they had a turnover of £11,000 which dropped to £4,795 the following year, and finally plummeted during the terrible winter of 1947 when Shetland lost half its sheep and lambs and there was practically no trading for the first five months of the year. By this time the Stewarts were in deep trouble with purchase tax payments and in a mess with their coupons, owing traders and knitters 1,601 coupons. In an attempt to extricate themselves from this financial mess, E.C. Stewart hit on the idea of a propaganda magazine, *The Shetland Monthly*, and in March 1947, launched his new socialist magazine, aimed at winning over the Shetland worker.

Stewart started by proclaiming himself champion of the people, particularly the knitter, eager and willing to create a new post-war Shetland full of opportunity for its working people. The first edition, which was also to be the penultimate, opened with a flourish - "With the publication of the first issue of *The Shetland Monthly* a new era of journalism starts in Shetland".[30] Knitters were to have fair and stable prices for their hosiery, fishermen were to be guaranteed reasonable prices seasonally in advance, and:

> ...those who create the wealth of Shetland shall benefit in direct proportion to their efforts. In the past, as most Shetlanders know to their cost, the exact opposite has applied - the wealth of the community has gone into the pockets of those who produced nothing. It will be the privilege of *The Shetland Monthly* to keep a watchful eye on industry with these points in view.[31]

The magazine continued in this tone and was full of grandiose but facile statements. However, knitters may have felt some concern when the April edition of *The Shetland Monthly* failed to appear. The May edition was the last in this "new era of journalism"!

In his first edition, Stewart informed his readers that he was a fully trained journalist with a lifetimes experience in Glasgow, London and elsewhere. This edition also carried a long and reasonably informed article on the Shetland hand knitting industry. In this, he explained how he and his wife had started a knitting business whilst waiting for the Ministry of Supply to relax the paper restrictions. Stewart analysed the buying and selling of hosiery and came to the conclusion that knitters should be paid an hourly rate for their work, that

MODERNISATION 1918-1950

prices for both buying and selling of hosiery should be fixed and that hosiery buyers should always be prepared to buy hosiery - all very utopian and impracticable. The little business acumen which he did possess made him realise that it was useless to try and compete with mass-produced hosiery and that it was only by selling hand knitted Shetland hosiery as a luxury item that sales could be maintained and that to obtain satisfactory prices, he had to by-pass wholesalers and sell direct to the retailer through his agents. He claimed that by a policy of carefully selecting the right shop in a certain area, and by giving it the sole rights for his hosiery, prices could be maintained as there was no danger of another shop undercutting it. Marketing in this way, Stewart claimed that although he was selling in 300 cities and towns in

STEWARTS OF SHETLAND
FREEFIELD, LERWICK

Inches	A.O.F.I. Jumpers	A.O.F.I. Cardigans	F.I.B Jumpers	F.I.B Cardigans	LACE Jumpers	LACE Cardigans
22	42/6	45/-	25/-	27/6	22/-	24/6
24	45/-	47/6	27/6	30/-	24/-	26/6
26	47/6	50/-	30/-	32/6	26/- Twin	28/6
28	50/-	52/6	32/6	35/-	28/- Sets	30/6
30	55/-	57/6	35/-	37/6	30/- only	32/6
32	60/-	62/6	40/-	42/6	32/-	35/-
34	90/-	95/-	50/-	55/-	45/-	52/6
36	95/-	100/-	52/6	57/6	50/-	55/-
38	95/-	100/-	52/6	57/6	52/6	57/6
40	100/-	105/-	55/-	60/-	55/-	60/-

PRICES ARE FOR LONG SLEEVES, WELL-SHAPED SHOULDERS, BUTTONS TO NECK

SPECIAL PRICES FOR WORK OF SPECIAL MERIT

Inches	A.O.F.I. PULLOVERS Sleeveless	Sleeved	Inches	FAIR ISLE Gloves	Mitts
22	35/-	42/6	$6\frac{1}{2}$	6.6	4/6
24	37/6	45/-	7	7/-	5/-
26	40/-	47/6	$7\frac{1}{2}$	7/6	5/6
28	42/6	50/-	8	8/-	6/-
30	45/-	52/6	$8\frac{1}{2}$	8/6	6/6
32	47/6	55/-	9	9/-	7/-
34	60/-	90/-	W	11/6	10/6
36	60/-	95/-			
38	65/-	100/-	BERETS (over $8\frac{1}{2}$"), 11/3
40	70/-	100/-	Sets as Prices Above
42	70/-	105/-	Combined

WHITE HAPS, 56", 40/- ; 60", 45/-

PRICES FOR GOOD HANDKNIT ONLY

Equally good prices for anything else you knit. Please send it on or bring it in.

We can sell any quantity of good handknit at these prices. They will not go down

Every parcel is acknowledged at once, with prices Please address them as above.

CASH & COUPONS IN 14 DAYS

Support the Firm which Advertises—and Pays—Firm, Fair, Prices

Fig 6.12 Stewarts of Shetland.

England, he had never lost a customer. E.C. Stewart, who traded under the name of "Stewarts of Shetland" promised to pay knitters within 14 days, although he allowed his retailers the usual one month's credit - this unusual promise was based on his "certain arrangements" and was topped by an even bigger and better promise, that of guaranteeing to sell "the whole output of Shetland at our present prices" (Fig. 6.12).

In the second, and final, edition of *The Shetland Monthly*, E.C. Stewart indulges in nauseating sycophantic messages of thanks to the Shetland knitters for their support, not only to *The Shetland Monthly*, but to his personal view as well. He seemed to revel in his new found, but much encouraged, role of the Shetland knitters' 'agony aunt', by personally answering knitters' letters. However, further down the same page there is an apology "but not on bended knees" to knitters. The inevitable had happened - knitters had not been paid within the 14 days advertised. Excuses of distance from markets and the time it took for parcels to reach London and cheques to be sent back etc. were given - quite feasible explanations but ones which any competent Shetland merchant was well aware had to be taken into the overall marketing picture.

E.C. Stewart does make some valid points, for instance, that knitters must be prepared to knit what the public want and not just what they themselves have always knitted, that knitters must put sleeves in pullovers as buyers have to part with the same number of coupons for sweaters and so forth. However, the bulk of the space is devoted to chatty drivel basically advertising to Shetland what wonderful people the Stewarts were, ending with a compliment from one of their knitters which they were thinking of adopting as their new motto - "The Stewarts dinna cheat".[32]

However, the Stewarts disappeared off the face of Shetland some time later the same year, seeking refuge in Orpington, Kent. No more copies of *The Shetland Monthly* appeared and the Glasgow printing firm, of Kirkwood (Printers) Ltd., were left with unpaid bills amounting to £243-11/- for 6,000 copies of *The Shetland Monthly*, whilst 136 Shetland knitters were owed £2,509-1/2d by them. The estates of Edward C. Stewart and Mrs. L. Stewart were sequestered on 22nd December, 1947. They failed to attend the Public Examination held at Lerwick Sheriff Court on 30th January, 1948, but were finally brought to trial at the High Court of Justice (for bankruptcy) in March 1948, where it was disclosed that after the realisation of assets, they owed £2,194-19/10d.

Realising the vastly increased demand for Shetland hosiery which had arisen due to war-time shortages, the Stewarts had ensured a steady supply of hosiery by paying their knitters in cash - an astute move when other Shetland merchants were failing to meet orders through lack of supplies. Shetland, exempt as it was from the national wool quota (this continued until 1951), and whose knitters were released from the Limitation of Supplies (Miscellaneous) Order 1940, were free to sell as they chose. Working on a profit margin of

17%, all went well until the beginning of the post-war slump made itself felt. The severe weather conditions of the winter of 1947, with heavy falls of snow well into the spring, not only destroyed half the Shetland flock but also played havoc with postal services, on which Stewarts of Shetland so heavily relied. Lack of working capital and withdrawals greater than profits warranted soon caught up on their business during this lean patch, and the Stewarts found themselves inextricably financially embarrassed.

The inability of the Stewarts to weather a lean patch in the hosiery trade highlights the underlying problems which Shetland hosiery merchants faced. On the whole, these merchants were not grasping capitalists, but seasoned dealers with years of experience in this unpredictable and volatile trade. They were well aware, that in order to remain in business, it was necessary to have sufficient capital to survive trade slumps. This they could accumulate only by charging hosiery at prices which the public would pay, but which represented a poor return to the knitter for her hours of labour. Competition from machines had rendered all but top quality hand knitted goods, uneconomic for the middleman-merchant to handle. Hand knitters were better off selling their hosiery privately or through the SHKA. However, if they sold through middle-men-merchants, like Stewarts of Shetland, many knitters found that it was prudent to accept the smaller, but reliable, sum paid by established merchants, than to risk no payment at all.

The Shetland Hand Knitting Industry in 1950

By 1950 the Shetland hand knitting industry was very much alive but on the brink of another attempt to have the word 'Shetland' kept exclusively for knitwear produced in the islands. The industry's application to the Board of Trade to this end, had been precipitated by the increasing competition from machine made imitations flooding the market. The trouble with the hand knitting industry was basically one of price. Hand knitted hosiery had sold very well during and immediately after the War when little else was available, customers being prepared to pay the high price charged for hand knitted goods for the sake of obtaining hosiery. With the relaxation of war-time restrictions and rationing, mass produced machine-made hosiery appeared on the market at a fraction of the price of Shetland hand knits, with the result that the market for hand knits collapsed. However, as the name 'Shetland' was regarded by the public as a symbol of quality, it followed that when the cheaper machine-made hosiery, produced within the Shetland Islands, appeared on the market, there was a good demand for it.

This preference for machine knitted Shetland hosiery also resulted from the old problem of poor quality hand knits appearing on the market and threatening the future of the hand knitting industry. Despite repeated reminders by the SHKA of the need for a united marketing policy - necessary to maintain high standards of quality and price stability - during the post-war depression in the hosiery trade, many knitters, anxious to make sales, sold their hosiery at suicidally low prices to merchants. Rather than wait until the market picked up, hosiery merchants responded by putting this hosiery on the southern market at cut prices. Almost immediately firms dealing in Shetland knitwear in the south, stopped buying expecting prices to stabilise at a lower level. For a considerable time, only cut price goods could be sold so that rather than the name 'Shetland' being a symbol of quality, it was in danger of becoming synonymous with bargain knitwear. And it was in this vulnerable position that the Shetland hand knitting industry entered the 1950s.

References - Chapter 6

1. Nicolson, J.R., Shetland, (London 1972), p. 116.
2. Mitchell, I., Johnson, A., Coghill, I., (editors) *Living Memory*, (Shetland 1986), p. 20.
3. Op. cit., p. 21.
4. *New Shetlander*, 1947, p. 16.
5. *The Shetland News*, 22nd April, 1943
6. SRO (WRH), DD16/18.
7. Ibid.
8. *Daily Express*, 14th July, 1932.
9. SRO (WRH), DD 16/18. Russell's report was entitled "Shetland Hand-knitting Industry. Summary of position disclosed by Inquiry made by the Department of Agriculture for Scotland" and dated 22nd February, 1933.
10. Ibid.
11. *The Scotsman*, 3rd April, 1933.
12. SRO (WRH), DD16/18 26843/53. Letter from the Board of Trade 12th April, 1932 to Scottish Office passing on Zetland County Council's letter of 28th March, 1932 re SWIA and trademark.
13. Op. cit., letter dated 28th March, 1933.
14. SRO (WRH) DD16/25, p. 6.
15. Mitchell, I., (ed.), *Ahint Da Daeks*, (Lerwick 1987), p. 18.
16. *The Scotsman*, 30th December, 1941.
17. *The Shetland News*, 26th October, 1939.
18. *The Shetland News*, 1940, 26th December.
19. *The Shetland News*, 1st January, 1942.
20. SRO (WRH) SEP12/30.
21. *The Shetland News*, 9th December, 1943.
22. SA, ZCC Minutes, CO3 1/15. Meeting of Post-war Reconstruction Central Committee for the County of Zetland, 25th January, 1943.
23. SA, ZCC Minutes, CO3 1/14. Meeting of Post-war Reconstruction Central Committee for the County of Zetland, 7th December, 1943.
24. *The Shetland News*, "Shetland in 1948".
25. *The Shetland News*, 1937 annual review.
26. Livingstone, W.P., *Shetland and the Shetlanders*, (London 1947), p. 181.
27. SRO (WRH), DD16/26. Letter from Miss Sutherland, Strathpeffer depot, 1936.
28. Ibid.
29. *The Shetland News*, 22nd April, 1943
30. *The Shetland Monthly*, March 1947, p. 1. The two editions of this magazine which were published can be found in the Shetland Room, Shetland Museum, Lerwick.
31. Ibid.
32. *The Shetland Monthly*, May 1947.

Chapter 7
Evolution or Repetition?

Conclusions (c.1600-1950)

From its earliest recorded beginnings in the seventeenth century to the present day, the Shetland hand knitting industry has always played an important role in the islands' economy. Initially this can be attributed to the quality of the native wool, to the dexterity of the islands' female knitters and to their ability to adapt to changing circumstances. Knitting as a home-based subsistence activity was well suited to the crofting-fishing way of life, being subsidiary to, and keeping in step with, other occupations. Thus, in times of hardship, knitters were able to adapt their output to meet the needs of the domestic economy. This knitters did so successfully that the true value of knitting to the domestic and island economy has been obscured - spinning and knitting being regarded merely as integral parts of women's work. This fusion of domestic chores with gainful employment within the home, has been a contributory factor in rendering valuations of the Shetland hand knitting industry of little worth and in obscuring the extent of women's role in the socio-economic development of the islands. Much of the hosiery knitted was for home use, thereby making a hidden rather than a quantifiable contribution to the domestic economy, or was sold or bartered privately, leaving no record or valuation of such transactions.

The difficulties of attempting to assess the true value of the Shetland hand knitting industry are further aggravated by the failure of census returns to record secondary occupations. For example, the 1911 census listed 2,782 women as knitters - that is, 18.15% of the female population - whilst Mr Anderson, a Lerwick hosiery merchant who had been in the trade for 61 years, estimated that no less than 90% of the women knitted for sale. Although Professor W.R. Scott regarded this estimate as too high, it does serve to emphasise the shortcomings of census returns in under-recording those engaged in seasonal and/or secondary employment. In the crofting counties, where pluralism of employment has always been an essential feature of the rural economy, this has led to an undervaluing of the importance of cottage industries and to the crucial role women played in a crofting-fishing community.

The significance of cottage and rural industries in helping to sustain rural life and curtail depopulation was stressed by Professor W.R. Scott in his Home Industries Report, published in 1914 - a point accepted and reinforced by subsequent Scottish Office Reports. In the crofting counties with their scarcity of alternative employment, rural industries have always been necessary as a source of income to supplement the returns from agriculture and fishing, and to act as a safety net in times of harvest failures, poor fishing seasons or disasters; without this additional source of income, rural life may have been unsupportable, or only so at a very low level. Shetland knitters had always taken advantage of the abundant supply of native wool and their adeptness at knitting, to turn spare, or available, time to good use in this way - a necessary measure with the produce from the over-small crofts, created by the splitting of outsets, being insufficient to meet the needs of the family, far less provide a surplus for sale. In consequence, as the population expanded during the nineteenth century, casual occupations such as knitting became increasingly important to supplement the domestic economy, as a means of buying, or obtaining by exchange, goods not provided for by crofting or fishing.

During the first half of the nineteenth century, when rising population figures, poor fishing seasons and the failure of the potato crop, caused widespread destitution throughout the Highlands and Islands, the resilience of the Shetland hand knitting industry as a dynamic force able to adapt to changing circumstances, was highlighted by the emergence of Shetland lace. This delicate form of open-work knitting developed in response to economic pressure and was able to find a market outlet in the south, thanks to hosiery dealers taking advantage of the increase in communications with Britain. The returns from knitting, whether in cash or truck goods, were sufficient to sustain life, albeit at a subsistence level, and unlike the Western Isles with their lack of established home industries, help curtail rural depopulation and mass emigration, by allowing the land and sea to support a greater population than its natural resources would otherwise have permitted.

The vulnerability of total dependence on the land and sea for food and income, was illustrated during the first half of the nineteenth century in the Western Isles, when the collapse of the all-important kelp industry, followed by the failure of the potato crop and poor fishing seasons, left the people of these vastly overcrowded islands starving and destitute, and dependent on Government relief or emigration for survival. Similar hard times, aggravated by the collapse of Hay & Ogilvy and the Shetland Banking Co., rather than the kelp industry, were also experienced in Shetland. Government relief was necessary, but not mass emigration; unlike the Western Isles, whose population peaked at 1851, census returns show no decline in Shetland's population until the 1871 census - see appendix 1.

Many reasons for Shetland's low pre-1870 emigration rate have been postulated. W.L.P. Thomson, when presenting a paper at a congress held in Shetland in 1969, suggested that it was only with the expansion of communications with the outside world from the 1830s onwards that Shetlanders became aware of the opportunities outwith the islands, whilst Hance Smith states in *Shetland Life and Trade 1550 - 1914* that people were too poor to leave and didn't turn to emigration until the better times of the

EVOLUTION OR REPETITION?

1860s, when during the inter-censal period 1861-81, 3,556 persons emigrated. Furthermore, statistics suggest that far fewer people were displaced by sheep clearances in Shetland than in the Western Isles.

But of greatest significance to this study is the trend for single women not to emigrate. For instance, although there had been a steady trickle of emigrants from Foula since 1800, by 1870 only one women had left, despite an average excess female population of 12.6% during this period. It has already been noted that Shetland women, unlike other Scottish fish-wives, did not follow the fishing fleets during the season, but remained within the islands. This reluctance to migrate, even temporarily, it will be remembered, was noted in 1906 by Henry Pearson Taylor, Medical Officer for the northern isles, when he failed to persuade Shetlander women to leave the islands to train as nurses; this resistance being attributable to the women being able to earn a living from fish work in the summer and knitting in the winter.

The isolation of, and the protracted lack of organisation in, the Shetland hand knitting industry until well into the twentieth century, have arguably, been major assets to the local, if not the islands', economy. As long as this industry remained home-based, employing knitters on a casual basis, it provided an invaluable source of employment to the islands' widely dispersed knitters, regardless of their age, mobility, or distance from Lerwick. This type of rural industry was particularly suited to the demography of the islands. However, lack of organisation invariably led to poor or non-existent quality control, so that whilst the loose structure of this industry created employment for home-based knitters, together with the economic consequences of trucking, it was also responsible for a deterioration in standards.

Undoubtedly the trucking of knitters throughout the nineteenth and early twentieth centuries, acted as a break in preventing emigration, but, pernicious as truck may appear by modern day standards, the facility, offered by local merchants, of exchanging goods for hosiery (and other home produce) and of extending credit in times of need, were both essential features in the islands' slow transition during the nineteenth century, from a primitive to a modern economy. Even when knitters were forced to resell the 'soft goods' obtained through truck sales, some income, no matter how small, was at their disposal. Left to their own devices it is unlikely that knitters would have been able to market their goods independently - a weakness pointed out by Sheriff Guthrie, Professor Scott and others. The individual knitter, particularly in isolated rural areas, had always been a weak seller, as she was out of touch with markets, current prices and trends. By marketing her hosiery through truck stores, she was able to turn spare time and available wool to some profit, and no matter how small these returns were, in economic terms they represented a net gain to the domestic economy. When the lot of the nineteenth century crofter-knitter is compared with that of her Western Isles counterpart, the appalling hardships of near starvation and destitution which the people of the Hebrides were experiencing during the 'Hungry Forties' were never as widespread or severely felt, as in Shetland. Many factors contributed to this situation, but it cannot be overlooked that the lack of a well established cottage industry at that time, undoubtedly aggravated a desperate situation, and recognising the importance of rural industries, Lord Dunmore virtually created the Harris Tweed Industry c.1844 to fill this void.

It was the returns from knitting, whether in truck goods or in small amounts of cash, which made a significant, albeit small, contribution to the local economy, sufficient to sustain rural life. For example, during the harvest failures of the 1870s and 1880s, when much of Shetland was destitute, Sheriff George Thoms pointed out in *The Shetland Times* in 1885 that there was no destitution appeal from Fair Isle thanks to the exertions of the women knitting, and interestingly as the men relieved them of their menial tasks to allow them more time to knit. Whilst the trucking of hand knitters played a major part in curtailing depopulation and emigration, it was however, responsible, for much poor quality hosiery, as such a system did not encourage quality work - economic necessity dictating maximum output. Moreover, from around 1860 onwards, the rise in Shetland imitations, mass produced cheaply by machines, highlighted the deficiencies in this type of work; and the story of the Shetland hand knitting industry in the twentieth century is characterised by attempts to overcome these problems.

The introduction of knitting machines to the islands from 1922 onwards, posed a new threat to the industry - that of imitation Shetland 'hand knits' from within the islands. Competition from these machines became so serious - machine-knits could be produced more cheaply and uniformly - that by the early 1930s, the volume of hosiery produced locally on hand-frame knitting machines, became the subject of a concerted attempt by all involved in the hand knitting industry, to protect the future of the Shetland hand knitting industry. This move to safeguard the future of the hosiery industry, became increasingly important during the inter-War years as the returns from fishing, the traditional cornerstone of the islands' economy, fell. The main problem with machine-made Shetland knitwear was that they were often taken for hand knitted hosiery, as they could carry, not illegally, a 'Hand-knit - Made in Shetland label'. This led to the SWIA, backed by the Zetland County Council, appealing to the Scottish Office in 1932, for assistance in their bid to have the term 'hand-knit' or 'hand-finished' banned from use on machine-made Shetland hosiery. Despite help from the Scottish Office, this attempt failed, and in order to compete on the international market more knitting machines were imported to the islands. The cussed determination of this traditional and reactionary industry to refuse to accept that it was their responsibility, and not the Government's, to overcome this problem, and that of 'Shetland imitations', by improving standards and creating a distinctive differentiation between hand and machine knitwear, was symptomatic of the industry's fear of the future. It was this external force which rid the hand knitting industry of its damaging jetsam, allowing superior hosiery, like Fair Isle knitwear, which machine could not emulate, to come to the fore and find its place in the luxury market.

With the outbreak of the Second World War, Shetland hand knitters found themselves in the advantageous position of having a large ready-made market in their midst, created by the influx of servicemen and wartime shortages, willing and anxious to purchase hosiery to send home. It was from these wartime conditions that Shetland hand knitters, for the first time, organised their own protective organisation and marketing co-operative - the Shetland Hand Knitters' Association. This move helped to establish set, realistic rates for knitwear, which in turn helped knitters free themselves from merchant domination and trucking; although it must be acknowledged that Tulloch of Shetland is credited by many, for establishing set realistic rates for knitwear. Shetland knitters enjoyed record sales during the War - the Shetland wool clip being exempt from the National Control. This boom came to an end with the havoc caused to Shetland flocks by the severe and protracted winter of 1946/47. Shetland lost approximately half its flocks, which coupled with the reappearance - now that wartime trade disruptions were at an end - of cheap mass-produced hosiery from the Continent, led to the bottom falling out of the market. Desperate for sales, knitters offered their hosiery to local merchants at low rates. In turn, some merchants put this knitwear on the market at cut-prices - a short-sighted move which undermined the stability of the industry and resulted in the name 'Shetland' becoming synonymous with cut-price, and not, quality hosiery.

Shetland hand knitters were fortunate that this partially self-inflicted slump in the hosiery market and their hostility to knitting machines, coupled with their reluctance to accept that, in a machine age, hand made goods must be of superior quality to justify the necessarily high prices charged for them, were not their downfall. The isolation of the islands, and the high reputation which Shetland hosiery had gained in the nineteenth century, combined to extend the life of this dying industry, and to halt temporarily the evolutionary process of the industry's inevitable transition to one based on the factory units. As shown overleaf (Fig. 7.1), the Shetland Hand Knitters' Association's policy of marketing only quality knitwear made from pure Shetland yarn, and at fixed rates, provided the stability which enabled the hand knitting industry to survive well into the sixties.

By 1950, the Shetland hosiery industry, regarded as the "sheet anchor of the islands"[1] and "the country's greatest source of income and wealth"[2], had split into two distinct spheres - the hand knitting and the machine knitting industries, the latter being regarded a having "transform[ed] the Shetland knitwear industry into a powerful and priceless cornerstone of the economy".[3] However, by this time many hand knitters had come to realise that it was possible for them to complement rather than compete with machines, as hand knitters were employed as outworkers finishing machine-made hosiery or as factory workers by local manufacturers.

S. H. K. A.

Was it a Good Investment?
IT STILLS STANDS

FOR	AGAINST
The highest economical price to the Knitter Steady markets at steady prices 100 per cent. Pure Shetland Yarn Profits and benefits for the greatest number	Low prices to knitters Alternate raising and cutting of prices Marketing of inferior goods Low Standards of Workmanship

THIS POLICY NEEDS STRENGTHENING
YOU CAN HELP BY INVESTING
It is a Better Investment than ever
TAKE OUT A £5 SHARE

Fig 7.1 SHKA advert 1949.

Thus, yet again, Shetland's women, were able to adapt to changing circumstances and continue to make an important contribution to the islands' economy. Therefore, it can be said that the protracted evolutionary development of the Shetland hand knitting industry from one based on hand knitting to the use of machines, has played an invaluable part in the islands' socio-economic development, by enabling knitters to remain in their own locality; whilst competition from machines has acted as a long-overdue catalyst, purging the industry of its poor quality hosiery, and leaving only the most skilled knitters to create quality products. Such quality products, whether made in Fair Isle or in Shetland lace knitting, ensure that the prestigious status which Shetland hand knitting undoubtedly deserves, is retained in the annals of traditional Scottish crafts and textiles.

Postscript 1950 - 1990

The Fifties

The first half of this decade was marked by a continued boom in the hosiery industry and by the arrival of the domestic knitting machine in many island homes. This led to division of labour, to an increase in factory outworkers and to men as well as women - and in many cases almost all members of the family - operating these machines within their own homes. Wages were low and long hours had to be worked if more than a supplementary income was to be earned. However, this transition from home-based hand knitting to home-based machine knitting, was of vital importance to the local economy, as it allowed many islanders to take advantage of modern technology whilst still following their traditional life style of crofting and fishing. The opportunities presented by the arrival of the knitting machine within the home, led to machine knitting - in addition to hand knitting - being taught in schools.

Despite increased competition from all over the world and the failure in 1953/4 of the ZCC's Trades Name Committee to have the word 'Shetland' kept exclusively for use on hosiery produced within the Shetland Islands, knitting continued to be a major source of employment. For example, in the Parish of Delting machine-knitting and tweed weaving were carried on side by side at Mossbank and Voe by the long-established firm of T.M. Adie and Sons. At Voe, this firm, in addition to textile manufacturing, also ran a bakery, shop and farm, and by 1955 was employing a total of 62 people. Unfortunately the tweed side of T.M. Adie and Sons was badly hit soon afterwards by changes in US - their chief buyer - marketing policy. This was followed by the hosiery side of their business being hit by the slump in the knitwear industry, a slump felt generally throughout the islands from the mid fifties onwards. (T.M. Adie and Sons ceased trading in the early 1990s).

The Sixties

The opening years of the 1960s saw the knitwear industry in decline with the subsequent consequences of a lag in living standards, scarcity of employment and rise in emigration. However, from the mid sixties, knitwear played an important part in the economic recovery of the islands. The recovery of both the fishing and hosiery industries was aided largely by grant assistance from the Highlands and Islands Development Board created in 1965. Local firms and individuals were not slow to take up the assistance offered by the Board, and although the old problem of an exclusive Shetland trade mark still had not been resolved, Shetland hosiery was widely marketed in America and Europe. An article in *The New Shetlander* stated that during the 1960s knitting, traditionally used to supplement the domestic economy, had become so lucrative, that some men found it more profitable than crofting. In the Parish of Delting, for instance, a major boost to the number of households engaged in home knitting had been provided by the firm of Thuleknit. Thuleknit was started in 1965 in a croft house on Muckle Roe by Peter and Chrissie Johnson. In 1968 they moved to a small factory on the Mainland at Brae. Four years later, the Johnsons expanded by installing modern machinery for washing and pressing knitwear. At the peak of their production, they employed 38 people on the premises, and approximately 300 knitters as outworkers. Their hosiery van, delivering yarn and collecting jumpers, ran as far as Scousburgh in the south, Yell in the north and over to the west side.

Interestingly, it was during the 1960s that Fair Isle hand knitters, unable to meet the demand for their products, turned to knitting machines. Initially, knitting machines were imported to produce self-coloured jumpers to which patterned Fair Isle-type yokes were added. However, as this form of knitwear was not eligible to carry the 'Hand made in Fair Isle' trade mark, it could not command the same high prices as traditional hand knitted Fair Isle jumpers. To the islanders, the obvious advantages of the knitting machine were that they could be operated by men as well as women; had a greater potential output timewise; could still be used to fit in with the rhythm of crofting life; and in an isolated place like Fair Isle, presented employment opportunities otherwise unavailable. And it was for these reasons that the islanders decided to direct their attention towards mastering the art of producing all-over patterned goods on punch card machines and to exploring the feasibility of setting up a knitters' co-operative. As a result, Fair Isle Crafts Ltd., was set up at Koolin in 1980. Initially eight knitters, two finishers and a packer/administrator were involved. A weekly workshop is held in the community hall and has become an established tourist attraction. In addition to seeing Fair Isle knitters at work in their native environment, visitors can purchase goods or place orders specifying the colours, size and style they require. Every garment is unique as each knitter uses his or her own individual choice of colours and patterns. Fair Isle Crafts Ltd. is a member of the Shetland Knitwear Trades Association (see below) and holds its workshop on Monday afternoons from April to September. By 1990, this craft co-operative had a full order book and provided invaluable part-time employment for 13 men and women.

Thus the sixties, having started in a depressed economic climate, was able to do an about turn thanks to private enterprise building on local skills and traditions and seizing favourable opportunities from external forces such as the Highlands and Islands Development Board.

The Seventies

This decade is characterised by two very important events which were to affect all aspects of Shetland life and trade. They were, of course, the exploration of oil in Shetland waters and the setting up of the Shetland Island

EVOLUTION OR REPETITION?

Council. This all-purpose local authority was one of the island authorities which avoided the two tier structure of modern government set up under the 1974 Act reorganising local government in Scotland. The SIC, aided by revenue from the oil boom, did much to help regenerate the Shetland economy - this was particularly true in the eighties. Although the hosiery industry benefited from grants made available through prudent management of the oil revenue, as has been shown, the industry as a whole was to suffer adversely with firms like Tulloch of Shetland losing such substantial numbers from their workforces that they were forced to contract or close down. Knitters seemed to prefer the more lucrative pay and working hours offered in oil related jobs.

Another knitwear victim of the oil boom was Shetland Fashions. In the late sixties a young English couple, the Caldwells, bought over a disused hosiery factory at Gudataing, Aith. Trading as Shetland Fashions, they expanded rapidly and eventually had a new purpose-built factory constructed at Aith. The dressing and packaging of hosiery was carried out mainly in their factory, whilst the actual jumpers were being produced by outworkers throughout the islands. At the peak of their success, they employed 24 factory workers and a great number of full and part-time home workers. However, the demand for workers from the oil industry and a recession in the knitwear trade affected Shetland Fashions so badly that by the end of the seventies their staff in the factory had been reduced to four. The Caldwells moved back to England and eventually managed to sell their factory in 1982.

Fig 7.2 Jamieson's logo.

The boom in oil-related jobs at the expense of the knitwear industry was felt to be so serious that in 1979 the OIO, recognising the relatively short-lived nature of the oil bonanza, commissioned a report on the knitwear industry. This report is generally referred to as the McNicoll Report. It pointed out that, as a result of oil related employment, during the mid-1970s the Shetland knitwear industry had declined by 30% or more. The report also stressed the need for a local spinning mill:

> The industry's impact on the local economy was, however, less than it might have been because of its relatively high tendency to import its production requirements. A major element of this was the substantial importation of wool yarn for transformation into knitted goods. Indeed, although perhaps not practical on other grounds, the creation of a spinning mill locally to provide these yarn requirements would significantly increase the activity generated by knitwear in Shetland.[4]

In 1985 Peter Jamieson set up a small experimental spinning mill in Sandness in West Mainland, trading under the name of Jamieson's Spinning Shetland Ltd. (fig. 7.2). The mill expanded in 1988 to double the number of carding and spinning machines; it now employs 12 people. Only Shetland wool is processed in the mill. As well as using natural coloured wools, the spinning mill also produces a wide variety of coloured yarns. Although there is little difference in price between home spun and Scottish spun wool, this locally produced yarn helps to diminish imports and ensures that real Shetland wool finds its way into garments produced on the islands. Jamiesons also have a knitwear factory and factory shop and are members of the Shetland Knitwear Trades Association. This family business has come a long way since it was originally established by Peter Jamieson's great grandfather - Robert - in the early 1890s.

Fig 7.3 SKTA's Shetland Lady trademark.

The Eighties

In 1983 Shetland knitwear producers formed the Shetland Knitwear Trades Association (SKTA) to protect genuine Shetland knitwear and to promote it world-wide. The Association was created with the financial help of the Shetland Islands Council, as the SIC was concerned that the North Sea oil boom might encourage Shetlanders to abandon their traditional industries. All SKTA members pay a registration fee and are licensed to use the Shetland Lady trademark, a mark which guarantees that the knitwear has been made in Shetland from the best quality yarns and to high quality specifications (fig. 7.

3). The trade mark shows a traditionally dressed Shetland woman knitting by hand with the aid of a knitting belt the colours are blue and gold. The SKTA is responsible for marketing 'Real Shetland Knitwear' and protecting the unique cottage industry from imitations.

The Association has its own quality assurance programme to ensure these high standards are maintained and uses top quality yarns - Shetland yarn is the main yarn used although cashmere, lambswool and cotton are also knitted. The SKTA has an agent and wholesale outlet in London and attends major European fashion exhibitions, such as SEHM in Paris and Herren-Mode-Woche in Cologne, as well as taking part in trade missions to Japan and the USA. The Association produce very attractive brochures showing the work of their members. Many of their garments are still made in the traditional way - knitted in the round without seams - and carefully finished by hand. In addition to hand and hand frame knitwear, the Association produces power machine-made knitwear adding to the diversity of knitwear available. Ironically history repeated itself during the latter years of this decade with the power knitting machine usurping the hand frame machine. For a time feelings were running high as hand frame knitters felt that they should be able to earn a living wage.

State of the Shetland Knitwear Trade in 1990

Designer/knitters such as the Shetland Trader, Margaret Stuart of Walls, Victoria Gibson and Hazel Hughson have done much to raise design standards for Shetland knitwear, thereby keeping Shetland knitwear in the forefront of the quality fashion market. For example, Margaret Stuart's firm Shetlands from Shetland, grew from a desire to produce well designed, fashionable knitwear in traditional Fair Isle patterns and colours. Her contemporary collection of knitwear is inspired by tradition and by the land and seascape of Shetland. Margaret Stuart also operates a small museum of Shetland knitwear.

Grants from the SIC and the strong marketing policy of the SKTA have led to full order books with trade booming. In 1990 the Association's members were having difficulty finding sufficient knitters to complete orders. Over half a million garments per year are knitted in the Shetland Islands by SKTA members. There is still much controversy over the question of home-based hand knitters and machine knitters working in factory units. It is generally felt amongst the older members of the community that, in the traditional way, knitters should be able to stay at home and knit. The SIC keeps a register of hand knitters and pays the SKTA a small fee for inspecting hand knitters' work. This is time consuming and not particularly satisfactory for either party. Some of the problems facing the inclusion of hand knitters in the Association are that:

1/ hand knitters, tension can differ from person to person, 2/ hand knitted ribs are not as firm as machine made ones, 3/ not infrequently, hand knitters when dressing their

KNITTING BY THE FIRESIDE

Style H1: *THE COBWEB LACE SHAWL*, by Margaret Peterson is a fine example of the knitter's craft. The patterns have been handed down through the generations and incorporated into the shawl according to the knitter's own preference. The patterns used in this shawl are, (starting from the middle and working outwards) "Diamonds" pattern, the "Small Tree", the "Fan" or "Tree", the "Steek Diamond" and the "Roche Diamond". The border pattern is called the "Brand Iron". The shawl measures approx. 54" square.

PRICE: £375.00

Fig 7.4 SKTA's Heritage Collection.

hosiery overstretch it so that on first washing the garment appears to shrink and the customer is dissatisfied.

It is generally felt that nowadays hand knitting is no more than a paying hobby or a supplementary income from which a full-time living can not be made. Hand knitted goods continue to be sold to private orders, but in general the home-based hand knitter sits uneasily in the matrix of the SKTA's marketing organisation - of which the registration fee alone may be prohibitive for small producers. The SKTA has made strenuous efforts to find market outlets for their hosiery and are aware that, in order to stay in the forefront of the market, they have to tailor their knitwear to fashion trends and the demands of the market. The days when knitters can stay at home producing the hosiery which they have always knitted have gone. With the exception of highly skilled knitters like Gema Ord, who produces beautiful one-off Shetland lace creations, and similarly skilled knitters selling to the top end of the luxury market, it is difficult to envisage a place for the home-based hand knitter, other than as outworkers knitting up Fair Isle yokes and cuffs to machine produced garments. Hand knitters do still knit cockle-shell scarfs, Fair Isle gloves and other relatively small articles for sale to retailers, but the financial returns are very small. Skilled hand knitters are fortunate in being able to market their work through the SKTA's mail order catalogue 'Real Shetland Knitwear', as this catalogue includes a 'Heritage Collection' (fig. 7. 4). Fine Shetland lace and traditional Fair Isle garments can be ordered from this collection.

Revenue from the oil industry ploughed back into Shetland's traditional industries has provided the opportunity for Shetland knitwear to continue to be a viable product in the 21st century. Thus, for the first time, if all concerned in this ancient - but by no means antiquated industry - capitalise on this advantageous situation and work together, Shetland can look to the future with confidence.

References - Chapter 7

1 *The Shetland News*, 26th December, 1948.
2 *The Shetland News*, 1st January, 1948.
3 Donald, Stuart, 'Economic changes since 1946', in *Shetland and the outside world 1469 - 1969*, edited by Withrington, Donald J., (Oxford 1983), p. 210.
4 SIC, 'The Knitwear Industry in Shetland', Report to the Shetland Islands Council, by I.H. McNicoll, November 1979, p. 8.

Appendix 1

Population statistics for Shetland.

Year	Male	Female	Total	% excess females of the total population
1755*	–	–	15,210	
1790s*	–	–	20,451	
1801	9,945	12,434	22,379	11.1%
1811	10,024	12,891	22,915	12.5%
1821	11,801	14,344	26,145	9.7%
1831	13 489	15 903	29 392	8.2%
1841	13 176	17 382	30 558	13.8%
1851	13 145	17 933	31 078	15.5%
1861	13 053	18 617	31 670	17.7%
1871	13 103	18 505	31 608	17.1%
1881	12 656	17 049	29 705	14.8%
1891	12 190	16 521	28 711	15.1%
1901	12 413	15 753	28 166	11.9%
1911	12 589	15 322	27 911	9.8%
1921	11 604	13 916	25 520	9.1%
1931	9 545	11 876	21 421	10.9%
1941	no census	-	-	-
1951	9 001	10 351	19 352	7%

(Source: Decennial censuses, except for the years marked by an asterisk, that is 1755 and 1790, are taken from the OSA -1978 edition)

Appendix 2

Valuations of the Shetland hand knitting industry.

Date	Valuation	Source
1767	£1,625	Cd. 7564, p. 15.
1797	£17,000	Edmondston, Vol. I, p. 224.
1809	£5,000	Edmondston, Vol. II, p. 3.
1871	£10 - 12,000	Cowie, p. 186.
1890	£30,000	O'Dell, p. 159.
1910	£50,000	O'Dell, p. 159.
1911	£30,390	Cd. 7564, p. 53.
1920	£100,000	O'Dell, p. 159.
1922	£33,000	*Scotsman*, 22nd December, 1922.
1926	£100,000 - 40,000	*Scotsman*, 28th December, 1926.
1929	£46,000	*Scotsman*, 27th December, 1929.
1930	£45,000	*Scotsman*, 27th December, 1930.
1930	£60,000	O'Dell, p. 159.
1932	£50,000	*Scotsman*, 24th December, 1932.
1932	£80,000	DD16/18.
1934	£80,000	*Scotsman*, 27th December, 1934.
1942	£80,000	SN 30th July, 1942.
1947	£1,000,000	SN 1st January, 1948*.

* This figure represents the gross value of the Shetland woollen industry, and includes, the Shetland wool clip.

GLOSSARY

Delling – To dig and turn over the ground with a spade.

Geo – A minor inlet of the sea; usually steep sided.

Haaf fishing – Fishing in deep or open ocean as opposed to coastal waters in open boats. The term comes from the Norwegian *hav*, meaning ocean.

Hairst – A Shetland term used for harvest time or autumn.

Hap – A wrap, similar to a shawl, worn by Shetland women outdoors as a protection against inclement weather.

Kishie – A straw basket used to carry peats etc., usually by slinging across the back.

Lodberrie – A type of 18th century house in Lerwick built with its foundation in the sea, combining pier, courtyard and house at which goods could be directly transferred to or from vessels or boats.

Merchant-tacksman – This composite term defines a merchant, usually in business as a fish curer but also running a truck store, who has the leasehold tenure of an estate, land, fishing station, with rights to collect the revenues in return for payment of a sum of money, commonly known as tack duty, to the proprietor. The heyday of the merchant tacksman was during the nineteenth century when fishing tenures were at their height.

Niddy noddy – This is a simple wooden reel on to which spun wool is wound. It is shaped like the letter 'H' with the cross bar measuring 18". Therefore, a full turn of yarn wound on to a niddy noddy would be 1 yard.

Outsets – Small holdings created by enclosing parts of the hill land during the period of population expansion, notably in the 18th century.

Pirn – Wooden reel used in spinning. Pirns were filled with one ply yarn as it was being spun. To form three ply worsted, three pirns would be filled with one ply yarn. The yarn from these pirns would then be twisted together to form a three ply yarn.

GLOSSARY

Shetland colour-stranded knitting – Native Shetland wool comes in many natural shades ranging from Shetland black through a range of browns and beiges to a variety of off-white tints. It is from this range of natural colourings that Shetland colour-stranded knitting has evolved. Traditionally this knitting is worked in colour-pattern bands which were repeated at regular intervals throughout the entire garment. These geometric patterns have similarities to those used in Fair Isle knitting. The overall effect is much more subtle than Fair Isle knitting as no dyed yarn is used.

Tambourers – Embroiders who worked with a tambour frame and hook on white muslin. The heyday of this work was between 1780 and 1850 when many dresses in white muslin as well as accessories like collars, cuffs, caps and pelerines were tamboured. Ayrshire tambourers came to be known as 'the flowerers'.

Voar – A Shetland term used for seed time/Spring.

Voe – A derivative of the Old Norse *vagr*, a term applied in Orkney and Shetland to inlets of the sea, generally relatively narrow and sheltered from the open sea.

Waulking Mill – A machine formed of ponderous wooden hammers and originally driven by water power, which beats the virgin woven cloth in a damp state, until the spaces between the warp and weft threads of the web are closely felted together, thus making it a more suitable protection against wind and rain, preventing further shrinkage and giving a firm cloth which will keep its shape during wear. This process could be done by hand or by machine.

Wool Cards – These are oblong pieces of wood with handles, covered on the operating side with leather stuck full of fine wire teeth. A pair of wool cards is used to card wool, that is to tease out the fibres prior to spinning.

Select bibliography

Bennett, Helen, *Scottish Knitting* (Shire Album 164), 1986.
Bennett, Helen, *The Origins and Development of the Scottish Hand-Knitting industry*, unpublished thesis, University of Edinburgh 1981.
Brand, Rev. John., *A New Description of Orkney, Shetland, Pightland Firth and Caithness*, (Edinburgh 1703).
Bremner, David, *Industries of Scotland*, (Edinburgh 1869).
Compton, R., *The Complete Book of Traditional Knitting*, (Batsford, London 1983).
Coull, James R.(ed.), *The Third Statistical Account of Scotland; The County of Shetland* (Edinburgh 1985).
Cowie, Robert, *Shetland : Descriptive and Historical* (2nd edition, Edinburgh, 1874).
Edmondston, Arthur, *A View of the Ancient and Present State of the Zetland Islands*, Vol. I & II, (Edinburgh 1809).
Edmondston, B., and Saxby, J., *The Home of a Naturalist*, (London 1884).
Edmondston, Mrs Eliza, *Sketches and Tales of Shetland*, (Edinburgh 1856).
Edmondston, Mrs Eliza, *The Poor Knitters of Shetland*, published under the name of 'A Lady Resident', (Paisley 1861).
Gaugain, Jane, *The Lady's Assistant for Executing Useful and Fancy Designs in Knitting, Netting and Crochet Work*, (Edinburgh 1840).
Gifford, Thomas, *Historical Description of the Zetland Islands in the year 1733*, (Thuleprint edition 1976).
HDBP *Planning for Progress. Shetland Woollen Industry - Special Report No. 1970*. (The Calder Report, 1945, is included in this publication).
Henshall, Audrey S., 'Early Textiles found in Scotland' - *Part I, In The Proceedings of the Society of Antiquaries of Scotland*, Vol 68, 1951-52).
Hibbert, Samuel, *A Description of the Shetland Islands*, (Edinburgh 1822).
Johnson, R.L., *A Shetland Country Merchant - a biography of James Williamson of Mid Yell 1800-1872*, (Lerwick 1979).
Livingstone, W.P., *Shetland and the Shetlanders*, (London 1947).
Loch, David, *Essays on the Trade, Commerce, Manufactures and Fisheries of Scotland*, Vol. I - III, (Edinburgh 1778).
Low, Rev. George, *A Tour Through the Islands of Orkney and Schetland*. Information collected in 1774 but not published until 1879 by William Peace and Son, Kirkwall, Orkney.
Manson, T., *Lerwick During the Last Half Century 1867-1917*, (Revised edition, Lerwick Community Council, 1991).
Mitchell, Isobel, (ed.), *Ahint Da Daeks*, (Shetland 1987).

BIBLIOGRAPHY

Mitchell, I., Johnson, A., Coghill, I. (editors), *Living Memory*, (Shetland 1986).
Martin, Martin T., *A Description of the Western Islands of Scotland*, (1703).
Munro, Lewis, *Scottish Home Industries*, (Dingwall 1895).
Nicolson, John, *Arthur Anderson, a Founder of the P. & O. Company*, (Lerwick 1914).
Nicolson, J.R., *Hay and Company, Merchants in Shetland*, (Lerwick, 1982).
Norbury, James., *Traditional Knitting Patterns*, (Batsford, London 1962).
O'Dell, A.C., *Historical Geography of the Shetland Islands*, (Lerwick 1939).
Official Descriptive and Illustrated Catalogue of the Great Exhibition 1851, Vol. II.
Peace's *Orkney and Shetland Almanac*, 1884.
Sandison, Charles, *Unst, My Island Home*, (Lerwick 1968).
Saxby, J., *Shetland Knitting*, (Lerwick - undated).
'A Scotsman', *A Trip to Shetland*, (1872).
Scotland of To-day and Edinburgh its capital, (Edinburgh 1890).
Sinclair, John, *The Statistical Account of Scotland 1791-1799, Vol. XIX Orkney and Shetland*. (1978 reissue, EP Publishing Ltd. England).
Smith, Brian, Shetland Archives and Sources of Shetland History, *History Workshop* (1977).
Smith, Hance D., *Shetland Life and Trade 1550-1914*, (John Donald, Edinburgh 1984).
Smith, Mary and Bunyan, Chris, *A Shetland Knitter's Notebook*, (Shetland Times, Lerwick 1991).
Standen, Edward, *The Shetland Islands*, (Oxford 1845).
Reid Tait, E.S. (ed.), *The Hjaltland Miscellany iv*, (1974).
Rutt, Richard., *A History of Hand Knitting*, (Batsford, London 1987).
Walker, Barbara, *A Treasury of Knitting Patterns*, (Batsford 1968).
Wheeler, P., *Geographical Field Group Regional Study no. 11, Isle of Unst*, (1964).
Wilson, J., *A Voyage Round the Coasts of Scotland and the Isles*, (Edinburgh 1842).
Withrington, Donald J. (ed.), *Shetland and the Outside World 1469-1969*, (Pb. for the University of Aberdeen by Oxford University Press, 1983).

Index

A

Aberdeen - 1, 4, 93, 101, 155
Aberdeen, Countess of - 55
Aberdeen stocking trade - 18, 19, 159
'acre' - 78
Adam, H.C. - 161
Adie, T.M. - 106, 120, 156, 157, 175
advertising - 139, 144, 151-153
agents - 22, 24, 28, 30, 35, 85, 101, 115, 121, 151, 154, 157
Agricultural Sir John - see Sinclair, Sir John
agricultural work (for women) - 37
agriculture - 131, 136, 140
Agriculture Credit Act (1923) - 63
Agricultural Marketing Act - 158
Ahint Da Daeks - 97, 134
air service - 133
Aith - 156, 162, 177
Aithsting - 14
Aitken, James - 108
Alexandra, Princess - 88
alpaca - 24
amenities - 95
America - 124, 125, 130, 138, 141, 151, 162, 175, 179
'Anderson & Co.' - 114, 118, 161
Anderson, Andrina - 35, 124
Anderson, Arthur - 73, 74, 88
Anderson, Margaret - 114
Anderson, Mrs - 46
'Anderson & Smith' - 161, 162
Anderson, Thomas - 59, 162, 169
Antigua - 10
anti-truck league - 55, 57, 107
anti-truck legislation - 50
'appro' (on approval) - 126, 162
'approved house mark' (of SHKA) - 151
Arcus, Ann - 28
Army - 62, 113
'Arnott & Co.' - 101
Arts & Crafts Movement - 86
auction (of hosiery) - 30, 127
Australia - 42, 47, 95, 125
awards (for knitting) - 58
Azores - 76

B

'Baabie' - 15
Baltasound - 127, 155
Barbados - 10
Barclay, Rev. Patrick - 18
barilla - 15
barley - 9
barter - 19, 28, 29, 40, 113, 114, 131, 146, 158, 170, 171
barter-truck - 40, 49, 50, 64
bedizened - 46
begging - 15
Bennett, Dr Helen - 138
bere - 9
'Bestway' - 78
black face sheep - 3
Black, John - 101
Blance, Ann - 121
Blance, Peter - 52, 53, 55
blankets - 126
Board of Agriculture - 62, 63, 106, 113, 139, 145
Board of Manufacturers - 14
Board of Trade - 105, 140, 142, 143, 146, 147, 148, 151, 158, 167
bonnetmakers - 4
book keeper - 30
booth, trading - 7, 8
Borders - 37
Borthwick, Catherine - 47
Bowie, Dr. - 144
Boyle, Sarah - 54
Bradford - 24
Brae - 52
branding system - 10
bread - 7
Bremner, David - 4, 5
brimstone - 126
British Wool Marketing Scheme - 158
brochures - 179
Brown, Agnes - 21
Brown, Catherine - 45, 88
Bruce, John - 9, 41, 67
Bruce, Rt. Hon. Robert - 148
burnous - 82
butter - 8, 10, 32

C

Calder Report - 153
Caldwells - 177
California - 42
Campbell, P. & P. - 30
Canada - 95
cap, christening - 70
caps, night - 8, 84
caps, woollen - 4, 5, 19, 80, 84
capital, lack of - 61, 62
cardigans - 156
carding - 24, 80, 112
carding mill - 106, 128
Carlyle, Thomas - 86
cars - 127, 133, 156
cash book - 30
cash payments - 27, 35, 45, 52, 54, 58, 59, 62, 110, 135, 172
cash shop - 48
cashmere - 179
'cat's paw' - 78
census - 25, 52, 95, 100, 122, 169, 170
charitable persons - 46, 86
charity - 13, 15, 35, 94, 112, 160
Cheshire - 122
Cheviot sheep - 3, 4, 145
Cheyne, Sir Watson - 105
Chicago Exhibition (1893) - 88
children - 135
children's frocks - 83
cholera belts - 126
chromate quarry (Unst) - 93
Church of Scotland - 7
circulars - 163
Clark, Fordyce - 60
clearances - 21, 94, 107, 171
Clerk, James - 121
clerks - 30
cloaks - 82
clothes - 17, 102
clouds - 82, 125, 126
Cochrane, Miss J. - 60, 112
cockle-shell scarves - 181
c.o.d. - 145
Collafirth - 47
Cologne - 179
colouring, natural (of wool) - 3, 83, 83, 178
Colvin, Margaret - see Currie, Margaret
comforters - 84
Commissary Records - 34, 49, 113, 116

Commissioners of Supply - 10, 36, 96
communications - 30, 31, 51, 55, 61, 63, 93, 95, 101, 102, 127, 128, 131-133, 156, 170
company store - 41
competition (in hosiery industry) - 54, 61, 103, 127, 128, 135, 136, 139, 142, 146, 154, 156, 160, 167, 172, 174
Complete Book of Traditional Knitting Patterns - 76
Compton, Rae - 76
congested districts - 96, 97, 104
Congested Districts (Scotland) Act (1897) - 97
Congested Districts Board - 102, 104, 127
consignment principle - 34, 49, 113, 117
Continent - 124
Cornwall - 161
cottage industry - 18, 21, 51, 86, 102, 104, 109, 136, 138, 140, 144, 153, 169, 171, 172, 179
cottars - 18, 36, 104
cotton - 179
coupons - 147, 148, 164, 166
Court Book of Shetland - 5
Court of Session Productions - 10
Coutts, Agnes - 21
Coutts, Mary - 45
Coventry cappers - 4
Cowie, Dr. Robert - 18, 46, 69, 70, 73, 76, 88, 101
Cowie, Mrs Robert - 35
Cracroft, Sophia - 46, 47, 71, 76, 79
crafts, rural - 86, 87
Cramer - 133
credit - 9, 34, 40, 41, 48, 51, 171
crinolines - 89
crofter - 18, 86, 132
crofter knitter - 24, 157, 171
Crofters' Commission - 96, 131
Crofters' Counties Scheme - 133
Crofters Holdings (Scotland) Act (1886) - 50, 51, 63, 95, 132
Crofter Wool Committee - 147, 153, 154
Crofters' Woollen Industry - 151
crofting - 4, 17, 18, 127, 129, 131, 132, 135, 136, 142, 146, 169, 175, 176
crofting counties - 95, 142, 144
crofting-fishing community - 2, 132, 169
cross-breeding - 3
cup, christening - 70

currency - see money [entries]
Currie, Margaret (nee Colvin) - 57
Customs Quarterly Returns - 10
cut price hosiery - 167, 173
cuts (of worsted) - 80

D

Daily Express - 140
Dale - 53
debt-bondage - 40, 96
debts - 34, 47, 116, 120
delivery vans - 176
delling - 100
Delting - 14, 52, 62, 121, 175, 176
Delting Truck Inquiry (1888) - 52, 107, 110, 112, 120
Department of Agriculture - 142, 145, 147
depopulation - 64, 75, 95, 100, 104, 134, 136, 142, 169, 170, 172
designer/knitters - 179
destitution - 9, 10, 13, 14, 40, 55, 62, 64, 68, 75, 86, 93, 94, 120, 128, 160, 170-171
deterioration in standard of knitting - 103-105, 110, 128, 136, 141-144, 167, 171-173
Diggs, Sir Dudley - 5
discounts for cash - 35, 48
Diss Lace Association - 86
division of labour - 156, 175
domestic service - 15, 47
Downham, Mrs Mary - 70
drapery trade - 29, 46-48, 54, 162
drawers - 126
drawing room sales - 86, 89
dressers - 27, 28, 108, 156, 157
dressing (of hosiery) - 26, 30, 126, 177
Duncan's Zetland Trade Directory - 20, 25
Dundas, Frederick - 70, 71
Dundee - 4, 5
Dunmore, Lady - 87
Dunmore, Lord - 172
Dunrossness - 13, 15, 96
dyeing - 30

E

Earl of Zetland - 108, 122
economic recovery (Shetland) - 175, 177

economy, domestic - 21, 28, 142, 169-172, 175
economy, Shetland - 2, 7-9, 11, 131, 136, 143, 169, 171-175
Edinburgh - 4, 10, 14, 16, 20, 32, 34, 35, 47, 57, 72, 85, 101, 111, 114-116, 122, 127, 134, 160
Edinburgh International Exhibition - 49, 55, 88
Edmondston, Dr. A. - 3, 19, 47, 80
Edmondston, Mrs Eliza - 70, 71, 75, 79, 80
Edmondston, Dr. T. - 42
education - 13, 95
Edward, King - 133
eggs - 29, 32, 51
emigration - 21, 40, 47, 64, 94, 96, 132-134, 170-172, 175
Empire - 135
employment - 13, 14, 50, 72, 84, 95, 97, 100, 129, 131, 132, 135, 136, 156, 175, 176
England - 4, 34, 144
enterprise - 55, 176
Established church - 13
Evershed, H. - 2
eviction - 40
exchange of goods - see barter
An Excursion to the Shetland Islands - 72
exhibitions - 86, 87, 112
exports - 14, 127

F

factory inspector - 48
factory shop - 178
factory system - 37, 156
factory units - see knitting units
Fair Isle - 1, 49, 57, 133, 172
'Fair Isle Crafts Ltd'. - 176
Fair Isle knitting - 6, 58, 84, 89, 118, 124, 126, 136-139, 156, 160, 162, 172, 174, 176, 179, 181
falls - 36, 82
family unit - 24
famine - 9
farming - 132
Faroes - 5
fashion - 87-89, 106, 137, 141, 156, 160, 162, 179, 181
feathers - 32

Fetlar - 20, 26, 46, 72, 133
finishers (of machine produced hosiery) - 156, 157
First Shetland Shawl - 69, 70
Firth - 53
fish - 7-10
fish curers - 8, 32, 40, 118, 127
fish wives - 15, 37, 100, 171
fishermen - 4, 7-10, 18, 40, 50, 61
fishing - 2, 7-9, 15, 16, 32, 95, 136, 140-142, 171, 172, 175
fishing accidents - 94
fishing stations - 118, 135
fishing-tenures - 9, 25, 40, 132
fleece weight - 3
Flett - 53
flock book - 106
'Fortnum & Mason' - 163
France - 125, 162
Franklin, Lady Jane - 46, 47, 71, 80
Franklin, Sir John - 47
Fraser, Daniel - 59
Fraser, Robert - 59
Free church - 13
free trade - 51, 61, 93
freighting (of wool, hosiery etc.,) - 36, 155
Foula - 1, 49, 171

G

galley mark - 139, 141, 151
Gareloch - 87, 104
Garriock, William - 35, 51
Garth estate - 32
gas - 96
Gaugain, Jane - 72
Germany - 4, 75, 76, 103, 125
Gibson, Victoria - 179
Gifford, Mrs John - 28
Gifford, Thomas - 8, 9
Gilbert Bain Hospital - 134
Glasgow - 4, 34, 89, 94, 101
Gloup - 94, 118, 120
gloves - 5, 8, 19, 80, 83, 89, 126
golf wear - 137, 138
grants - 62, 144, 175
Gray, Gifford - 60
Great Exhibition (1851) - 72, 73, 83, 84, 87, 88, 124
Green, Catherine - 21
Greenbank - 118

Greenland whalers - 47
Grierson, Mrs Alice - 15, 82, 111, 112
Grimond, Jo - 151
guild, trade - 4
Gunnister - 5
Gunnister Man - 5-7, 137
Gurkhas - 160
Guthrie, Sheriff William - 25, 28, 32, 42, 45-64, 171
gutters - 15, 100, 102, 118

H

haaf fishing - 120
Hamburg - 4, 8, 10, 20
Hamilton - 41
Hamilton, Dr - 35
handkerchiefs - 71, 82, 83
hand-made lace industry - 86
Hanseatic merchants - see merchants, Hanseatic
haps - 3, 81, 89, 122
harbours - 127
hardship (of knitters) - 37, 54, 64, 68, 93, 169, 171
Harris tweed industry - 55, 60, 87, 104, 105, 111, 129, 172
Harrods - 163
Harrogate - 115
hawkers - 46, 157, 160
hawking - 15
'Hay & Co'. - 15, 29, 32-34, 40, 42, 45, 97
Hay, A. J. - 42
'Hay & Ogilvy' - 70, 170
Hay, William - 32
health - 95, 101, 125, 127
Hebrides - 15, 129, 146, 171
Henderson, Mrs - 122
Henderson, R. & I. - 145
Henry, L.D. - 71, 77, 89, 138
Heritage Centre, Unst - 77
Heritage Collection (of SKTA) - 180, 181
Herren-Mode-Woche - 179
herring fishing - 32, 95, 127, 132
Hibbert, Samuel - 2, 19
High Court of Justice - 166
Highland & Agricultural Society of Scotland - 2, 18
Highland Development files - 140, 142
Highland Home Industries (HHI) - 103, 104, 112, 113, 142, 144, 157, 160, 161

THE SHETLAND METHOD

Highlands & Islands - 21, 86, 94, 96, 104, 131, 136, 153, 154, 160, 170
Highlands & Islands Development Board - 132, 175, 176
Highlands & Islands Home Industries Report (1914) - 62, 106, 127, 144, 169
Hillswick - 5, 47
A History of Hand knitting - 76
Hollanders - 5, 7
Home Industries Report - see Highlands & Islands Home Industries Report (1914)
Home of a Naturalist - 70
home workers - 62, 179, 181
Honiton lace - 103
hosiery shops - 101, 157, 161, 181
hosiery trade - 10, 20
Hoswick - 156
housing - 77
Hughson, Hazel - 179
'hungry forties' - 171
Hunter family - 68, 79
Hunter, Mrs - 16
'Hunters of Brora' - 81, 101, 108, 145, 158
Hutchison, Miss - 35

I

Iceland - 19
idle persons - 94
illicit sales of hosiery - 147, 148
imitations - 61, 62, 101, 103, 105, 106, 128, 138, 139, 140, 153, 158, 167, 172
import-export agents - 20
imported hosiery - 63
imports - 15, 20, 103, 127, 178
improvers, agricultural - 3, 13
Incorporation of Bonnetmakers & Dyers - 4
Industrial & Provident Act - 148
industrialisation - 86
Industries of Scotland - 5
Inkster, Mr - 52
inter-war years - 89, 131, 135, 145, 162, 172
International Wool Secretariat - 2
Inverness - 112, 115
Ireland - 13, 126
ironmongery - 34
Irons, Mrs - 122
Irvine, Gilbert - 59

Irvine, Miss - 16
isolation - 93, 95, 98, 110, 127, 143, 158, 159, 171, 173
Italy - 4, 162

J

Jack, Rev. William - 16
Jaegar, Dr. - 101
Jakobsen, Jakob - 5
James, Richard - 5
Jamieson, Margaret - 45
Jamieson, Mr - 24
Jamieson, Peter - 178
Jamieson, Robert - 178
Jamieson sisters - 79
'Jamieson & Smith' - 158
'Jamieson's Spinning Shetland Ltd.' - 177, 178
Japan - 179
Jaw Bone Stand - 55
jerseys - 160
Johnson, Peter & Chrissie - 176
Johnson, R.M.Y. - 164
Johnson, William - 31
Johnston, Charlotte - 47
Johnston, Margaret - 52
journalism - 164
jumpers - 156, 177

K

'Kays of Shetland Ltd.' - 150, 151, 161-163
kelp - 10, 15, 20, 21, 37, 93, 170
kelp gathers - 9, 40, 100
Kennedy, John - 59
Kent, Duchess of - 74
Kirkhouse - 53
Kirkland Galloway, James - 60
'Kirkwood (Printers) Ltd.' - 166
knee caps - 84, 126
knitter, employed by merchant - 26, 30, 40, 109, 110, 118, 122, 127, 155, 157, 158, 160, 165, 171
knitter, self-employed - 25, 26, 28, 30, 31, 35, 102, 109, 110, 111, 115, 127, 147, 155-158, 160, 165, 171, 173, 175
knitters' co-operative - see SHKA or Fair Isle Crafts Ltd.
knitters, old & infirm - 54, 62, 80, 128

knitting (definition of) - 4
knitting machines - 21, 61, 111, 128, 130, 136, 140-142, 143, 146, 151, 156, 157, 159, 172, 173, 176, 179
'Knitting Madonna' - 4
knitting needles - 4, 7, 80
knitting (origin of) - 4
knitting patterns - 71, 72, 76-79, 138, 159
knitting units - 156, 157, 161, 162, 173, 176-179
'The knitting years' - 146
'Knox, Samuel & Dickson' - 115, 116

L

lace knitting - see Shetland lace
lace yarn - 80, 81, 88, 158
ladies sleeves - 82, 84
A Lady's Assistant for executing useful and fancy
   designs in knitting netting and crochet work - 72
'A Lady Resident' - see Edmondston, Mrs Eliza
Laing, Alexander - 101, 105
Laing, Samuel - 69
lambswool - 179
land reform - 95
Land Settlement (Scotland) Act (1929) - 132
land tenure - 50, 96
landlord - 7-10, 15, 94
Laurenson, Arthur - 29, 30, 34, 35, 37, 45, 49, 73, 107, 113
'Laurenson & Co.' - 22, 28-31, 34, 45, 49, 73
Laurenson, Lawrence - 20, 29
Laurenson, Morgan - 47
Leask, James - 59
Leask, Robert - 59
Leeds - 155
leggings - 84
Leicester - 31
Leisk, Robert - 32
leisured classes - 72
Leith - 20, 95, 115
Lerwick - 1, 5, 7, 8, 10, 11, 14, 15, 19, 20-21, 25, 32, 40, 42, 49, 59, 79, 80, 96, 97, 100, 104, 114, 127, 138, 148, 149, 155, 156, 158, 162

Lerwick Harbour Trust - 96
Lerwick Local Committee - 84, 88
Lerwick Sheriff Court - 166
letter book - 30
Limitation of Supplies (Miscellaneous) Order (1940) - 147
'line' book - 118
linen - 7, 8, 14, 15, 20, 89
'lines' - 28, 30, 31, 45, 46, 117, 118
Linklater, Hugh - 31
Linklater, Peter - 59
Linklater, Robert - 20, 25, 29, 30, 35, 107, 113-116
'Linklater, Robert & Co'. - 31, 34, 36, 84, 87, 101, 114
Lisbon - 10
Liverpool - 115
living conditions - 13, 93, 97, 131, 133
Living Memory - 97, 134
Local Government (Scotland) Act (1889) - 96
Loch, David - 2, 14
lodgers - 21
London - 14, 34, 35, 46, 47, 74, 94, 111, 122, 131, 179
London Exhibition (1870) - 88
Louise, Princess - 57, 111
Lower Brouster - 28
Lubeck - 4
Lyall, Lady - 111
Lyall, Leonard - 52, 53

M

McBrair, Eliza - see Edmondston, Mrs Eliza
Mackenzie, Sir Kenneth - 87
MacKenzie, Sheriff-substitute David - 52-55, 121
Mackenzie, William - 35, 72, 82, 84, 87, 124
McLaughlin - 59
MacNeill, Lady Emma - 57
McNicoll Report - 178
Machine Age - 86
machine made hosiery - 62, 63, 140, 156, 158, 167, 172, 175, 179
Madeira - 10, 75, 76
mail order - 118, 123, 125, 126, 133, 157, 162, 163, 181
Mainland (Shetland) - 1, 20, 79

makers of home spun cloth - 52
makkin - 5
Malta - 75, 75
Manchester - 115
Manpower Services - 134
Manson's Shetland Almanac - 57, 108, 109
Manson, T. - 29, 116, 145, 153
market, Southern - 14, 33, 144
marketing of hosiery - 34, 36, 37, 63, 75, 80, 85, 86, 101, 102, 110, 111, 125, 127, 136, 139, 146, 148, 151, 154, 156, 159, 160, 161, 164, 171, 173, 175, 181
marriage - 9, 13
'Marshall & Snellgrove' - 115, 163
Martin, Martin - 7
Mary, Princess - 138
mass production - 31, 37, 138, 143, 146, 156, 165, 167, 172, 173
meal - 13, 45
'meal' roads - 62, 127
medal, gold - 88
men, Shetland - 2, 4, 16, 175, 176
Menzies, Rev. John - 13
Merchandise Marks Act - 142
merchants, country - 24, 32, 34, 48, 156
merchants, general - 32, 41, 48, 114, 162
merchants, Hanseatic - 4, 7, 9, 19, 28
merchants, Lerwick (town) - 34, 35, 162
merchant, middleman - 62
merchants, Shetland - 20, 24, 25, 28, 36, 48, 55, 61, 63, 95, 101, 107, 113, chapters 5 & 6, 128, 129, 146, 147, 154, 155, 156, 157, 160, 161, 162, 169, 173
merchants, southern - 8, 30, 60, 61, 103, 154, 157
merchants, visiting - 10, 25
merchant-laird - 8, 18, 19, 40
merchant-tacksman - 40
merchant, wool - see wool broker
Midland Lace Association - 129
migration - 80, 94, 127, 129, 171
Mill of Aden - 108
Mill, Rev. John - 13
mitts - 6, 83
modernisation - chapter 6
mohair - 24, 32, 115
money, foreign - 7, 8
'money item' - 24, 48
money, 'ready' - 8, 24, 35, 37, 45

moorit - 3
Morris, William - 86
Morrison, Betty - 46
Moscow - 76
Mossbank - 25, 52, 118, 175
Motherwell - 41
Mouat, Joan - 77
Mouat, Thomas - 3, 10, 14
Muckle Roe - 52, 176
Muir, Mrs - 57
Munros - 158
museum - 179

N

Napier Commission - 51, 96
Napier, Lord - 50
National Farmers Union (NFU) - 148, 151, 155, 158
natural dyes - 136
navy, merchant - 16, 21, 95, 132
navy, royal - 16
necktie - 82, 125
Nesting - 22
New Pitsligo - 86
The New Shetlander - 73, 136, 175
New Statistical Account (NSA) - 72
Newgord - 32
Newlands, Archibald - 48, 60, 110
New Zealand - 32, 95, 107
Nicholson, Thomas - 31
niddy-noddy - 80
Nisbet, Marion - 88
nobility - 57
Norbury, James - 68, 69, 79
Norn - 5
North Bank - 123
North Isles - 20, 93
Northmavine - 5, 16, 22, 48, 122
Norway - 2, 19, 49
nurses - 100

O

oats - 9
occupation, male - 4
occupation, part-time }
          secondary } 18, 26, 129, 169, 170, 176, 177
          spare-time }

O'Dell, A.C. - 2
Ogilvy, Charles - 70
Ogilvy, Frederick John - 70
Ogilvy, Ginny or Jenny - 70
Ogilvy, Jessie - 35, 88
Ogilvy, Joan - 35, 45
Oil Age - 61, 163, 176-178, 181
oil-related jobs - 178
old age pensions - 63, 96
Old Haa' - 101
The Old Lore Miscellany of Orkney...Sutherland - 81
'old shale' - 78
Old Statistical Account (OSA) - 10, 13, 14, 16, 19
open-work - see Shetland lace
opera cloak - 88
oppression - 40, 96
oral history - 134, 135, 153
Ord, Gema - 181
organisation of labour - 22, 107, 110, 141, 146, 148, 158, 161, 171, 176
origin of Shetland lace - chapter 4
Orkney - 7, 8, 15, 35, 45, 85, 86, 96, 146
outsets - 9, 13, 132, 170
outworkers - 22, 156, 157, 173, 175-177, 181
Out Skerries - 1
Oxford - 35, 70

P

packaging (of hosiery) - 177
Pacquette - 133
A paper on the Shetland Islands...choice specimens of Shetland knitting - 73
Park, Mrs - 26
parliamentary reform - 95
Paris - 179
Parochial Board - 42, 115
pass book - 30, 117
Paterson, Mary - 60, 61
'Patons & Baldwins' - 78, 79
patronage - 55, 58, 86-89, 122
'Peace & Low' - 115
Peace, Thomas - 35
peddlers - 36
'peerie flea' - 78
Peterhead - 16
petition, Delting - 52, 53

Petrie, Catherine - 26
Petrie family - 109
Petrie, Peter Edward - 35
philanthropy - 36, 55, 86, 87, 89, 102, 111, 112, 129
photographs - 97
piece-rates - 156, 164
pirns - 80
pluralism of employment - 18, 94, 100, 159, 169
'Pole, Hoseason & Co.' - 52, 59, 114, 115, 118, 119, 121, 122, 156
Pole, William - 29, 52, 59, 114, 118-121, 128
Poor house - 40, 64, 96, 129
Poor Knitters of Shetland - 71
Poor Law Commissioners - 68
Poor Law Inquiry - 7, 20, 21,
poor quality hosiery - 37, 60, 61, 64, 121, 172, 174
poor rates - 94
Poor roll - 15
population, female - 21, 25, 37, 75, 100, 102, 104, 134, 135, 169, 171
population, increase - 9, 13, 40, 170
population, Shetland - 9, 13, 14, 21, 52, 95, 128, 134, 140, 170, 182
Portugal - 75
post office - 54
post, letter - 20, 133, 163
post, parcel - 55, 94, 101, 102, 107-109, 127, 133, 145, 163
postal order - 123
post-war reconstruction - 151, 153, 154
post-war years - 89, 136, 166
potato - 9, 93, 104, 170
poverty - 8, 40, 96, 110
pricing (of hosiery) - 31, 37, 52, 54, 60-63, 147, 151, 158, 165, 167, 173
'Pringles of Inverness' - 81, 108, 158
'print o' waves' - 78
private people - 24, 25, 35, 36, 47, 85, 157, 160, 161
Procurator Fiscal - 52
profit (on hosiery) - 34, 36, 37, 47, 48, 51, 121
profiteering - 147
prosecutions - 59, 62
prostitution - 46
provisions - 34, 45, 46, 47, 54
purchase tax - 163

purchasing depots - 160
purse - 5, 6
Pyrenees - 24, 81

Q

quality hosiery - 61, 161, 162, 165, 174, 179, 181
Quarff - 45
quartering of poor - 96
Quebec - 122

R

Rae, Miss - 112
raising of standards (i.e. of knitwear) - 152, 153
Rampini, C. - 70
Ramsay, Mr - 124
rationing - 100
Rattar, J.D. - 109
'Real Shetland Knitwear' - 179, 181
recipes (knitting) - see knitting patterns
Reform Act (1832) - 95
religion - 13
Rennie, Alexander - 108
rent - 4, 8-11, 18, 35, 41, 46, 50
Report on Social and Economic conditions in the Highlands & Islands (Congested districts of Scotland - 105
retail business - see hosiery shops
Ridlon, Mrs - 121
roads - 2, 128, 133
Robertson, Miss - 26
role of women - 14, 100, 134, 169
Roman catholic church - 13
rooing - 2
Rose, Mr. - 143
Rosebery, Countess of - 111
Rothesay - 115
Royal Commission on the Poor Laws & Relief of Distress (1907) - 100
Royal Highland Show - 77
Royal Museum of Scotland - 5
royalty - 57, 88
rugs - 126, 139
rural industries - see cottage industries
Rural Industries Bureau - 142-144
Ruskin, John - 86
Russell, John C.- 140, 141, 143

Russia - 5, 76
Rutt, Richard - 76

S

St. John's Day - 7
St Kilda - 86
sail drifter - 132
salt tax - 7, 8
Sandison, Alexander - 34
Sandison, Charles - 155
Sandlodge - 73
Sandness - 45
Sands, Rev. John - 14
Sandsting - 22, 40
Saxby, Jessie - 70, 71, 76, 89, 111
Scalloway - 25, 156
Scandinavia - 1, 4, 5, 93
Scanlon, Jessie - 68, 69, 70
schools - 134
'Schoor & Co.' -57-59
Schoor, Mrs - 57
Scotch wool - 81
Scotland - 4, 14, 95
Scotland To-day & Edinburgh its capital - 123
The Scotsman - 59, 61, 62, 84, 88, 89, 93, 127
Scott, Sir Walter - 17, 21
Scott, Professor W.R. - 62, 104, 106, 127, 139, 144, 154, 169, 171
Scottish Council of Industry - 153
Scottish Home Industries - 80, 111
Scottish Home Industries Association (SHIA) - 60, 62, 82, 87, 102, 105, 109-112
Scottish National Development Council (SNDC) - 144
Scottish Office - 63, 70, 113, 136, 140-144, 160, 169, 172
Scottish Rural Industries Bureau - 144
Scottish Secretary - 55
Scottish Women's Rural Institute - see Women's Rural Institute
Scousburgh - 176
seamen's frocks - 72
service industries - 131, 135, 146
servicemen - 62, 62, 110, 131, 146, 147, 156, 173
shaela - 2

Shaw, Thomas - 60, 62
shawls - 29, 36, 67, 69, 71, 75, 76, 81, 83, 84, 88, 114, 125
shawl, wedding ring - 76, 81, 89
shearing - 2
sheep (Shetland) - 2, 7, 136, 145, 173
sheep scab - 3, 93
Sheffield Daily Telegraph - 89
Shetland - 69
'Shetland Banking Co.' - 45, 170
Shetland Chamber of Commerce - 148
Shetland colour stranded knitting - 3
'Shetland Fashions' - 177
'Shetland Fishery Co.' - 73
'Shetland Fishing Co.' - 51
Shetland fishing industry - 40, 44, 50, 128, 131, 135, 175
Shetland Flock Book Society - 136, 139, 144, 145, 151, 153, 155
'Shetlands from Shetland' - 179
Shetland Hand Knitters Association (SHKA) - 63, 110, 136, 146, 148, 149, 151-153, 155, 157, 160, 167, 173, 174
Shetland hand knitting industry - 18, 39, 44, 52, 60, 61, 89, 93, 100, 102, 104, 107, 127, 129, 135-139, 142, 143, 145, 146, 153, 154-167, 169, 170, 171, 175, 177, 178
Shetland housewives - 21, 64, 102
Shetland Islands Council (SIC) - 134, 177-179
Shetland Islands, demography - 1, 95, 96,
Shetland Knitting - 71
Shetland Knitters Repository - 55, 111, 112
Shetland knitwear trade - 179
Shetland Knitwear Trades Association (SKTA) - 176, 178-181
Shetland lace - chapter 4, 21, 32, 100, 104, 107, 114, 124, 136, 138, 158, 170, 174, 181
Shetland Lady trademark - 178, 179
Shetland Life and Trade 1550-1914 - 7, 170
Shetland machine knitting industry - 173, 175, 177, 178
'Shetland Method' - 9, chap. 2, 40, 93, 96
The Shetland Monthly - 164, 165, 166
Shetland Museum - 67, 97
Shetland News - 2, 116, 137, 146, 147, 155, 158
Shetland Spinners & Weavers - 155
Shetland stocking trade - 10, 68
The Shetland Times - 51, 55, 73, 88, 93, 127, 143, 147, 161, 164, 172
'Shetland Trader' - 179
Shetland Truck Inquiry (1872) - see Truck Inquiry (1872)
Shetland Warehouse - 35
Shetland Woollen Industries Association (SWIA) - 136, 137-145, 148, 151, 155, 160, 162, 172
shirts - 84
shopmen/women - 30
shortages - 100, 166, 167, 173
silk - 84, 118
Sinclair, Mr of Graven - 52
Sinclair, Sir John - 3, 10, 13, 14, 145
Sinclair, Robert - 21, 25, 26, 28, 30, 35, 45, 96, 107, 114, 116-118
Sinclair, Robert & Co. - 31, 34, 36, 45, 48, 101, 114, 116
Sketches & Tales of Shetland - 71
Small Work on Fancy Work - 72
Smallholders (Scotland) Act (1911) - 132
smallpox - 9
Smith, Brian - 50
Smith, Ellen - 88
Smith, George - 25, 42
Smith, Dr. Hance - 7, 10, 20, 170
Smith, James - 137, 138, 162
Smith, John & Co. (Wools) Ltd. - 127
Smith, Mrs Mary - 114, 122
Smith, Prophet - 2, 145, 151, 153
smuggling - 15
socks - 62, 84, 126
'soft goods' - 25, 29, 32, 34, 37, 45, 46, 54, 171
Some Impressions of the Shetland Woollen industry - 148
South Africa - 103
Spain - 10, 20, 75
Spence, Catherine - 49
'Spence & Co.' - 32, 34
Spence, John - 59
spencers - 89, 126
Spiggie - 145
spinning - 16, 24, 79, 80-82, 84, 103, 105, 107, 112, 128, 158
spinning, by machine - 81, 84, 101, 107, 156

spinning mills - 30, 81, 101, 108, 136, 147, 148, 157, 158
spinning mill (in Shetland) - 145, 151, 153-157, 178
spinning sets - 145, 153, 155
spinning wheels - 80, 81, 108
SRO - 52
Staithes - 16
'Standen & Co.' - 73, 84, 87, 122
Standen, Edward - 18, 35, 46, 70, 71, 73
Standen, Mrs - 73, 74
starvation - 13, 40, 62, 170, 171
Statement regarding the Poor in Shetland - 94
steam drifters - 94, 127
steamer service - 20, 25, 35, 86, 93, 97, 101, 108, 127, 133
Stewart, E.C. - 163-166
Stewart, Mrs L. - 166
'Stewarts of Shetland' - 161-165
stockings - 2, 5, 7, 8, 10, 11, 14, 15, 16, 18, 19, 21, 37, 72, 74, 80, 82-84
stocking frame - 18, 19
stocking trade - 7
stoles - 82
store system - 28, 31, 34, 117
Strathpeffer - 160
straw plaiting industry - 14, 47
Stuart, Margaret - 179
subsistence activity - 2, 14, 18, 50, 109, 132, 169
Suffolk - 122
Suffragette Movement - 100
Sumburgh - 1
supplementary income - 18, 102, 136, 142, 162, 175, 181
Susetter - 53
Sutherland, Charlotte - 45
Sutherland family - 79, 158, 159
Sutherland, Millicent, Duchess of - 60, 62, 87
Sutherland, Miss - 160
Sutherland, Rev. James - 48

T

tabling down the money - 54
Tait, Andrew - 145
tambourers - 22
Tarbet - 86, 104

Taylor, Henry Pearson - 100, 171
tea - 20, 25, 46, 47, 48, 60, 102
teaching of knitting - 175
technology - 128
telegraph system - 59, 95, 126, 133
telephone - 133
tenants - 9
Tennant, Mrs - 60
Third Report on Highland Destitution - 17
Thoms, Sheriff George - 55, 57, 111, 172
Thomson, W.L.P. - 170
Thule Hotel - 93
'Thuleknit' - 176
Tingwall - 14
Toft - 54
tourists - see visitors
Town Planning (Scotland) Act (1919) - 133
trade depressions - 51, 130, 131, 166, 167, 175-177
trade disruptions - 14, 15, 62, 147, 173
trade mark - 106, 130, 139-143, 148, 151, 154, 155, 175, 176
traders, early - 7
Traill, Mrs A. - 72, 111
trains (for court dresses) - 82
transport - 1
Treasury of Knitting Patterns - 68
Treaty of Union (1707) - 14, 41
trucking - 8, 9, 24, 28, 40-64, 87, 93, 95, 96, 102, 107, 113, 121, 128, 129, 135, 148, 152, 160, 171-173
Truck Act (1831) - 26, 42
Truck Amendment Act (1887) - 51, 52, 54, 55, 59, 61, 62, 95, 107, 121
Truck Commission Act (1870) - 42
Truck Commission, Shetland (1872) - 25, 28, 41, 57, 121
truck-free shops - 57
truck goods - 48, 170, 172
Truck Inquiry (1871) - 32, 87, 97
Truck Inquiry (1872) - 24-26, 28, 30, 34-37, 40-64, 73, 81, 84, 87, 88, 93, 95, 97, 100, 101, 107, 110, 114, 116, 118
Truck Inquiry (1908) - 59, 60, 97, 107, 110, 121
Truck Inquiry, Delting - see Delting Truck Inquiry
truck shop - 48, 59, 116
Tulloch, A.I. - 161, 163
Tulloch, James - 31
Tulloch, Margaret - 46

'Tullochs of Shetland' - 163, 173, 177
'Tullochs of Urafirth' - 157
tweed, Shetland - 4, 139, 153, 175
two-price system - 48

U

underwear, woollen - 21, 30, 37, 100, 114, 126
unemployment - 21, 75, 97, 113, 131, 136, 155
uniformity - 31, 37, 141, 162, 172
United Free Missionary - 46
United States of America - see America
Unst - 3, 10, 14, 18, 20, 22, 24, 35, 68, 79, 80, 88, 115, 127, 138, 155
Urafirth - 156
Uyeasound - 32, 34

V

valuation (of knitting industry) - 10, 19, 101, 113, 154, 169, 183
veils - 32, 37, 82, 83, 84, 88, 101, 114, 115, 125
vests - 126
Victoria, Queen - 52, 57, 68, 74
Victoria & Albert Museum - 76
View of the Ancient and Present State of the Zetland Islands - 19
Virginia - 10
visitors - 21, 25, 35, 86, 93, 101, 110, 161
Voe - 53, 156, 175
Vogue - 137

W

wadmal - 4, 19
wages (of knitters) - 37, 84, 85, 102, 135, 146, 152, 154, 179
waistcoats - 126
Wales - 144, 156
Wales, Prince of - 88, 138
Wales, Princess of - 88
Walker, Mr John - 42
Walker, Mrs John - 35
Walls - 22, 28, 45, 116, 179
war, First World War - 62, 63, 88, 89, 94, 97, 100, 106, 113, 127, 129, 135, 139, 146, 148, 156, 162

War, Napoleonic - 15, 19, 20
war, Second World War - 63, 131, 133, 135, 146, 154-158, 173
war risk insurance - 147
Wason, Cathcart - 101, 105, 110, 112
water - 96
waulking mill - 4
weaving - 4
wedding veils - 82, 84, 88
Weisdale - 21, 22
welfare system - 41
well-to-do - 55, 80, 86, 89, 94
West Register House - 52
Western Isles - 15, 16, 94, 96, 170, 171
Westminster, Marchioness of - 84, 88
whaling - 16, 20, 94
Wheeler, Professor - 2
White, John & Co. - 35, 114, 123-125, 127
White, J.R. - 140
Whiteness - 22
wholesale, prices - 24, 115
wholesale, trade - 35, 110, 113, 121, 125, 162, 163
Wick - 115
widows - 18, 122
wigs - 84
Williamson, Agnes - 114
Williamson, Christina - 114
Williamson, C.G. - 59
Williamson, James - 29, 41, 42
Williamson, Lawrence - 114
Williamson, Mrs - 76
Wilson, James - 15
'wires' - see knitting needles
Womanhood - 57
women, unmarried - 15, 18, 37, 100, 171
women's book - 31
Women's Rural Institute - 141, 142, 144
wooden patterns - 11
Woods, Mr - 53
wool (Shetland) - 2, 4, 8, 10, 11, 24, 25, 29, 72, 79-83, 101, 106, 114, 120, 127, 129, 132, 135, 138, 140, 145-147, 153-158, 162, 169, 178, 179
wool broker - 101, 102, 127, 132, 145, 157, 158
wool cards - 80
wool clip - 154, 158, 173
Wool College (Galashiels) - 156
wool control (wartime) - 146, 147
wool marketing board - 155

Wool Order - 146
wool/worsted imported - 93, 106
wool winder - 80
woolleners - 101
work book - 30, 114
work ethic - 86
Working Women's Association - 100, 110
workshops - 176
worsted - 8, 11, 24, 32, 48, 84, 95, 145, 156

Y

Yates, Jean - 46
Yell - 14, 20, 29, 94, 162, 176

Z

Zetland - 1, 2, 8
Zetland County Council (ZCC) - 96, 140,
    146, 147, 151, 153, 154, 162, 172
ZCC Trade's Names Committee - 175
Zetland, Lord - 94, 105